NO MASTER

Libertarian Educa...
in Bri...

1890 - 1990

Libertarian Education is a small independent publishing collective, which for the past quarter of a century has been campaigning for the development of non-authoritarian initiatives in education. As well as books, they publish the termly magazine, *Lib ED*.

Also in this series:

Free School, The White Lion Experience, by Nigel Wright, ISBN 0-9513997-1-3.

Freedom in Education: A do-it-yourself guide to the liberation of learning, ISBN 0-9513997-2-1.

NO MASTER
HIGH OR LOW

Libertarian Education and Schooling in Britain 1890 - 1990

John Shotton

Libertarian Education

Published by:

Libertarian Education
Phoenix House, 170 Wells Road, Bristol, BS4 2AG.

ISBN 0-9513997-3-X

Copyright: Libertarian Education 1993

Printed and bound by:
BPCC Wheatons Ltd., Hennock Road, Marsh Barton, Exeter, EX2 8RP. (Tel: 0392-74121, Fax: 0392-217170)

Front cover by **Cliff Harper**.

Photographs:

page 48:	Origin unknown, *Lib ED* archive.
pages 53, 110:	*Lib ED*.
page 126:	Roger Fidler.
pages 150, 153, 184:	*Lib ED*.
pages 230, 232:	Chris Draper.
page 268:	*Lib ED*.

Table of Contents

Foreword v

Preface vii

Introduction 1

PART ONE
The Thirst for Knowledge - Libertarian Schools And Sunday Schools, 1890-1930 21

    1.   TOWARDS UTOPIA
         The Movement for Libertarian Education in Europe,
         1890-1920 23

    2.   LIBERTY, FRATERNITY, EQUALITY
         The International School, (Fitzroy Square, London, 1890) 33

    3.   NO-ONE TELLING US WHAT TO DO
         The Anarchist-Socialist Sunday School, (163 Jubilee Street,
         Mile End, London, 1907) 36

    4.   TEA PARTIES AND LECTURES
         The West London Sunday School, (83 Charlotte Street,
         London, 1908) 41

    5.   TURNED OUT IN THE COLD
         The Liverpool Anarchist-Communist Sunday School,
         (Toxteth Co-operative Hall, Smithdown Road, Liverpool,
         1908) 43

    6.   THE TORCH OF LIBERTY
         The Ferrer School, (New King's Hall, 135 Commercial Road
         East, London, 1912) 49

    7.   YOUNG REBELS
         The Modern School, (24 Green Street, Cambridge Road, E.
         London, 1915) 54

    8.   FANNING THE FLAMES OF DISCONTENT
         The International Modern School, (62 Fieldgate Street,
         Whitechapel, London, 1921) 57

    9.   THE COMMON THREADS
         England and the Movement for Libertarian Education,
         1890-1930 61

    NOTES 63

PART TWO
Rural Retreats - The Libertarian Private Adventures In Education, 1890-1990 67

    1.   BEYOND THE CRANKS
         Private debates for private adventures, 1890-1960 69

2. MAKING MISTAKES WITHOUT FEELING STUPID
   Summerhill School, (Lyme Regis, Dorset, 1924-1927;
   Leiston, Suffolk, 1927-Date) 77
3. GOING HOME TO SCHOOL
   Dartington Hall School, (Totnes, Devon, 1920-1987) 82
4. A SCHOOL ON A HIGH HILL
   Beacon Hill, (Telegraph House, Harling, 1927-34; Boyles
   Court, Warley, 1934-37; Kingswell Hall, Brickwell, 1937-40;
   Tresidder Mill, Porthcurno, 1940-43) 88
5. THE WORLD THEY WANT
   The Forest School, (Godshill, Fordingbridge, Hampshire,
   1929-38; Whitwell Hall, Reedham, Norfolk, 1938-40) 92
6. A COLLECTIVE HEAD
   Burgess Hill School, (Burgess Hill, Hampstead, 1936-39;
   Redhurst, Cranleigh, Surrey, 1939-45; Hampstead again,
   1945-53; Boreham Wood, Hertfordshire, 1953-62) 95
7. URBAN TO RURAL RETREAT
   Monkton Wyld School, (Charmouth, Dorset, 1940-82) 100
8. FREE AS A BIRD
   Kilquhanity House School, (Castle Douglas,
   Kircudbrightshire, 1940-Date) 109
9. SUMMERHILL IN THE CITY
   Kirkdale School, (186 Kirkdale, London, 1965-1990) 117
10. DISTINCTIVE BUT EXCLUSIVE?
    The Libertarian Private Adventures in Education, 1920-90 120
NOTES 122

PART THREE
On the Edge - Libertarian Schools For The Unschoolable,
1910-1990 127

1. SCHOOLING THE UNSCHOOLABLE
   Libertarian Ideas on Special Education, 1910-1990 129
2. THE WHOLE CHILD
   The Caldecott Community, (26, Cartwright Gardens,
   London, 1911-17; Charlton Court, East Sutton, Kent,
   1917-25; Cuffley, Hertfordshire, 1925-41; Egdon Heath,
   London, 1941-5; New House, Mershan Le Hatch, 1945-Date) 133
3. FREE TO WORK OR LOAF
   The Little Commonwealth, (Flowers Farm, Evershot, Dorset,
   1913-1918) 135
4. THE RESIDIUM
   Sysonby House, (Riverside Village, Melton Mowbray,
   1914-19) 138
5. THE TESTING GROUND FOR PROGRESS
   Red Hill School, 1934-Date, (East Sutton, Nr. Maidstone,
   Kent) 140
6. THE HORRORS OF PERSONAL SELF-DISCIPLINE
   Hawkspur Camp, 1936-1940, (Hawkspur Green, Great
   Bardfield) 143

7. FROM TRUANTS TO CITIZENS
   The Barns Experiment, 1940-1944, (Peebles, Scotland) 146
8. CONTINUING THE LINE
   New Barns School, 1965-Date, (Church Lane, Toddington, Gloucester) 147
9. CHILDREN UNDER STRESS
   Rowen House School, 1979-1992, (Holbrook Road, Belper, Derbyshire) 149
10. A CONTRADICTION IN TERMS?
    Libertarian Schooling for the Unschoolable, 1910-1990 154
NOTES 156

PART FOUR
Inside the State - Libertarian Education And State Schooling, 1918-1990 159

1. EFFECTING CHANGE
   Libertarianism and the debate about education, 1918-1990 161
2. OUT WITH THE 3 Rs
   Prestolee Elementary School, (Farnworth, Lancashire, 1918-51) 164
3. A KEYSTONE OF CO-OPERATION
   St. George-in-the-East School, (Cable Street, Stepney, London, 1945-55) 167
4. IN JOHN KNOX COUNTRY
   Braehead School, (Buckhaven, Fife, Scotland, 1957-67) 169
5. THE REBEL HEAD
   Summerhill Academy, (Aberdeen, 1968-1974) 172
6. A TEAM APPROACH
   Countesthorpe College, (Winchester Road, Blaby, Leicester, 1970-Date) 175
7. AN AFFIRMING FLAME
   The Sutton Centre, (Sutton-in-Ashfield, Nottinghamshire, 1973-Date) 185
8. A NON-FRONTAL APPROACH
   William Tyndale School, (Islington, London, 1974-6) 189
9. BEYOND PROGRESSIVISM
   Libertarian Education and State Schooling, 1918-90 194
NOTES 196

PART FIVE
City Freedom - The Free School Movement, 1960-90 199

1. TOWARDS ALTERNATIVE SCHOOLING
   The Libertarian Debate and Movement, 1960-1990 201
2. FREEDOM WORKING BOTH WAYS
   The London Free School, (Notting Hill, London, 1966-71) 205
3. INTO THE REALM OF REALITY
   Liverpool Free School, (University of Liverpool, Liverpool, 1969-72) 208

4. A VANGUARD FOR SOCIAL CHANGE
   The Scotland Road Free School, (Vauxhall Community
   Services Centre, Silvester Street, Liverpool, 1970-72) 210
5. FIVE FREE SCHOOLS
   Durdham Park Free School, (Bristol, 1971-8); Saltley Free
   School, (Birmingham, 1972-4); Nottingham Free School,
   (Nottingham, 1972-4); Freightliners Free School, (Camden,
   London, 1972-6); Brighton Free School, (Brighton, 1972-3) 215
6. OUT OF URBAN DECAY
   Balsall Heath Community School, (Birmingham, 1972-Date) 218
7. THE MANCUNIAN EXPERIENCE
   Parkfield Street Free School, (Parkfield Street, 1972-3);
   Manchester Free School, (Burlington Street, 1973-9) 220
8. THE LION OF ISLINGTON
   White Lion Free School, (Islington, London, 1972-90) 226
9. NEIGHBOURLY LESSONS
   Leeds Free School and Community Trust, (Eldon Chapel,
   Woodhouse Lane, Leeds, 1972-4; 7, Marlborough Grove,
   Leeds, 1975-82) 239
10. FROM BARE CHURCH HALL TO THRIVING SCHOOL
    Barrowfield Community School, (Glasgow, 1973-8) 245
11. AN UNSTRUCTURED TYRANNY
    British Free Schooling, 1960-1990 251
NOTES 254

CONCLUSION
A Century of Libertarian Education - A Theory, A Practice, A Future 257

1. A THEORY AND A PRACTICE 259
2. A FUTURE
   Blackcurrent, (Northampton); Sands School, (Ashburton,
   Devon); Lady Jane Grey School, (Groby, Leicestershire);
   Bath Place School Unit, (Leamington Spa, Warwickshire) 264
3. A CHALLENGE
   Alternatives to the New Educational Orthodoxy 270
NOTES 274

Bibliography 275

Section 1: Archival Materials 275
Section 2: Books, Pamphlets and Articles 276
Section 3: Journals, Newspapers and Periodicals 280

Index 281

FOREWORD

Who reads histories of education? The only people who are **obliged** to do so are students in colleges, polytechnics and universities seeking degrees or diplomas to qualify them as teachers or as sociologists. A whole series of standard texts meets this need and most of them can be recognised as having a political bias, either towards the Right, with a belief in hierarchy, or towards the Left, with a belief in equality.

But in practice both celebrate a series of landmarks, not in education but in legislation, from the Education Act of 1870 which was alleged to have made elementary schooling free, compulsory and universal, down to the Education Act of 1944, providing secondary education for all. The authors of the standard histories are no doubt working at this moment on updated versions to incorporate the Education Reform Act of 1988 and its imposition of a National Curriculum on all schools controlled by the government.

The irony of this most recent landmark in the officially perceived history of education is that its instigators on the political Right ensure that their own children attend schools which are described as "independent" and consequently are not obliged to follow the National Curriculum. The response of the political Left is not to oppose the idea of a National Curriculum but simply to demand that it should be made obligatory in the "independent" sector too. (Labour Party policy document *Looking to the Future*, 1990).

Yet, as John Shotton shows in his Introduction, it is two hundred years since William Godwin set out with deadly and prophetic accuracy precisely why we should all oppose the very idea of a National Curriculum, regardless of its content. Indeed, part of my pleasure in the book before you is its establishment of Godwin, who is never mentioned in the textbooks for students of education, as an immensely significant philosopher of libertarian education.

But this is almost incidental to the main function of this book. To me it is the final part of a trilogy of books of the past ten years which, through painstaking and impeccable research, have turned the standard histories of education and their assumptions upside down. The first was Stephen Humphries' *Hooligans or Rebels? An Oral History of Working Class Childhood and Youth 1889-1939* (Blackwell 1981). The second was Philip Gardner's *The Lost Elementary Schools of Victorian England* (Croom Helm 1984). I found both these books really exciting, which itself is a remarkable thing in the histories of education.

John Shotton is right to stress the importance of those suppressed Victorian working class schools which provided "an education that was fully under the control of its users." The historian Paul Thompson commented on the lessons of Gardner's research that "Victorian middle class experts regarded this distinctive educational system as inefficient. They had their way. The price was the suppression in countless working class children of the very appetite for education and ability to learn independently which contemporary progressive teaching seeks to rekindle. Universal education, in short, is not a good thing in itself. It has to be genuine education."

The search for genuine education is the theme of John Shotton's book. Its importance is that it surveys all the missing historical connections; the buried history of libertarian working class schools, the progressive school movement of the 20s and 30s, the attempts in the 60s and 70s to introduce the lessons of the progressive experiments into the official school system, and the "free schools" of the same period which sprang up as alternatives.

He makes no claims that cannot be backed up by evidence, and he looks especially for the evidence provided by children rather than by propagandists. He draws us into unexplored territory and reminds us that experiment is the oxygen of education. It dies without it. Plenty of people would claim that this death has already happened. Teachers could hardly have been more demoralised than they are in the 1990s, buried by a mountain of form-filling imposed by a government elected with slogans about "setting the people free", and with a policy described with incredible cynicism as "local management of schools."

Yet every year a new cohort of five-year-olds can't wait to get into school, while another of fifteen-year-olds can't wait to get out. Something has happened in the years between. Dare we call this process education?

John Shotton's book provides a response to this challenge, and it also ensures that all those textbooks on the history of education have to be seen as conspiracies to conceal the really significant happenings.

Colin Ward

PREFACE

I detested school. Right from the start, until I managed to leave with enough qualifications to get into a university, my schooling was, in the teachers' eyes, unblemished by achievement. For me it was a nightmare of coercion and constraint. My memories of school in the 1960s focus specifically around the cane, detention and marks, and generally on the humiliation that accompanied these devices.

Imagine then the joy with which I, as an undergraduate in the early 1970s, discovered a dissenting tradition in British education. This discovery led to me working in a number of alternative education projects. Those experiences in their turn formed the inspiration for this book.

Whilst many historians have examined Britain's progressive educational history, little consideration has been given to the influence of libertarian ideas and practice in education. My research has revealed a rich tradition of libertarian educational theory and practice in Britain since 1890. The theory is highly distinctive, and the practice unique.

The libertarian critique of education is distinctive in the first place because of its emphasis on the right of learners to be recognised, treated and respected as autonomous individuals.

Secondly it emphasises the development of non-authoritarian pedagogies.

Thirdly it stresses the necessity of recognising the relationship between government and education as one determined by any government's need to subdue and repress its learners.

This critique and analysis is evident in the unique libertarian schools that have existed between 1890 and 1990, and in the pockets of libertarianism in other more generally liberal or progressive schools.

This book, then, is essentially an historical one which focuses attention on a lost history. Lost in the sense that what is known of libertarian education is rarely considered as such, and also in the sense that there have been a number of libertarian projects in education which require a very localised study in order to unearth them. This is hardly surprising as many such projects defied and resisted government controls and were related to the needs of individuals and individual communities.

However, this book is not simply an historical narrative where initiatives are merely described. I have attempted to place the various debates, analyses and projects within the socio-economic circumstances of their particular era, as well as more generally within the framework of a capitalist society. In this sense I would argue that the context in which experimentation and development actually took place is crucial to any real understanding.

Further, I have tried, where possible, to evaluate the various libertarian initiatives and their impact as alternatives to, and for, the national state system of education.

Whilst researching and writing this book I have been fortunate to receive generous amounts of help and support. First and foremost my thanks go to all those who have enjoyed a libertarian education, who allowed me to pester them with my tape recorder. Thanks too, to the many people who talked to

No Master High or Low

me about relatives who had either taught in or attended libertarian schools, and who supplied me with letters and diaries that took me right into the tradition. This research was a privilege for me.

A considerable number of poorly paid library staff in the British Library gave me enormous amounts of their time, retrieving uncatalogued journals and periodicals. I would particularly like to thank Edgar Weston and Caroline Williams.

I would also like to thank Ian Lister, Roy Carr-Hill, Colin Ward, Jan Bartholomew and Richard Musgrove for their reading of the script and their many observations.

Finally, special mention is due to Anthony George and Elaine Lee who helped type the script, and to the members of the *Lib ED* collective for their support, especially George Shaw, who undertook the considerable task of editing and typesetting this book. His advice and expertise have been invaluable.

John Shotton

INTRODUCTION

The Authoritarian Tradition in British Education since 1870 and its Libertarian Critique

Britain presents a paradox to historians of modern education systems. The first to industrialise, it lagged way behind other Western European countries in terms of government intervention in the education enterprise. Compulsory universal education was founded in Calvinist Geneva in 1536. Friedrich Wilhelm I of Prussia made primary education compulsory in 1717 and regular school attendance was required in France as a result of a series of ordinances of Louis XIV and Louis XV. In 1833 the British government set aside money from the Treasury which was paid to philanthropic groups for the purpose of educating the poor. However, the government was reluctant to become directly involved. This is borne out in a Parliamentary Committee report on the State of Education in 1834. In a section entitled *Education as a Private Venture with Public Help: The Case against Free Compulsory Schooling*, the response of the Lord Chancellor to a series of questions about establishing a national state system of education is quoted at length:

> "I think that it is wholly inapplicable to the present condition of the country, and the actual state of education ... suppose the people were taught to bear it, and to be forced to educate their children by penalties, education would be made absolutely hateful in their eyes, and would speedily cease to be endured ... I don't well perceive how such a system can be established, without placing in the hands of the Government, that is of the ministers of the day, the means of dictating opinions and principals to the people ..."[1]

The ministers of the day clearly agreed with the Lord Chancellor, for it was not until 1870 that the necessity of a national state system had become clear.

Between 1834 and 1870 Britain was faced with a growing population, a decrease in child labour, a massive increase in deprivation, and, by 1870, the first indications of world competition and industrial depression. It is no coincidence that the demand for a national state system of education accompanied these developments. By 1870 education was seen as the panacea for the social problems of the Victorian era:

> "There was a chorus of voices ... raised in favour of the doctrine that education is the great panacea for human troubles, and that, if the country is not shortly to go to the dogs everybody must be educated."[2]

No Master High or Low

Poverty and crime were of special concern:

> *"Pauperism cannot be checked until the children are nurtured in habits of self-reliance, independence and morality, and these qualities are only to be cultivated by a proper system of education."* [3]

> *"Would not the policeman be better employed in assisting the work of the schoolmaster by collecting together, for school attendance, the wilfully neglected children, who are springing up into recruits for the great army of crime."* [4]

Education administered by the state was also seen as the means of producing the required labour force. The relationship between such a system and the economy became clear:

> *"The more thorough primary instruction of such countries as Prussia ... afford to foreign workmen advantages which ours must have in order to maintain a successful competition."* [5]

In addition, an educated worker would realise that strikes were not in her/his own interest:

> *"What would prevent the working classes from engaging in those vain strikes which end in ninety-nine out of a hundred leaving them in a worse condition than before; what would keep them from habits of waste and improvidence, but some knowledge of the succession of events in life, such as education could supply."* [6]

The provision of education also had to keep pace with the extension of the franchise. So-called democracy apparently needed an educated electorate. The Second Reform Act of 1867 enfranchised some men of the urban working class. Robert Lowe expressed his concern:

> *"Political power is henceforth to reside in the poorest class of householders. We dare not place it in the hands of men who cannot read and write. The most ordinary principles of self-preservation will soon make popular education the first and highest of political necessities."* [7]

It was also believed in certain influential quarters that the provision of elementary education would improve the efficiency of the army and the navy. Here it is important to be clear as to the meaning of the term "elementary education". It was not simply education for all those of a particular age group: it was not synonymous with first stage or primary education. Rather it was education for a class, for the "labouring poor" as they were known for most of the century. The success of the Public Schools in producing Gentlemen had led to an increased awareness of the type of individual that other schools might produce:

> *"It is a great satisfaction to think that, though the distraction of momentous events now occurring abroad may continue ... the machinery*

Introduction

will have been definitely constituted for a system of National Education and thus rendering our people better fitted for any purpose and for any struggles, whether friendly or hostile which may await us in the future ... We have been rather backward in our efforts to improve this elementary material of war." [8]

Putting all these tendencies together, the desire was clearly for more direct and successful means of social control. The massive movement of population from the country to the towns had the effect of displacing the church from its position of influential dominance at the same time as creating urban ghettos where subversive ideas could thrive. Whilst artisans lived in cottages scattered over moors and wolds there was only limited danger to the state. But in the concentrated populations of the towns danger lurked:

"In the concentrated populations of our towns, the dangers arising from the neglect of the intellectual and moral culture of the working classes are already imminent and the consequences of permitting another generation to rise without bending the powers of the executive Government and of society to the great work of civilisation and religion, for which the political and social events of every hour make a continual demand, must be social disquiet little short of revolution." [9]

When he introduced the Elementary Education Bill in the House of Commons on February 17th 1870, W. E. Forster bore testament to the government's fears and change of will since 1833:

"We must not delay. Upon the speedy provision of elementary education depends our industrial prosperity. It is of no use trying to give technical teaching to our artisans without elementary education; uneducated labourers - and many of our labourers are utterly uneducated - are, for the most part unskilled, notwithstanding their strong sinews and determined energy, they will become over-matched in the competition of the world. Upon this speedy provision depends also, I fully believe, the good, the safe working of our constitutional system." [10]

It may well be that men like John Stuart Mill believed that liberty depended upon the greatest possible degree of diffused social intelligence, but the intentions of the government in establishing a national system of education were clearly rooted in the belief that chaos would prevail over culture unless the populace was brought under the disciplines of schooling.

As a result of the 1870 Act the country was divided into about 2500 school districts. In each district School Boards were to be elected by ratepayers with the brief to examine the provision by Voluntary Societies of elementary education in the district. Where provision was lacking an individual Board's responsibility was to levy a School Rate and build and maintain a Board School. The Board could insist on attendance if they wished. The London Board, for example, made attendance compulsory for children between the ages of five and thirteen. Only in 1880 did the Mundella Act make attendance compulsory, and only for children aged between five and eleven. Subsequently an Act of 1893 fixed the school-leaving age at eleven and in 1899 this was raised to twelve. Since then the school-leaving age has risen to fourteen in 1918, fifteen in 1947 and sixteen in 1971.

The fact that schooling became compulsory in 1880, and has remained so ever since, is critical in understanding the authoritarian nature of the national state education system. It also indicates how serious the state was in its intention to create a structure which aimed principally at social control and social engineering. School Boards and teachers did not need to look very far for appropriate models; there was the family and a series of existing schools.

Historians seem to agree that it is difficult to generalise about the nature of the family in Victorian Britain. But, as James Walvin has demonstrated, from 1800 to 1914 more often than not the family was a tiny kingdom, an absolute monarchy.[11] Currently most of those people who talk angrily about saving the family, or of bringing back the virtues of the family, do not see it as an instrument of growth and freedom, but of dominance and slavery; a miniature dictatorship in which the child learns to live under and submit to absolute and unquestionable power. Such was the Victorian family. It was a training for slavery. As Bernard Mandeville wrote:

"It is our Parents, that first cure us of natural wildness and break in us the Spirit of Independency we are all born with. It is to them that we owe the first Rudiments of our Submission and to the Honour and Deference which children pay to parents, all societies are obliged for the principle of Human Obedience." [12]

Children in Victorian England owed their parents total obedience.

It was hardly surprising that schools after 1870 would be constructed upon such family values. In the early Victorian Age young ladies were told:

"When you go to school your teachers take the place of your parents ... They ought therefore to be obeyed accordingly." [13]

This image of adult authority and its corollary, children's obedience, cast a shadow across most schools in England before 1870. That shadow was to lengthen steadily after 1870.

The state's main intention in introducing the 1870 Education Act was to nationalise the process of education in schools. The Board Schools became havens of order and obedience. Power was invested in adults over children, through unsophisticated means of reward and punishment, and children were treated as passive objects condemned to be meek, submissive and deferential. As early as 1793 William Godwin had warned of the dangers of a national state education system. It is worth quoting him at length:

"The injuries that result from a system of national education are, in the first place, that all public establishments include in them the idea of permanence ... public education has always expended its energies in the support of prejudice; it teaches its pupils not the fortitude that shall bring every proposition to the test of examination, but the art of vindicating such tenets as may chance to be previously established ... even in the petty institution of Sunday Schools, the chief lessons that are taught are a

Introduction

superstitious veneration for the Church of England, and to bow to every man in a handsome coat ...

Secondly, the idea of national education is founded in an inattention to the nature of the mind. Whatever each man does for himself is done well; whatever his neighbours or his country undertake to do for him is done ill ... He that learns because he desires to learn will listen to the instructions he receives and apprehend their meaning. He that teaches because he desires to teach will discharge his occupation with enthusiasm and energy. But the moment political institution undertakes to assign to every man his place, the functions of all will be discharged with supineness and indifference ...

Thirdly, the project of a national education ought uniformly to be discouraged on account of its obvious alliance with national government ... Government will not fail to employ it to strengthen its hand and perpetuate its institutes ... Their view as instigator of a system of education will not fail to be analogous to their views in their political capacity ..." [14]

In the Board Schools after 1870 Godwin's predictions came to fruition. Attendance became compulsory; there was no right to dissent. Mobility in school was regulated by timetables and bells. Actions were monitored and either rewarded or punished. All autonomy of the individual was undermined by the pedagogue. Only a particular set of values - religious, moralistic and capitalist Euro-centric - were allowed.

However, it would be a mistake to assume that the 1870 Education Act established the authoritarian national state education system. On the contrary, it only planted its seed. Already we have noted that compulsory schooling came later. Similarly it was the Education Act of 1902 that really established the kind of system that the twentieth century required. Further, it was this Act which condemned children to a never-ending life of misery at school. This Act was Arthur Balfour's contribution to domestic Unionist policy, and was unquestionably one of the most important pieces of legislation passed by the Unionist government. As far as Balfour was concerned the education system at the turn of the century was chaotic and ineffectual. The old Voluntary Schools run by religious societies had more children than did the country's Board Schools. Further, although the Board Schools had local rates for their support, the standard of equipment and furniture was much lower in these schools. There would have to be a change in their financing. Higher classes were being run by some Boards and schools to cater for more able children whose parents were willing to let them stay on after the school leaving age. This was an illegal use of the School Rate, as was proved by the Cockerton Judgement of 1901. Something had to be done about these illegal classes. County Councils set up in 1888 provided technical education out of funds obtained from the Science and Art Department attached to the Kensington Museums, and from the Board of Agriculture. But there was no link between Board and County Technical Schools. There had to be a reform to provide this link. Most worrying of all, not enough children were attending school and there was little central control over the curriculum.

Balfour was clear in his own mind that it was not consistent with the duty of an British government to allow that state of things to continue without adequate remedy. This was very much the language of the movement for "National Efficiency". This aspect of the educational question was most aptly represented by Sidney Webb, who, as chairman of the London County Council's Technical Education Board, was strategically placed to influence the London Education Board, and Robert Morant, an intensely ambitious officer of the civil service who, since 1895, had been preparing a coup d'état inside the Education Department to gain effective direction of its policies.

Webb and Morant agreed on the necessity of putting all forms of education under the direction of a vigorous central authority, not merely for the purpose of efficiency in administration, but as a means towards a more successful propagation of a national ideology. They deplored the elective School Board system, with its assumption that education should be subject to democratic popular judgement instead of being controlled by informed expert opinion. To Webb and the Fabians, compulsory education was one of the elements in their project of a "National Minimum", a set of standards in every sphere of life below which no member of society should be allowed to fall in the interests of the general social good. This was a view widely shared by those who stressed the need for a more coercive and authoritarian mode of governmental guidance in a well-meaning but ill-informed democracy.

What the Act did, in 1902, was to abolish School Boards and create 140 Local Education Authorities. These were run by county councils and county borough councils, which were to be responsible for elementary education, technical education and secondary education and to provide some of the money needed by the Voluntary Schools. The Act caused controversy for a variety of reasons. For the authoritarian tradition in British Education the Act did one thing and one thing alone - it established that a national compulsory education system, controlled centrally by codes of regulations and a system of inspection which was to propagate the interests of central government, was here to stay. For children the picture was bleak. The government was to decide what they were to do. They were to be compelled to do it. The best they could hope for were humane pedagogues, but with teachers being paid according to their results it was the spectre of punishment and control which loomed.

It is impossible to deny that significant changes have been wrought on the system of national education since 1902. John Lawson and Harold Silver represent the consensus amongst historians of education when they write about schools in the modern age being more open, having more flexible school and timetable design, using more integrated curricula and developing more humane approaches to teaching and learning.[15] It is, though, impossible to get away from the fact that, in schools in Britain today, children are expected to be submissive, passive, obedient, deferential to authority and to conform to the values inevitably implicit in any school controlled by the government. In this context it is illuminating to consider an article written by Brian Simon for *Marxism Today* in September 1984. Simon analyses the reasons behind Keith Joseph's strategy for centralising control of education during Margaret Thatcher's second period of premiership. He points out that the centralising tendency of government is nothing new in the history of education. He argues that what is new is the mode of control rather than the practice. His case is irrefutable, and supported comprehensively by a series of extracts from statements by Department of Education and Science officials, the most significant of which reads:

> "We are in a period of considerable social change. There may be social unrest, but we can cope with the Toxteths. But if we have a highly educated and idle population we may possibly anticipate more serious social conflict. People must be educated once more to know their place." [16]

Although there have been many changes in education since 1870 the essential power relationship between government, its teachers and children has not changed.

This is not to suggest, however, that there have been no radical critiques of the development of state education during the twentieth century. Nor is it to suggest that radical critiques have not had an impact on schools and schooling. There is a strong social democratic critique, an influential progressive one, and varieties of socialist critique. They are, though, bound together by one fundamental flaw; a failure to address the issue of authority in education and the power relationship between adults and children. They focus on state education provision, but not on the authoritarian nature of that provision.

At the beginning of the 1920s the Labour Party established an Advisory Committee on Education (ACE). It was a non-elected body consisting of experts from academic and so-called 'progressive' educational life. ACE became the mouthpiece of the Labour Party's philosophy of education and was rooted in an intention to transform education through raising mental and moral standards, and through programmes of education built on justice, rationality and wisdom. In 1922 Allen and Unwin published an ACE production, R. H. Tawney's *Secondary Education for All*, which claimed that:

> "Labour's policy is not for the advantage of any single class, but to develop the human resources of the whole community." [17]

It was this claim and this philosophy which underpinned the development of the social democratic critique of state education based on the principle of equality of opportunity.

It is of interest, then, that the 1944 Education Act, which established the tripartite system of education, was welcomed by the Labour Party, which called it "a giant progressive step".

They were able to do this because state education was no longer to be separated into elementary and secondary sectors, a division based on class, but into grammar and secondary modern schools, a system of selection by ability based on testing and selecting at the age of eleven. As Ken Jones has written:

> "... this seemed to displace the issue of failure from a class to an individual level. The eleven-plus took into each family the traumas of success or failure at school." [18]

The Labour government of 1945-51 rested on these laurels. Somehow this does not seem to have represented a commitment to equality of opportunity, never mind any intention to challenge the relationship of the state to education, or the basis of the pedagogy which existed in schools; the dominance of adults over children.

The Labour Party eventually became committed to the principle and practice of comprehensive education. This was embodied by Circular 10/65, which was issued by the new Labour government in 1965. This was an important document, as it asked local government to submit plans for the comprehensivisation of state schooling. But what has social democracy bequeathed to educational radicalism? Despite a commitment on paper to the principle of equality of opportunity, Labour effectively rejected any attempt to enforce it. They have also stopped campaigning for it, and have chosen instead to focus on the relationship between education and economic expansion.

In the 1970s the social democratic educationalists began to demand a general restructuring of education to produce new skills for the new economically stringent world. What this has meant is that, in 1978, Chief Education Officers received a document setting out the part that schools were to play in the Labour government's industrial strategy. This included:

"... preparing pupils more effectively while at school for the transition to adult and working life, in particular by equipping them with a basic understanding of the functioning of the economy and of activities, especially manufacturing, which create the nation's wealth." [19]

Such is the bequest of social democracy to educational radicalism. It has failed in any way to address the authoritarianism that afflicts the national state education system.

Whereas it is possible to identify the social democratic critique of Britain's national state education system in and around the Labour Party, the progressive critique is more diverse. W. A. C. Stewart traces progressive critiques of education and progressive initiatives back to the eighteenth century.[20] For the most part, though, he indicates that progressivism has been identified with middle class independent schools. There is a sense in which this is true, but there have been many progressive schools inside the state system. R. J. W. Selleck, Ken Jones and, more recently, Tuula Gordon have demonstrated this.[21] The need is really to consider what is meant by progressivism. Essentially it is a philosophy of teaching and learning which is child-centred. Many progressive thinkers are inspired by John Dewey, who argued strongly that the child was to be the sun around which schools would revolve. He also argued that teaching and learning should engage the whole child, and that teachers should see themselves as facilitators to learning. This philosophy, in practice, led to the emergence of certain characteristics in certain schools. Gordon has summarised the characteristics thus:

"1. Mixed ability, flexible, vertical groupings working together and/or individually in an open plan classroom under a team of teachers.

2. The day is integrated, the curriculum problem- or concept-based.

3. A wide range of resources is drawn upon (audio visual equipment etc., but also the local community in various ways).

4. The teaching-learning is child-centred, based on the pupils' interests, needs and skills.

5. The teacher is a guide and supporter in the child's pursuit of learning.

6. Academic learning is balanced by social and emotional learning, emphasising creativity and self-expression.

7. Decisions in the school are made by all those involved in it." [22]

The schools which developed some, but not necessarily all, of these characteristics were independent schools, like Bedales, Abbotsholme and King Alfred's in the early twentieth century, a wide range of primary schools throughout the century, and a number of secondary schools in the 1960s and 1970s. It should also be noted that there is a considerable overlap between progressivism and libertarianism, but this has more to do with the rhetoric of progressivism rather than its practice. This is because, while claiming to be child-centred, in reality progressivism was and is teacher-centred.

Admittedly many progressive initiatives have explored the ways in which children learn. They have also demonstrated the pedagogical superiority of processes which are rooted in the child's own experiences, but in the end the focus for radical change has been essentially on the role of the teacher. Michael Armstrong has noted those interpretations of the changing role of the teacher which seem to be implicit in many discussions of progressive theory and practice.[23] The first sees the teacher as a resource provider and as the manager and monitor of children's learning. The second sees teachers abandoning their traditional authoritarianism by letting the pupil decide whether or not to attend lessons or courses, without changing their style of teaching when courses and lessons are attended. The third sees the teacher abandoning all forms of control in the progressive name of licence. Armstrong correctly identifies the hidden authoritarianism that lurks in all three of these roles but, when he counterposes the need for teachers to develop genuinely mutual relationships with children in order to further their learning, he falls victim to his own criticisms of the other models. He writes:

"Guidance is paramount. Without the systematic help of tutors or pedagogues only a few students are likely to direct their own learning successfully." [24]

Armstrong remains in the progressive camp, and as such he represents the failure of progressivism to identify the overwhelmingly authoritarian nature of the national state education system. That system is not merely constructed on the foundations of what the state desires, but is cemented by the maintenance of adult superiority over children.

A comprehensive socialist critique of state education was first developed by the Socialist Sunday School movement. This movement commenced in 1892, when the first school was started in London by Mary Gray, a member of the Social Democratic Federation. However, the movement really developed in Glasgow, when four or five schools opened in the late 1890s, inspired by Caroline Martyn. From here it spread, to London, Yorkshire and Lancashire in particular, bringing together socialists of many faiths. The schools adopted the form and methods of traditional schools, but transformed the content. Instead of hymns there were songs and poems carrying a socialist and secular message, a song book being compiled.[25] The place of the ten commandments was taken by ten precepts, preceded by a declaration based on justice and love. The intention was to bring children to an understanding of the meaning of socialism, as well as of the structure and nature of existing society.

By focusing on the need to change the content of what was to be taught in schools, the Socialist Sunday School movement set the tone for future socialist critiques of state education. Two such critiques which warrant consideration are those developed by the Centre for Contemporary Cultural Studies (CCCS)[26] and by Ken Jones[27]. The research and analysis undertaken by the CCCS constitute a devastating indictment of the social democratic educational tradition. Working from the sound base that schools are more determined than determining, their analysis and prognosis identify the problem as being that of developing a politics of schooling on two fronts. The first front is indicated by a modified understanding of a Marxist functionalism; schooling performs various tasks for the Capitalist mode of production and for patriarchal relations, but this is not necessarily guaranteed. The key, then, to transforming schools in the first instance is to identify:

"... how and what and from whom will children learn about industry in a school." [28]

In the second instance the need is to construct a counter-politics of schooling that:

"... tries to discredit and stand outside the specific class and gender nature of the processes currently presented as natural and eternal." [29]

Sadly such a programme has little to say about the way in which the power relationship between adults and children can be similarly transformed.

Ken Jones' analysis and strategy for change are similarly incomplete. He argues that, in the first instance, the main means of purchase of any attempt to gain support and initial momentum for a socialist strategy for educational reform lies in the trade union organisation of teachers. This may or may not be true, but a glance at the issues which Jones considers to be important reveals the weakness in his analysis of the nature of authoritarianism in education. He writes:

"Three issues are important to the developing of a strong socialist current: the content of education, the winning of popular support, and the related tasks of accomplishing a further trade unionisation of the National Union of Teachers, while at the same time achieving a closer political relationship between the union and the labour movement as a whole. In each of these areas, a challenge to present attitudes is necessary." [30]

The lack of any perspective of the experience of children at school is conspicuous.

A consideration of the social democratic, progressive and socialist critiques of national education together reveals a common thread. All three fail to consider the experience of state schooling from the viewpoint of the child, the user, the learner. There is an agreement about the purpose behind such schooling, a kind of consensus that is rooted in an awareness of the controlling and engineering tendencies of government. And yet, without a rejection of the meekness, submission and deference that is expected of children in schools, any transformation of schooling on social democratic, progressive or socialist lines will always be incomplete. In this context it is worth noting the final paragraph of the review of *Beyond Progressive Education* by *Lib ED*, a magazine for the liberation of learning:

"In the end it seems that Ken's, task (and that of others on the non-Libertarian left) is not so much to transform the education system as to gain control over it. As if power and authority are not themselves a problem, only who wield them." [31]

It is with this in mind that attention should now turn to the libertarian critique of national state education in Britain, a critique which chooses as its reference point the authoritarian nature of such education. Firstly, though, it is worth considering the wider theory of libertarian education as it has emerged through libertarian thinkers and practitioners.

A libertarian approach to education is highly distinctive for a number of different reasons, but it is based upon an awareness of, and opposition to, the controlling tendencies of state education systems. There is a compatibility here with the other critiques that have already been discussed. Again it is William Godwin who articulates the feelings held by libertarians in this area:

"It is not true that youth ought to be instructed to venerate the constitution, however excellent; they should be led to venerate truth; and the constitution only so far as it corresponds with their uninfluenced deductions of truth. Had the scheme of national education been adopted when despotism was most triumphant, it is not to be believed that it could have for ever shifted the voice of truth. But it would have been the most formidable and profound contrivance for that purpose that imagination can suggest." [32]

However, for libertarians, education has to be freed from the authority of the teacher as well as from the state. It is here that their critique takes on a fundamental significance.

It was Francisco Ferrer, founder of La Escuela Moderna in Barcelona in 1900 and of the International League for the Rational Education of Children in 1908, who described the relationship between the nation state and its teachers, and was to be a great inspiration to the movement for libertarian education in Western Europe in the first two decades of the twentieth century:

> "Much of the knowledge actually imparted in schools is useless; and the hope of reformers has been void because the organisation of the school instead of serving an ideal purpose, has become one of the most powerful instruments of servitude in the hands of the ruling class. The teachers are merely conscious or unconscious organs of their will, and have been trained on their principles ... Teachers have inspired themselves solely with the principles of discipline and authority, which always appeal to social organisers ... The children must learn to obey, to believe and to think according to the prevailing social dogmas." [33]

Indeed a number of Modern Schools were established in Britain between 1907 and 1921, based on a completely alternative approach defying all such conceptions of state and teacher control. These schools were amongst the first libertarian initiatives in Britain in the twentieth century.

Inevitably the libertarian critique of national state education is also rooted in a total opposition to all forms of coercion. For thinkers like Godwin and Ferrer, learning could only flourish in a libertarian environment. Libertarianism sees education as a spontaneous process rather than something to be imposed on the child. Rote, memorisation, routine and the staples of conventional learning which characterise national state education systems, these do nothing but destroy the imagination and inhibit the natural development of children. A libertarian education is one which rejects such forms of coercion. Coercion enters into adult relationships with the young to a greater extent than adults suppose. It is evident in the peremptoriness and unkindness with which children are all too commonly treated, as it is in the profound lack of respect by adults for the young. As Godwin wrote in 1783:

> "All education is despotism. It is perhaps impossible for the young to be conducted without introducing in many cases the tyranny of implicit obedience. Go there; do that; read; write; rise; lie down; will perhaps for ever be the language addressed to youth by age." [34]

However, whilst the libertarian critique might begin with perspectives on the intentions of the state in creating a national system, on the controlling urges of teachers, and on the pernicious nature of coercion, it is really underpinned by a fundamental respect for children as individuals. Adults usually approach other adults with certain assumptions, namely that each are accorded powers of initiative, a capacity for discretion, a right to reject, an ability to think for themselves. Libertarians accord children the same respect. Godwin captures the essence of this respect brilliantly:

> "There is a reverence that we owe to every thing in human shape. I do not say that a child is the image of God. But I do affirm that he is an individual being, with powers of reasoning, with sensations of pleasure and pain, and with principles of morality; and that in this description is contained abundant cause for the exercise of reverence and forbearance. By the system of nature he is placed by himself; he has a claim upon his little sphere of empire and discretion; and he is entitled to his appropriate portion of independence." [35]

Introduction

This is not a charter for children's rights, it is a belief in equality, including girls as well as boys! Libertarians were perhaps the first educational theorists to regard children as being equal to adults, with the same need for freedom and dignity. Children belong neither to their parents nor to the government. They belong to themselves. Accordingly they must not be looked down upon as inferior beings, but treated with respect:

"As creators and not creatures ..." [36]

as Max Stirner has put it. This means that the libertarian critique of national state education is also determined by a faith in the essential goodness of human nature, and by a belief in the capacity of the young to direct their own learning. Writing in the nineteenth century, James Guillaume anticipated many of the libertarian educational initiatives that were to emerge in Britain after 1890:

"No longer will there be schools arbitrarily governed by a pedagogue, where the children wait impatiently for the moment of their deliverance when they can enjoy a little freedom outside. In their gatherings the children will be entirely free. They will organise their own games, their talks, systematise their own work, arbitrate disputes, etc. They will easily become accustomed to public life, to responsibility, to mutual trust and aid. The teacher whom they have themselves chosen to give their lessons will no longer be detested as a tyrant but a friend to whom they will listen with pleasure." [37]

Libertarian educational theory also extols the virtues of an integral education that cultivates physical, as well as mental, skills and develops all aspects of the child's personality. This notion appears to have originated with Charles Fourier, whose theories exerted a powerful influence on the anarchist movement. Taking his cue from Fourier, the French anarchist Pierre Proudhon advocated a combination of physical and intellectual learning, whose elements would both complement and reinforce each other. He wrote:

"Labour and study which have for so long and so foolishly been kept apart will finally emerge side by side in their natural states of union. Instead of being confined to narrow specialised fields vocational education will include a variety of different types of work ..." [38]

After Proudhon the same idea was taken up by many radical thinkers, socialist and anarchist alike. The leaders of the Paris Commune of 1871, for example, sought to inaugurate an integral education, so as to remedy the over-specialisation caused by the emergence of large-scale industry and the division of labour. During its brief life the Commune launched a number of educational experiments. It established schools of industrial arts, workshop schools, schools for orphans and schools for women. As far as its educational commissioner was concerned:

"The main lines of an egalitarian education had been sufficiently mapped out for the idea to start to spread." [39]

And spread it did, with Louise Michel, a Paris Communard, establishing an international libertarian school in Fitzroy Square in London in 1890.

Libertarian educational theory, then, is based upon resistance to the notion of a national state education, because of its natural servitude to state ideology. Thereafter it has a fundamental respect for, and belief in, the autonomy of children and their ability to control and direct learning. It considers all forms of teacher and structural control to be illegitimate, and sees education as a widely ranging, integral process. In the final analysis it assumes a capacity on the part of the young, their parents, and libertarian educational practitioners, to decide and organise the kind of education they want. In practice in Britain this has meant the emergence of initiatives both inside and outside the national state system, and it is a brief survey of these initiatives that is now required in order to understand the nature of the libertarian critique of Britain's authoritarian national state system of education.

Throughout the nineteenth century the working class was characterised as being apathetic towards education. This was one of the many justifications for the 1870 Education Act. More significantly it was the justification for later legislation which made schooling compulsory and subsequently pushed up the school-leaving age. However, before and after 1870, the structure and speed of educational development were affected by conflicts of cultural value, understanding, significance and experience between those who provided education and those who were to receive it. This was evidently the case because there was a deeply rooted and important working class educational culture, with its own values, aims and initiatives. Phil Gardner has drawn this out.[40] He maintains that, before 1870, there was a resistance to institutionalised schooling, fed by the currents of this alternative culture which had its own network of independent practical activity. This was the tradition of working class private schooling. After 1870 this tradition was challenged, and slowly working class private schools were put under pressure and eventually closed, but the process took a long time.

Briefly, what were these schools, what were their characteristics and what is their significance to this survey? Where these schools have been discussed by educational historians they are "dame schools", "inferior schools", "common day schools" and "adventure schools". As Gardner, states:

"They are denied the generic title of the independent schools of a distinct class - the people's schools." [41]

The schools were private through the absence of financial aid and bureaucratic regulation, and working class by the distinctive background of the children, their parents and usually the teachers. They were self-financing, beyond the reach of central government, and their fortunes fluctuated according to demand, not supply. The schools were rarely in a building designed for the purpose, usually being in the home of the teacher. The significance of these schools, and of Gardner's important book, to this brief survey lies in the fact that they constitute a forerunner to the libertarian initiatives of the twentieth century. They were not libertarian schools themselves, as they did not necessarily have an explicit self-governing philosophy, nor a stated belief in the autonomy of the child. They were, however, products of a culture that despised formality, were secular, and had little time for compulsory, regular attendance. They manifested:

> "... an education that was fully under the control of its users, it was an education truly of the working class and not for it." [42]

Many held out against the government, as the School Boards and Inspectorate closed in after 1870, but all were eventually consumed.

The history of libertarian education and schooling in Britain since 1890 lies in three areas. Firstly, it is to be found in a variety of free-standing alternatives, which were born of a particular culture and occupied the ground between the public and the private sector. They represent a challenge to the national state education system. Secondly, it exists in a series of "private adventures" in education, usually the inspiration of an individual or group of educational thinkers, many of which for a variety of reasons were recognised by government. The history of these schools, though, is complex, largely because it is mostly lost amidst the history of the more general independent progressive school movement. Thirdly, it awaits discovery inside the state system, again similarly lost amongst more general histories of liberal and progressive education.

As far as the free-standing alternatives are concerned they belong mostly to the early part of the twentieth century and to the 1960s and 1970s. The school that Louise Michel established at Fitzroy Square in 1890 does not seem to have had a long life, but between 1907 and 1921 a series of International Modern Schools, influenced by the educational ideas of Francisco Ferrer, emerged in London and Liverpool. Most were in London in the Jewish East End, and grew out of a working class culture that was turning its back on orthodox Judaism and on the demands made by the national state education system. One such school was established in 1907 in Whitechapel by a group of children led by a young girl of thirteen named Naomi Ploschansky, later called Nellie Dick. She was born in the Ukraine in 1893 and became demoralised by national state schooling and by the lack of facilities for young people in the working men's institutes of the East End. To begin with she helped to set up a Sunday School, which was to grow into a larger and more regular International Modern School later on. The history of such schools is largely unrecorded and yet is a major part of the dissenting tradition against national state education.

The history of the Free School movement of the 1960s and 1970s is also largely unrecorded. In the early 1970s there were over twenty such schools, mostly in inner cities. They were rooted in working class culture, although they were usually the inspiration of educationalists and teachers who were dissatisfied with the national state school system. The most famous of these schools was the White Lion Street Free School. It was born in 1972 in an old derelict house near London's Kings Cross Station. From the beginning the idea was to create a space in which local children could learn without the regimentation, boredom and fear that, by the 1970s, were the usual experience for most children in traditional schools. Many local children were involved in renovating the building, and when the school opened in September 1973 a lot of the children had not only discovered the school themselves, many having just "wandered in", but to some extent had physically created it.

In the second area of libertarian education and schooling, the private adventures in education, there are a number of schools of interest. When the Little Commonwealth, a self-governing colony for so-called "delinquent adolescents" appeared in July 1913 under the guidance of Homer Lane, the inspiration for various initiatives took root.

Even before he broke away from the New Education Fellowship and the magazine *New Era* to eventually set up Summerhill, A. S. Neill recognised the influence that Lane had on him:

> *"There are two ways in education: Macdonald's with Authority in the shape of School Boards and magistrates and prisons to support him, and mine with the Christlike experiment of Homer Lane to encourage me."* [43]

Lane's was a private adventure, as was Neill's, and there was a link between the two. Lane's initiative also had a great influence on a series of other initiatives which emerged after the 1920s. These were the "schools for the unschoolable", self-governing communities like Red Hill School, where libertarian philosophy and practice developed for the supposedly "maladjusted" children who attended them. These were private adventures in many cases, but they warrant separate consideration for there is a continuing tradition and, furthermore, they were frequently in receipt of state approval. There is something interesting about a state which will resist dissent in education at all costs, except when there apparently seems no alternative. Other private adventures which warrant consideration are Dartington Hall, Beacon Hill, the Forest School, Burgess Hill, Monkton Wyld, Kilquhanity and Kirkdale. Some of these initiatives have had their histories written, others have not, but what is certain is that they represent a series of libertarian initiatives which deserve to be differentiated from the more general progressive tradition with which they are normally associated.

The history of libertarian education in state schools belongs mostly to the 1960s and 1970s, at Braehead, Summerhill Academy, Countesthorpe College, the Sutton Centre, and William Tyndale, but here the issues are complex. None of these schools could be described as libertarian, and in the main these schools were really the slightly unacceptable face of progressivism. However, all of them developed libertarian practices, and more significantly the experiences of children at the schools often appears to have been libertarian. There is a sense in which all of these schools stand outside mainstream progressivism. The same is true of Prestolee School in the 1920s and St. George's-in-the-East School in the 1940s and 1950s. It is therefore impossible to deny that there has been a certain amount of libertarian dissent within the state system as well as outside it.

An enduring problem in a study of the history of libertarian education and schooling is the nature and availability of source materials. There is an abundance of worthwhile secondary material on some of the private adventures in education. The histories, for example, of Dartington Hall, Beacon Hill and Summerhill are well documented, and there is little point in going over ground that has already been adequately covered. The secondary source material is useful only insofar as it is possible to quickly construct a picture of what the initiatives were like, and to make a viable assessment as to how, and with what success, they challenged the state in its intention to control the process of education. Similarly there is considerable secondary material available about the state school initiatives. Prestolee, Summerhill Academy, Countesthorpe, the Sutton Centre and William Tyndale have all received the attention of an array of educational writers. Much of the writing available, though, is concerned with the politics of the campaigns that developed in those schools and the conflict that occurred between the schools and the authorities. It is difficult to build up a picture of what the experience was like for children in the schools.

It is in this sense that the available primary material has to form essential source material for any study of the history of libertarian education and schooling. The primary material available for a study of recent state school initiatives and some private adventures and free schools mostly takes the form of internal documents, Inspectors' reports and internal and external enquiry reports. However, journals and newspapers and some local archives often throw up interesting and relevant material. It is these sources that reveal the true nature of many of the free standing alternatives. Especially significant here is the large number of labour annuals and newspapers from the beginning of the twentieth century. These contain considerable information about the working class libertarian schools which existed before the first world war. It is in this area of study that local investigation is important. This also applies to research about the majority of Free Schools of the 1960s and 1970s. The difficulty with most evidence from local sources is that it is often completely de-personalised and takes a "distant" view. Nevertheless this material has to be greatly valued.

A major research problem is that there are few records of personal experiences. There are some personal accounts of the libertarian-influenced state schools, written mostly by heads and teachers. There are some personal accounts from children in the same schools, and in some of the free-standing alternatives. The need for oral testimony is critical. Most of the initiatives in the early years of the twentieth century lie beyond the reach of old age, but there are some accounts now available through the magazine *Lib ED*, which has conducted several interviews with people who founded or who attended the schools. For the majority of other initiatives it is possible to obtain interviews with those involved, with concerned parties outside the schools, both hostile and supportive, and most important with the children themselves. Any study of the libertarian critique of Britain's national state education system, and by implication of the history of libertarian education and schooling, would be inadequate if it were not rooted in the experiences of children. It is the absence of such experiences which weakens the majority of the more generalised histories of education.

With this in mind it is significant that much recent feminist research has led to a new and viable methodology, which has implications for the study of children, especially in schools. Ann Oakley has written of the need for, and the process, problems and consequences of, using the personal accounts of women as source material in feminist research.[44] She demonstrates effectively that most research processes in the social sciences indicate that the motivation for carrying out work lies in theoretical concerns. In consequence the research process appears orderly, coherent and mostly objective. By implication the personal tends to be, at best, negated, but usually completely removed. Oakley argues that a feminist methodology, which seeks to legitimise personal experience and to make it possible by an awareness on the part of interviewers of the powerlessness of interviewees, applies to social science research in general. It is certainly applicable to a study of the history of libertarian education and schooling in Britain. For Oakley the requirement is that:

> "... the mythology of hygienic research with its accompanying mystification of the researcher and the researched as objective instruments of data production be replaced by the recognition that personal involvement is more than dangerous bias - it is the condition under which people come to know each other and to admit others into their lives." [45]

If children are to be a valuable source of material for understanding the experience of schooling then they have to be empowered. This means that an observation of them in school, and a critical review of their work, is utterly inadequate in revealing the nature of their experience. A history of libertarian education and schooling in Britain requires that the children who have experiences of either are able to give their account, on their terms, of how it is or was.

It is undeniable that there is a very distinctive history of libertarian education and schooling in Britain since 1890, and that it represents a critique of considerable importance of the national state system. The temptation is to begin to talk of a movement. With a few exceptions there is little evidence of definite links between any of the initiatives. What is more important is to consider the context in which each initiative emerged, the influences behind it, the nature of the experience for its users and how much success each had in constructing and sustaining a viable alternative to the state education system.

NOTES

1. Stuart Maclure, J., *Educational Documents. England and Wales 1816-1968*. Methuen, London 1965, pp39-40.

2. Huckley, Sir T., *Address to the South London Working Men's College*. London 1868.

3. The Earl of Devon, *Hansard. Third Series, Vol. CLXIV Col. 634*. London 1862.

4. Cartwright, T., *Address to the National Association for the Promotion of Social Science*. London 1867.

5. Kay-Shuttleworth, Sir James, *Memorandum on Popular Education*. London 1868.

6. Fox, W.J., *Hansard. Third Series, Vol. CXII Co. 1243*. London 1851.

7. Lowe, Sir Robert, *Quarterly Review. Vol. 123*. London 1867, p274.

8. *The Times*. 22nd July 1870.

Introduction

9. Kay-Shuttleworth, Sir James, *Four Periods of Public Education*. London 1867, p204.

10. Stuart Maclure, J., op.cit., pp104-5.

11. Walvin, James, *A Child's World*. Penguin, London 1982.

12. Quoted in Hall, J., (ed), *Children's Rights*. Penguin, London 1972, p54.

13. Quoted in Walvin, J., op.cit., p104.

14. Godwin, William, *Enquiry Concerning Political Justice and its Influence on Morals and Happiness. (2nd ed., 2 vols., 1796; 3rd ed., 2 vols., 1798)* Oxford 1971, book VI, Chapter viii.

15. Lawson, J., and Silver, H., *A Social History of England*. Routledge and Kegan Paul, London 1973.

16. Quoted in Simon, B., *Breaking School Rules. Marxism Today*. London, September 1984.

17. Tawney, R.H., *Secondary Education for All*. Allen and Unwin, London 1922, p64.

18. Jones, K., *Beyond Progressive Education*. MacMillan, London 1983, p64.

19. Department of Education and Science, *Progress in Education*. H.M.S.O. London 1978, p15.

20. Stewart, W.A.C., *Progressives and Radicals in English Education 1750-1970*. MacMillan, London, 1972.

21. Selleck, R.J.W., *English Primary Education and the Progressives 1914-39*. Routledge and Kegan Paul, London, 1972; Jones, K., op.cit.; Gordon, T., *Democracy in One School*. Falmer, London 1986.

22. Gordon, T., op.cit., p29.

23. Armstrong, M., *The Role of the Teacher*, in Buckman, P., (ed), *Education Without Schools*. Souvenir Press, London 1973, pp51-52.

24. Ibid., p55.

25. *The Socialist Sunday School Tune Book*. London 1912.

26. Education Group. Centre for Contemporary Cultural Studies, *Unpopular Education. Schooling and Social Democracy in England since 1944*. Hutchinson, London 1981.

27. Jones, K., op.cit.

28. Centre for Contemporary Cultural Studies. op.cit., p260.

29. Ibid.

30. Jones, K., op.cit., p147.

31. *Lib ED*, Leicester 1986, Vol.2, No.2, p19.

32. Godwin, W., op.cit., Book VI, Chapter viii.

33. Ferrer, F., *The Origin and Ideals of the Modern School*. Watts, London 1913, p49.

34. Godwin, W., *An Account of the Seminary that will be opened on Monday the Fourth Day of August at Epsom in Surrey. (1783)* Gainesville, London 1966, pp24-25.

35. Godwin, W., *The Enquirer. Reflections on Education, Manners and Literature in a Series of Essays. (1797)* New York 1965, pp88-9.

36. Stirner, Max., *The False Principle of Our Education*. Ralph Myles, Colorado 1967, p11.

37. Quoted in Dolgoff, Sam., (ed), *Bakunin on Anarchy*. New York, 1972, pp373-4.

38. Quoted in Edwards, Stewart, (ed), *Selected Writings of Pierre-Joseph Proudhon*. Garden City, New York 1969, pp80-87.

39. Edwards, Stewart, *The Paris Commune, 1871*. London 1971, p275.

40. Gardner, P., *The Lost Elementary Schools of Victorian England*. Croom Helm, London 1984.

41. Gardner, P., op.cit., p4.

42. Gardner, P., op.cit., p100.

43. Neill, A.S., *A Dominie Dismissed*. Herbert Jenkins, London 1916, p53.

44. Oakley, Ann, *Interviewing Women: A Contradiction in Terms, in Roberts, H., (ed) Doing Feminist Research*. Falmer, London 1972.

45. Oakley, A., op.cit., p58.

PART ONE

The Thirst for Knowledge

LIBERTARIAN SCHOOLS AND SUNDAY SCHOOLS

1890 - 1930

1. TOWARDS UTOPIA

The Movement for Libertarian Education in Europe, 1890 - 1920

Between 1889 and 1898 three new independent schools were established in England: Abbotsholme (1889), Bedales (1893) and King Alfred's (1898). Allied together, if only in spirit, they formed what became known at the turn of the century as the New Schools Movement. Their inspiration had largely been a reaction against the narrowness of the classical education and ethos of muscular Christianity which were the hallmarks of public schools in Britain in the second half of the nineteenth century and which were translated with little essential change into the grammar schools. These new schools were started by men and women whose minds were open to new ideas and they soon widened their reforms to constitute a serious challenge to many of the hitherto secure values of orthodox education. This challenge was perhaps most impressively articulated by Edmond Holmes, at one time Chief Inspector of Elementary Schools.[1]

Holmes was a man of vision but found himself at odds with most of the ideas that lay behind the policies of the Board of Education which, since 1902, had been charged with administering the development of a national system of education in Britain. In the state schools, which he had observed as an Inspector, he had castigated the path of mechanical obedience that children were forced to tread. He noted that education was based on the thesis that the only way to salvation for a sin-ridden humanity was through strict adherence to rules and complete suppression of any instinctive learning or behaviour. Scripture lessons, rote learning, payments-by-results, rewards, punishments and examinations were the means by which the state sought to mould what it saw as being its 'children'.

In contrast, Holmes set out what might be by describing a school in a village called Utopia, run by an enlightened head teacher called Egeria. Here the whole pedagogical emphasis was on self-realisation where there was no need for punishment and reward or other forms of repression. Needless to say Holmes' outpourings provoked scorn and criticism. Some measure of this can be gauged from his publication, in 1914, of a second book which was almost entirely devoted to answering attacks on the first.[2] His defence was strengthened by the addition of the theories and practice of Maria Montessori to his intuitive approach. He declared:

> "I write as one who is championing a revolutionary movement ... which in its attempt to get to bedrock, threatens to undermine the very foundations of our western scheme of life."[3]

Holmes became one of the key figures in a small group which discussed these ideas, informally at first, and which later initiated a series of conferences out of which eventually grew the New Education Fellowship. The first of these conferences was held in 1914, under the title "New Ideals in Education", and its debates centred upon the work of Montessori.

The issue of freedom in schools seemed alive. In 1914 the editorial board of *The Times* decided to publish a monthly supplement, which very soon became weekly, devoted entirely to educational matters. This was not to be a radical tract, yet the early issues of the *Supplement* suggest that the question of freedom was treated with great seriousness. In a lengthy letter that was printed in the *Supplement* in March 1916 Professor Culverwell wrote:

> *"The most important of all educational questions hinges on that of freedom."* [4]

In January 1920 Beatrice Ensor, a founder member of Holmes' Ideals in Education group, began a quarterly journal, *Education for the New Era*, which was to propagandise more widely and deeply for freedom in education. Its opening editorial proclaimed that:

> *"Freedom, Tolerance and Understanding have burst the doors so carefully locked upon them in the secret chambers in the souls of men ... in all realms of thought and action they move: not least in education."* [5]

However, whilst trying to propagandise for a more open, humane and autonomous pedagogy in education in schools, in reality the *New Era* became the mouthpiece of the New Schools Movement and the Montessori method. This restricted its focus essentially to independent, fee-paying schools which were attended only by those whose parents could afford to pay fees. Furthermore, to many interested in freedom in education, Montessori's method had little to offer. Montessori believed that no child should be compelled to learn and that children should be free to cease work when they liked. But Montessori was no apostle of autonomy and believed strongly that there was a need for children to be patiently and lovingly directed at every step until, through knowledge, they could direct themselves. To many, including A. S. Neill, at one time a co-editor of the *New Era*, this was a contradiction in terms. The New Ideals Group had become a broad church, and when Summerhill (1924), Dartington Hall (1926) and Beacon Hill (1927) were established it became clear that Holmes' old group was really splitting up.

There were many differences between these three new schools and the older progressive schools like Abbotsholme which cannot concern us here, but still there were things that bound them together. In the first place they were fee-paying, and mostly drew their children from privileged backgrounds. Secondly, they have been presented by historians of education as the only libertarian educational initiatives worthy of consideration in the early part of the twentieth century. This latter perspective is grossly misleading. Primarily it is highly debatable whether or not schools such as Abbotsholme and the other Montessori influenced schools warrant consideration as libertarian initiatives, but more importantly such a narrow perspective is really only a product of academia's inability to undertake research that reaches beyond certain boundaries. The histories of most independent schools are well documented. Similarly journals like the *New Era* and the *Times*

Educational Supplement were read by many interested in, and able to afford, a private education. They were not widely read by working class people. Consequently there was not much incentive on the part of their respective editors to look beyond the narrow confines of what was essentially a bourgeois interest in alternative education.

And yet there is a rich history of other initiatives between 1890 and 1930. With the exception of some experiments which emerged in state schools, the most significant of which was at Prestolee in Lancashire, most of these initiatives require localised study. Further, it is the journals and newspapers of the working class that require close scrutiny if anything is to be discovered about working class ideas on, and initiatives in, education. Hitherto, most historians of education have not found it relevant to seek out such publications. And yet, between 1890 and 1930, working class areas in London and Liverpool witnessed the emergence of a series of Libertarian Sunday Schools. These schools were the product of a broad working class culture, attuned in personnel, atmosphere and organisation to the demands of that culture. They were under the control of their users, and in this sense were an education of the working class and not for it. In some cases the schools were the creation of children and children alone. During their existence they challenged the intention of the state to establish a particular type of education for all children in the aftermath of government legislation. Today they challenge the historical view that the majority of libertarian initiatives in education have only served a privileged few.

Most of the schools were in the East End of London and were the creation of Jewish anarchists. However, whilst only being few in number in comparison to the number of Socialist Sunday Schools, and the state's own day schools, they were in fact part of a much broader European movement for libertarian education.

When a popular revolutionary movement seized control in Paris after France's defeat in the Franco-Prussian war and ran the city as a Commune, a series of experiments in education were established. Attempts were made to construct an "integral" education, with the aim of remedying the over-specialisation caused by the emergence of large-scale industry and the division of labour. The experiments included schools of industrial arts, workshops, schools for orphans and schools for women.

The concept of integral education was close to the hearts of most libertarian educators in France in the last twenty years of the nineteenth century.[6] After the destruction of the Paris Commune, Paul Robin took up the ideas with vigour. In 1867 he had drafted a report on integral education for the First International's Second Congress at Lausanne. In 1879 he took the opportunity to put his ideas into practice when Ferdinand Buisson, the director of primary education in France under Jules Ferry, the Minister of Education, invited him to become an Inspector of Schools, and then in 1880 to take charge of an orphanage at Cempuis. He was to remain in this post for fourteen years. While there he developed a programme of integral education that was co-educational, and designed to develop both the physical and intellectual capacities of the pupils in a non-coercive atmosphere. Emma Goldman has summarised his approach and concept of integral education:

"He believed that whatever part heredity may play, there are other factors equally great, if not greater, that may and will eradicate or minimise the so-called first cause. Proper economic and social environment, the breath and freedom of nature, healthy exercise, love and sympathy, and above all, a deep understanding for the needs of the child - these would destroy the cruel, unjust and criminal stigma imposed on the ignorant child." [7]

In 1894 Robin was removed from his position in the aftermath of a wave of criticism. Benjamin Tucker, editor of the American periodical, *Liberty*, suggested that this was because he had:

"... refused to teach the orphans that France is bigger than the world or that God is bigger than man." [8]

However, Robin did not have a monopoly of the ideas concerning integral education. The school at Cempuis continued to function. Further, in 1897 Marcel Degalves and Emile Janvion formed a League for Libertarian Education which aimed to start a school in Paris similar to Robin's original experiment. Jean Grave, the editor of the periodical, *Les Temps Nouveaux*, lent his support, as did Louise Michel, Elisée Reclus, Peter Kropotkin and Leo Tolstoy. The League intended that:

"The sciences will be studied at the same time as letters, by practical illustration, even before reading is learned. The children will be brought face to face with Nature, and excursions will be made into the fields and Zoological Gardens to promote this end." [9]

The school was never formed, but at the turn of the century two libertarian schools were founded in the vicinity of Paris, Sebastien Faure's La Ruche and Madeleine Vernet's L'Avenir Social. Little is known of Vernet's initiative, but at La Ruche the principles of integral education were practised. Faure sought to develop all aspects of children's potential, physical, emotional, intellectual and imaginative, which would equip them with a range of entry skills into various industrial and craft occupations. After a visit to La Ruche in 1907, Emma Goldman wrote of Faure as having discarded the old methods of education and:

"... established understanding for the needs of the child, confidence and trust in its possibilities and respect for its personality." [10]

The French libertarians, then, had developed ideas and initiatives which were rooted in a rejection of the government's intention to produce a particular kind of fodder for industry, one that was specialised, disciplined, obedient and God-fearing. The concept of integral education was essentially a product of its time. Robin and Faure wanted to give the future worker more practical independence in the labour market, and to them integral education was part and parcel of the broader workers' struggle for emancipation. At the beginning of the twentieth century, though, libertarian ideas about education were also developing in Spain under the inspiration of Francisco Ferrer. He brought to the movement an even wider and in some ways more significant concept of liberation.

Francisco Ferrer y Guardia was born near Barcelona in 1859, the son of peasant parents. The family was devoutly Catholic but Ferrer developed a spirit of revolt in his youth which saw him reject Catholicism. In his early twenties he became a Freemason and a radical Republican. He became friendly with Manuel Ruiz Zorilla, the leader of the Progressive Republican Party, and, in his job as a conductor on the railway between Barcelona and the French frontier, he was able to act as a courier for Ruiz and to help political refugees to find sanctuary across the border. In 1885 he was involved in an abortive Republican uprising led by General Villacampa and was compelled to take refuge in France with his wife and three daughters. He earned a living by teaching Spanish in Paris and committed himself to many radical causes. He became an ardent defender of Dreyfus and a delegate to the 1896 Congress of the Second International in London. He was later to make other visits to England, which proved inspirational to many, particularly Jimmy Dick who was to be instrumental in establishing a Libertarian Sunday School in Liverpool.

Ferrer's years in Paris brought him into contact with new people and new ideas. After the death of Ruiz in 1895 he began studying anarchist literature and visiting anarchist clubs. He became a close friend of Jean Grave, editor of *Les Temps Nouveaux*, and spent time with Louise Michel, Elisée Reclus and Sebastien Faure. By the end of the 1890s he had come to believe in the supreme sovereignty and autonomy of the individual, and as a teacher he began to develop a special interest in the movement in France for libertarian education. He wrote to his friend Jose Prat:

"I intend to form a school of emancipation which will be concerned with banning from the mind whatever divides men, the false concepts of property, country and family, so as to attain the liberty and well being which all desire and none completely realises." [11]

In March 1900 Ferrer inherited a large sum of money, about £30,000, from Ernestine Meunie, a former student of his in Paris. In 1901 he returned to Barcelona to found a libertarian school, La Escuela Moderna, which opened in September of the same year. Ferrer did not simply bring new ideas about education to Spain on his own. His years in Paris had been very influential and he owed a great debt to Paul Robin. Further, the 1890s had seen a rising tide of revolt against traditional forms of organisation in education in Spain, as well as in industry and government. Ferrer contributed to this revolt with his deep hatred of the church and its domination over education. He believed in an education that would be rational, where pupils would not be tied down by religious dogma and would be able to organise their own lessons without compulsion. It must be stressed again that Ferrer was not alone in Spain with such beliefs. A large number of anarchist and secular schools had been created in Spain in the 1870s and 1880s, and Ferrer also owed a debt to Elias Puig in Catalonia and Jose Sanchez Rosa in Andalusia, who had responded earlier to the desire of Spanish workmen for independent secular schools.[12]

Ferrer, though, did bring his own ideas to the movement for rational secular education in Spain, as indeed he also did to the wider European movement for libertarian education. As Michael Smith has pointed out, the organisation of La Escuela Moderna represented a movement away from the position of the French libertarians. Concerning the concept of integral education he writes:

> *"Robin and Faure certainly believed that this meant the development of all sides of the human being, but they also believed that an important practical expression of this was the polytechnical apprenticeship which would give the worker more practical independence in the labour market. Ferrer was as wedded to the concept of integral education as they were but the emphasis for him was on the development of the whole human being and not on the preparation of children for roles in the economy."* [13]

What Ferrer was doing was moving towards a wider concept of libertarian education, which emphasised reason, observation, science, independence, autonomy and self-reliance.

From the outset Ferrer was determined that the children in La Escuela Moderna would control the process of learning:

> *"... education is not worthy of the name unless it be stripped of all dogmatism, and unless it leaves to the child the direction of its powers and is content to support them in their manifestations. But nothing is easier than to alter this meaning of education, and nothing more difficult than to respect it. The teacher is always imposing, compelling and using violence; the true educator is the man who does not impose his own ideas and will on the child, but appeals to its own energies."* [14]

Beginning in 1901 with 30 children, the numbers at La Escuela Moderna increased to 126 in 1905, and the figure was still rising when the school was closed by the authorities in 1906. Further, the school was an active and varied enterprise, containing an adult educational centre and a radical publishing house. Moreover, in October 1905 Ferrer opened a branch of La Escuela Moderna in Villanueva y Gettru. Other schools adopted his textbooks and methods of instruction. In this way his influence was felt in Seville, Malaga, Tarragona and Cordoba, as well as in smaller villages and towns. By the end of 1905 there were fourteen Ferrer-type schools in Barcelona alone, and thirty four in Catalonia, Valencia and Andalusia. His influence also extended to the wider movement for secular education. Indeed Ferrer himself led 1700 children in a procession and picnic in support of secular education in Barcelona on Good Friday, April 12 1906.

However, Ferrer's influence reached far beyond Spain. In April 1908, undeterred by the closure of La Escuela Moderna in 1906 after the Spanish authorities attempt to implicate him in an attempt on the life of King Alfonso XIII, he founded the International League for the Rational Education of Children in Paris. This organisation of free thinkers, radicals and reformers, which also published a journal, *L'Ecole Renovée*, had an international committee, which included Lorenzo Portet of Liverpool and William Heaford of Surrey. Both men were to be involved in some of the Libertarian Sunday Schools created in Liverpool and London between 1907 and 1914. So we can see that there were libertarian thinkers and educational initiatives in England which were part of a European movement for libertarian education.

Ferrer was executed in October 1909 after being charged with and found guilty of being the author and chief of a rebellion in Barcelona during the so-called tragic week in July of the same year. Ferrer was undoubtedly innocent, but his martyrdom led to his ideas about education spreading even wider. In England many schools were created after Ferrer's execution.

There was an avid interest in libertarian education amongst anarchists and other free thinkers in Britain. Louise Michel had realised this when she found support for her libertarian school in Fitzroy Square, London, in 1890. Ferrer had visited Liverpool on 15th August 1907 and had also received a warm and large reception.[15] Furthermore, in June 1908 *Freedom* published a letter from Peter Kropotkin to Francisco Ferrer. Parts of it are well worth quoting for it gives an indication of the type of educational thinking that anarchists in Britain were engaged in:

"*Dear Comrade and Friend,*

I am very glad that you are about to issue L'Ecole Renovée (the Reformed School) regretting but one thing: that I am unable to give it all the assistance I would. Everything has to be begun over again in the schools of the present day. Above all, education in the true sense of the word: that is to say, the formation of the moral being, the active individual, full of initiative, enterprise, courage, freed from that timidity of thought which is the distinctive feature of the educated man of your period - and at the same time sociable, communistic by instinct, equal with and capable of feeling his equality with every man throughout the universe; starting emancipated from the religious, narrowly individualistic, authoritarian, etc., principles which the schools inculcates ... In our present schools, formed to make an aristocracy under the supervision of priests, the waste of time is colossal, absurd. In English secondary schools two years of the time reserved for the instruction of mathematics are given up to exercises on the transformation of yards, perches, poles, miles, bushels, and other English measures. Everywhere history in schools is time absolutely wasted on the memorising of names, of laws incomprehensible to children, wars, admitted falsehoods, etc. ... Well, it is easy to foresee that we shall be compelled to adopt integral instruction - i.e. teaching which, by the practice of the hand on wood, stone, metal, will speak to the brain and help to develop it. We shall arrive at teaching everyone the basis of every trade as well as of every machine ... We must come to the merging of manual with mental labour as preached by Fourier and the International ...

My best wishes for the success of L'Ecole Renovée.

With fraternal greetings,

P. Kropotkin."[16]

Quite clearly Kropotkin was much influenced by Robin's and Faure's ideas about integral education.

Broadening the debate in August 1908, *Freedom* published a circular issued by the Paris Group of the International League for the Rational Education of Children. It addressed the whole question of teachers and teaching:

> "... The school-teacher should not only instruct, he should educate in the largest sense of the word. At no point in his work can he remain neutral; that is without conviction, without sincerity, without assent. However hard the truth may seem to established powers, this is only the right of the child. Who wishes to withhold the truth of this? Certainly not we. Yet there are certain truths common to the man in the street which no-one dares put to the children. Let this at least let us dare to stop teaching children what we know to be untruths, and then a great thing will have been done.
>
> For example, who believes in these days that a worker ought to be grateful to his employer simply because he gives him work? Yet is not this still being taught in schools? Who is there these days who seriously believes that a God outside the world created it as a toy and sits watching it go? Yet from how many of our 'secular' schools has this 'God above' creator been definitely expelled? Whatever may be the truth of these matters, the teacher should be able to show his true self to the children, his own ideas, his own convictions, such as he has himself acquired by experience and reflection, - and not in the hypocritical and awkward attitude of one who simply recites a State doctrine ..." [17]

And then, in the years leading up to the outbreak of war in 1914, *Freedom* began to address the whole issue of pedagogy and Children's Rights. In February 1910 it began a column specifically aimed at young people and carried articles castigating parents and teachers for their abuse of children. Typical is the introduction to a short piece by J. M. Guyan taken from his book *Education and Heredity*:

> "Flaubert says that life ought to be an incessant education, that 'from speaking to dying' everything has to be learned. Left to chance, this long education is every moment deviating. Even parents, in most cases, have not the slightest idea of the aim of education, especially when the children are still very young. What is the moral idea set before most children in a family? Not to be too noisy, not to put the fingers in the nose or mouth, not to use the hands at table, not to step into puddles when it rains, etc.
>
> A reasonable being! In the eyes of many parents the reasonable child is a marionette, which is not to stir unless the strings are pulled; he is supposed to have hands which are meant to touch nothing, eyes which are never to sparkle with desire for what he sees, little feet which must never trot noisily on the floor, and a silent tongue." [18]

Even more incisive is an article by Herbert Spencer on the issue of Children's Rights:

> *"The main obstacle to the right conduct of education lies rather in the parent than the child ... They do not recognise in these much-scolded, often-beaten little ones so many looking-glasses wherein they may see reflected their own selfishness ... 'I won't have that noise' exclaims a disturbed (sic) father to a group of vociferous juveniles: and the noise ceasing, he claims to have done something towards making his family orderly. Perhaps he has; but how? By exhibiting that some evil disposition which he seeks to check in his children - a determination to sacrifice to his own happiness the happiness of others."* [19]

Spencer goes on to argue for adults to try to gain some sort of insight into youthful emotions and to sympathise with them. Further, he puts the moral case for the political enfranchisement of youth, but is at pains to point out that this is only a right within the context of the moment where government actually exists. He argues strongly that an absence of government is essential for the full achievement of youth's autonomy.

These letters and articles from *Freedom* illustrate how in Britain, too, as well as in France and Spain, a debate was taking place, mostly amongst anarchists, about libertarian education.

After Michel's experiment in 1890 this debate initially found practical outlets in Sunday Schools established on Jubilee Street and Charlotte Street, London, in 1907 and 1908 respectively, and on Smithdown Road, Liverpool, in 1908. Thereafter two schools known as Ferrer Schools were established on Commercial Road, and again Charlotte Street, London, in 1912. These schools later became known as Modern Schools. In 1914 a new Modern School was established on Cambridge Road in London, a breakaway from one established on Commercial Road in 1912. And finally, in March 1921, a Modern School was founded on Fieldgate Street, also in London. However, before turning to look at these schools in detail it is necessary to consider the wider context in which they emerged.

Thus far the debate about libertarian education would appear to have been largely the preserve of anarchists. This was not strictly true. Mention has already been made of the New Ideals in Education Group, but a debate about freedom in education was also taking place amongst reformers of many dispositions. In 1900 the *Labour Annual*, a journal of the Independent Labour Party which subsequently changed its name to the *Reformers' Year Book* carried an article signed by Alfred Russell entitled the *Social Teaching of Children*. It is worth quoting at length:

> *"... Teaching, to be effective, should take growth of the child mind into account. Teachers need to pay attention to the child's mode of looking at things. Use of graphics, simple language conveying word-pictures and expressing thoughts within the child's ordinary knowledge and experience leads the child naturally, almost inevitably, to more far-reaching conclusions. All mental force, as it may be called, should be carefully avoided. Children are thus enabled to think for themselves, and really possess and value their opinions. They are in this way likely to become*

consciously intelligent. Such intelligence is a sure and effective conquering weapon for Truth. General principles which involve no dogmas and are the planting of the seed, should form the scope of the teaching. Let the child-mind develop its own conclusions. Leave experience room to teach later on. Plant the seed well. On that depends the nature and strength of growth. The subjects taught should be such as appeal to the child mind, while conveying the truth aimed at. Teaching should be free from bookishness and elaboration and should be human and direct." [20]

Subsequently the *Reformers' Year Book* carried articles about children's rights and child abuse. It also publicised the activities of the Society for the Reform of School Discipline, a body committed to the abolition of corporal punishment. Moreover it attacked the 1902 Education Act as:

"... a reactionary measure ... a serious set-back to the progress of free, unsectarian and democratic education ..." [21]

Anarchists and individual adventurers, then, were not the only people in Britain questioning the whole national system of education at the beginning of the twentieth century. Yet, on the other hand, it was mostly anarchists who sought to launch libertarian initiatives. However, they did not necessarily speak with one voice. The European movement for libertarian education was a diverse one which reflected different situations in different countries, as indeed it reflected differences of approach between individuals. Britain was no exception. The Libertarian Schools and Sunday Schools which were established in Britain at the beginning of the twentieth century were in many ways all very different, even though they were bound by a belief in the autonomy of the individual to control the learning process. It is to an examination of those schools that we can now turn.

2. LIBERTY, FRATERNITY, EQUALITY

The International School, (Fitzroy Square, London, 1890)

Louise Michel, born in 1830 in Vroncourt, France, is best remembered as a revolutionary who fought and struggled on the barricades of the Paris Commune, being lucky to survive after a trial before the War Council of France. There is a sense in which her name is associated with sainthood in most left wing circles. Edith Thomas has tried to get beyond such a romantic view and examine her life carefully and critically.[22] We owe Thomas a great debt for she has illustrated how important a cause education was for Louise Michel.

In fact she trained as a school teacher and, in 1865, began running a small day school in Paris. She was held in high esteem by her pupils, and Georges Clemenceau wrote of the school in Paris:

"It was a strange school anyway this school of Louise's, with its white mice, its tortoise, its grass snake and its beds of moss. It was something of a free-for-all, with some highly unusual teaching methods, but taking everything into account you had to agree that instruction was being offered."[23]

The "highly unusual teaching methods" of which Clemenceau wrote were considered unusual because they lacked coercion. Louise Michel had no time for disciplined learning and punishment; on the contrary she encouraged her pupils to think for themselves, to explore diverse areas of interest. She was later to draw inspiration from the lives of Sebastien Faure and Paul Robin, both of whom she considered to be ahead of their time in attempting to broaden the educational experiences of working class children.

These were the ideas that she brought with her when she came to London in 1890. They were ideas which were to be put into practice, for in the same year she opened a school for the children of political refugees. Its address was 19 Fitzroy Square, London, and it was to be known as the International School. Henry Betloff printed a delightful prospectus for the school, the cover of which bore an illustration of a woman wearing a Liberty Cap and lighting her lamp from the Sun of Truth with one hand, while feeding children the fruits of knowledge with the other. There was a caption in French "La Solidarité Humaine", and in English:

"From each according to his capacity, to each according to his needs. Liberty, Equality, Fraternity."[24]

Louise Michel also acknowledged a debt to Michael Bakunin when she included a statement by him, concerning education, in the prospectus:

> "The whole education of children and their instruction must be founded on the scientific development of reason, not on that of faith; on the development of personal dignity and independence, not on that of piety and obedience; on the worship of truth and justice at any cost, and above all on respect for humanity, which must replace always and everywhere the worship of divinity ...
>
> All rational education is at bottom nothing but this progressive immolation of authority for the benefit of liberty, the final object of education necessarily being the formation of free men full of respect, and love for the liberty of others." [25]

The idea of an education that was both rational and integral which had taken root so firmly amongst French libertarians, had arrived in Britain. It found a welcome audience.

There were many free thinkers in the vicinity of Fitzroy Square, including many exiles from the European anarchist movement. They found Britain, at this stage, the most accommodating of states, and they wished to take their children out of state schools because of the harshness of the regimes and the patriotic and religious nature of the curriculum. The prospectus acknowledged this as well:

> "Comrades wished to keep their children out of the hands of those professors of modern schools divinely inspired and licensed by the State or Church who teach, consciously or unconsciously, the doctrine of popular sacrifice to the power of the State and Church, and to the profit of the privileged classes." [26]

The school was run by a committee which consisted of the following, J. Barber, W. Hoppe, C. Franck, H. Koch, H. Schirmer, R. Gundesen and E. Ahlquist. The secretary of the school was Cyril Bell and the treasurer one H. Strenzleit. The teaching staff included Louise Michel herself, Miss A. Henry, Mrs Wilson, C. M. Dryhurst, Mrs Hyde, Mrs Podmore, Mlle Henery and Cyril Bell. The teaching was entirely voluntary and the school maintained by donations and parental contributions.

There was a broad curriculum in the school, and no subjects were compulsory. A lot of importance, though, was attached to foreign languages, and it appears that some of the most popular classes were in French and German. The prospectus is valuable here, for it stated:

> "He who has acquired one or more foreign languages commands a capital of which no one can deprive him, and which will at all times assure him a safer and more abundant return than any investment." [27]

Classes were also available in English, Science, Music, Drawing, Geography, Needlework, Gymnastics, Dancing, Singing and Technical

Education. This broad curriculum made the Board Schools of the day appear dull in the extreme.

However, it was the way in which learning took place that was important. Children were taught in very small groups and were rarely lectured as such.

Sometimes teachers would offer particular classes or courses, but it was not unusual for groups of children, of different ages, to come to teachers with their own idea of what they wanted to study. There was no requirement that the children had to have a balanced and varied timetable. On the contrary, children were encouraged to go into subjects in depth, spending as much time as their interest determined. Records were kept, though, of what children studied, and the teachers apparently tried to strike a balance between encouraging and developing diversified interests and the autonomy of the individual child. A strong emphasis was put on teaching children to reason for themselves and not to accept facts blindly.

The history of the school is shrouded in mystery. Edith Thomas has suggested that it was opened on the advice of a M. Coulon, an agent provocateur, who had hit on the idea of a school as a relatively easy way to keep political exiles under surveillance.[28] What is clear, however, is that the school was closed by the authorities in either 1892 or 1893. This was after the police apparently discovered bombs and bomb-making equipment in the basement of the school. Louise Michel was not implicated, but three anarchists, Jean Battola, Victor Cailes and Fred Charles, were sentenced to ten years hard labour in the famous Walsall Anarchist show trial in 1892, partly as a result of the International School 'evidence'.

The importance of the International School is considerable. It was probably the first libertarian school to be founded in Britain. Further it illustrates the way in which ideas concerning libertarian education, which were flourishing on the continent, attracted attention and took root in Britain, admittedly in this first instance largely amongst political exiles. Probably most important of all, the school and its ideas were to have a lasting effect. As late as 1921 a group of anarchists were to recognise the debt they owed to Louise Michel and her school in Fitzroy Square when they opened a Sunday school on Fieldgate Street also in London.

3. NO-ONE TELLING US WHAT TO DO

The Anarchist-Socialist Sunday School, (163 Jubilee Street, Mile End, London, 1907)

If the International School was something of a private adventure born of revolutionary exiles, the Libertarian Sunday School, which developed at the Workers' Friend Club and Institute on Jubilee Street in 1907 was very different.

Between April 1881 and June 1882, 225,000 Jewish families fled the pogroms of Tsarist Russia.[29] It was the first, but not the last, mass exodus from the land of persecution. Many set their sights on a future in the United States, but a substantial minority sought immediate refuge in a nearer land of promise. So began the immigration of Jewish families into East London.

Work was not easy to find and those who acquired it mostly ended up in East End sweatshops. The reasons for this were straightforward; high seasonal unemployment compounded by language and cultural differences which created suspicion and hostility. Furthermore, rigid union rules restricted entry into certain occupations and many Jewish families were forced to eke out a pitiful existence in cabinet making or tailoring.

In July 1885 a monthly socialist paper, *Arbeter Fraint* (Workers' Friend), began publication. It immediately attacked the terrible working conditions in the sweatshops and served as a focus for the hostility that had been created by their mushrooming growth. A Workers' Club was established on Berner Street and soon became associated with the paper. Slowly Jewish workers became organised into small but active and determined trade unions. In 1889 there was a wave of strikes in London with some of the Jewish unions playing their part. In the next decade agitation increased to end the sweatshops.

The *Arbeter Fraint* became more and more identified with anarchists and anarchist thinking, as did the Jewish trade unions. This occurred because the Social Democratic Federation began to turn its back on the developing militancy of Jewish working people. Further, the Jewish people found the free-thinking ideas of anarchists a source of liberation from the cultural oppression that they had suffered for generations and the racism that they were experiencing in the so-called land of the free. Around the turn of the century, Rudolf Rocker, born in Mainz in the Rhineland in 1873, made contact with the East End Jewish movement and became editor of the *Arbeter Fraint*, now a weekly . This paper became a vehicle for libertarian ideas. Rocker campaigned tirelessly against the sweatshops calling for workers to organise themselves in non-hierarchical unions. He urged people to educate themselves, to embrace new ideas and to try and break the chains of their Ukrainian past, where only one person in every hundred had been allowed to attend school. Thus a new Club was established on Jubilee Street in 1906, open to all workers, with a library, a reading room and canteen. Here debates and discussions were held on subjects ranging from Darwinism to parliamentary reform, and lectures were given by Goldman, Kropotkin, Malatesta, Morris, Michel and many others on the widest range of subjects.

It was to this club that a young girl of thirteen, Nellie Dick, born Naomi Ploschansky, was taken by her father to listen to lectures, particularly those of Rocker. Nellie had been born in 1893, in the Ukraine in a village near Kiev, but had come to Britain at the turn of the century with her parents and her younger brother. Two elder sisters had remained in Russia with their grandparents. Her father was a cabinet maker who quickly became involved with the *Arbeter Fraint*. One of her earliest recollections was living in a house in Stepney Green:

> "I can remember how, when the door opened there was a flight of stairs right in front of us and we walked up and upstairs there was a small printing press where the Jewish working men's paper, The Workers' Friend, was printed. This was done by many of the comrades. Rudolf Rocker, who later became very well known as a leader and speaker for the Jewish population, although he was German and a gentile, he was always there and he and his Jewish wife set type with all the others." [30]

She also remembers tea and discussions going on, hand-in-hand, and how as a young girl she became absorbed with the talk of freedom and struggle. She remembers vividly one family discussion after a meeting her father had been to:

> "When father worked as a cabinet maker he told us about a strike and how if he went on strike it would be hard times, worse than now and it might last a long time and there would be no bread but how if he stayed on the job, he would get double pay and we would be better off but then he would be a scab. We asked him what was a scab? He explained and painted a picture of the lowest kind of creature that crawls on its belly and we shuddered and said, 'Oh, we don't want a father like that' and that we didn't mind doing without. Until this day I can't cross a picket line." [31]

The Ploschansky family, like many others, shared decisions, as they tried to live their lives in a libertarian manner. The children were encouraged to think for themselves. Nellie remembers:

> "I became very interested in anarchism. I listened to all the discussions that went on about various ideas. We lived opposite a pub and synagogue and I used to watch the people coming and going. I used to wonder about freedom and why people went to the synagogue. I read Peter Kropotkin's pamphlet, 'An Appeal to the Young'. I also read his 'Mutual Aid'. They both had an effect on me. Not having any money I would stand at the wheelbarrow on Mile End Road, sometimes for hours, and just read and read. Mixing with people, reading, living in an environment where there were always workers, always questions of strikes and unions - this was how I became an anarchist, I suppose." [32]

Throughout 1906, as she attended the club in Jubilee Street, Nellie began to notice the absence of women and children:

> "I noticed that the hall was always filled with men, very few women and definitely no young people, no youngsters. That bothered me for quite a while." [33]

It was this that determined her to ask the Workers' Friend Club and Institute to set up a school in the club. She remembers vividly what happened:

> "I got up at a meeting in the club and suggested that we ought to try and have a little school of some kind for working men's children. The answer came from the chair (and I know who was in the chair at that time, it was Alexander Schapiro), that we didn't need a school. I had heard about Ferrer's school in Barcelona and that was what I wanted. Schapiro said that they had to have such schools in Spain because children there didn't get anything but a religious education and they were not taught science. Schools in Britain were not like that. And besides there was no money." [34]

Nellie agreed neither that schools in Britain were unlike Spanish state schools, nor that money should be a problem. She asked her parents if she could organise a school every Sunday in their house:

> "We were still living at the house in Stepney Green where there was a large room with centre doors which could open out. I asked could I have children come there on Sunday? My parents agreed." [35]

And thus began the first of a series of schools that Nellie was to be associated with in the East End of London. In 1917 she was to leave for the USA and spend most of her working life in the Modern School movement there.[36] However, it was in the East End schools that her educational ideas really developed. Further, it was in these schools for working class children that the theory and practice of libertarian education began to develop in Britain for the first time.

The school in the house in Stepney Green was much influenced by Ferrer. Nellie was determined that it be a school that, however small, was run freely. She remembers:

> "Various comrades sent their children along and we read poetry and stories. We sang songs and talked about anarchism. We used to sing a poem written by William Morris, the great artist, and an anarchist of course in his ideas. It was called 'No Master High or Low'. Gradually the children got other children to come along and living opposite the synagogue the Rabbi would come out and stand in front of the door and when the children left he would follow them home and tell their parents they should not allow them to go there because it was a very bad place. But the children made no mind. They came. They liked it, these working class children who had nothing." [37]

No-one telling us what to do

Soon the number of children coming to the house became too many and the Workers' Friend Club and Institute agreed to take it over, fund it and accommodate it at Jubilee Street. This was announced in the *Voice of Labour* in September 1907.[38]

The school remained at Jubilee Street until June 1912, when it moved to Commercial Road where it was to begin a new life. Until then the school grew and grew at the club. The emphasis was put on allowing the children to organise themselves every Sunday and to discuss issues and topics which they felt to be important. The Workers' Friend Group used to organise many trips as well. Nellie remembers several to Epping Forest:

"Children that had never been out in the woods and so on came to Epping Forest. My brother came too and my little sister. I remember my father saying to her, 'Did you have a good time?' 'Yes', she said, 'wonderful, there were no parents, no-one telling us what to do.'" [39]

The aim was to open up children's minds, and allowing them the independence to develop their own ideas. This was in stark contrast to the state schools, and Nellie admits that the Workers' Friend Group became convinced of the importance of the school as a means of taking children out of the cultural and authoritarian bondage that existed in these schools. Nellie often talks of how the school politicised children and legitimised their hostility to the state schools:

"For instance when I took some children from Jubilee Street to a 1st May demonstration, one time it happened to be on a week day when they should have been in public school. I told them that if the teacher asked why they were away they were to tell them why they were not at school. They did. They were punished. I don't know what the punishment was but they said, 'We went because it was a Workers' Labour Day, it was a Workers' holiday and my father is a worker and we went, so there.'" [40]

The school also began to develop an adult section. The Jubilee Street Club had always organised lectures and some classes for adults. After the success of the school for children, more and more classes in literacy, in poetry and in languages, especially Esperanto, were organised for adults. Nellie remembers that Thursday evenings at the Club became a school night. She remembers too that many children from the Sunday School used to go and join the adults, and the barriers between adults and the young began to be broken down as both learned together. The school had become a genuine community venture.

The Sunday School that opened on Jubilee Street in 1907, and had its origins in the Ploschansky house in Stepney Green, is part of the unwritten history of libertarian education in Britain. Small the school might have been, but implicit in its aims, organisation and operation was a devastating critique of the national system of education. It was an illustration of the way in which children, and eventually a wider working class community, could and did develop the kind of educational institution they desired and that was attuned to their culture. The school was created by a young person; there have not been too many of them. It was controlled by its users. It ran on libertarian lines and it sought to develop a curriculum which was relevant to those who attended it. That curriculum was to develop considerably when the school moved to Commercial Road in 1912.

> ANARCHIST-SOCIALIST SUNDAY SCHOOL.
>
> *AUGUST 22nd, 1906.*
>
> Bethnal Green Junction
>
> to
>
> Chingford.
>
> CHILD.
>
> Outward)   (half.
>
> ---
>
> ANARCHIST-SOCIALIST SUNDAY SCHOOL
>
> *AUGUST 22nd, 1906.*
>
> Chingford
>
> to
>
> Bethnal Green Junction.
>
> CHILD.
>
> Return)   (half.

Tickets to ride: for a Sunday School outing

4. TEA PARTIES AND LECTURES

The West London Sunday School, (83 Charlotte Street, London, 1908)

Sadly not an awful lot is known about the Charlotte Street School. *Freedom* heralded its existence in December 1908 with an advertisement underneath a notice about the Jubilee Street School:

> "The West London Sunday School meets at 2.00 prompt at the Club, 83, Charlotte Street, w. Children over six years of age invited." [41]

However, exactly when the school opened is not clear. Neither is it clear who was involved in running the school and how it operated.

In an article about Thomas Keell, in the centenary edition of *Freedom*, Heiner Becker casts some light on who was involved in the school when he points out that Keell's wife, Lillian, became involved in running a Ferrer School in Charlotte Street. However, this was probably some time after 1908.

A little more about the school's later history can be gleaned from the pages of *Freedom*. On May 5 1912 it moved premises to 99 Charlotte Street, by then known as the Ferrer School rather than the West London Sunday School. This is important for it indicates the impact of Ferrer's ideas and death on the movement for libertarian education in Britain.

The school's curriculum seems to have been based mostly around lectures. There is a reasonably detailed report of the school in the June 1912 edition of *Freedom*:

> "On May 9th Mat Kavanagh gave an interesting address on Ghosts. This subject never fails to arouse the curiosity of the youngsters. The following two Sundays comrade Cook, a South Wales miner, gave interesting accounts of the way in which mines are worked. The description of the boys' hardships in the mine was vividly given by our comrade. The attention of the youngsters was soon arrested during these graphic accounts and if we continue to have such admirable lectures we bid fair to progress." [42]

The school apparently grew during the latter months of 1912. Funding was a problem but tea parties and socials were held in the school to raise money. On Sunday September 8th 1912, Malatesta gave an address there, on "Ferrer and the Modern School Movement", and there was an evening of recitations, songs and instrumental music by the school children. [43]

Although so little is known about it, the West London school seems to have been slightly different to its East London counterpart, there being a lot more emphasis on lectures and not necessarily so much on discussion. In part

No Master High or Low

this may have been due to the influence of James Dick, an anarcho-syndicalist from Liverpool, who had been responsible for the setting up of a Libertarian Sunday School in that city in 1908, but who moved to London in 1912. He eventually married Naomi Ploschansky, and became very involved in the East London school when it moved to Commercial Road in June 1912, and then to Stepney Green in March 1913.

5. TURNED OUT IN THE COLD

The Liverpool Anarchist-Communist Sunday School, (Toxteth Co-operative Hall, Smithdown Road, Liverpool, 1908)

James Hugh Dick was born in Liverpool on 7th October 1882. His parents were Scottish (his father was a policeman) and as a young man he became a tea-taster and the manager of a grocery store. Frustrated with his job in the store he began attending classes at the University of Liverpool, where he met Lorenzo Portet, a comrade of Francisco Ferrer. The two became friends and Jimmy, as he became known, became interested and active in anarchist politics and the anarchist movement. In his book on British Syndicalism, Bob Holton illustrates Jimmy's growing involvement with the anarcho-syndicalist movement in Liverpool.[44]

When Ferrer visited Liverpool in 1907, Jimmy met him, and in August 1908 reported in *Freedom* on the emerging movement in Liverpool:

"Our comrades here, the ever fresh and green, have set themselves the task of building up an industrial organisation, appealing to all who can act in sympathy from a class-conscious and nonparliamentary viewpoint to assist. On the lines of an open conference, several meetings for the discussion of same have already been held on the Tagus Street I.L.P. (Independent Labour Party) rooms, and the heartiness with which both I.L.P. and S.D.F. (Social Democratic Federation) comrades entered into the spirit of the idea would raise the hopes of the veriest pessimist." [45]

It was in this context that the Liverpool Anarchist-Communist Sunday School was founded in November 1908. It began meeting in the Toxteth Co-operative Hall on Smithdown Road, but in January 1909 moved to the ILP rooms on Tagus Street. By now there were thirty-eight children attending the school, and Jimmy affiliated it to the International League for the Rational Education of Children, which had been founded earlier that year. Lorenzo Portet was one of the British delegates to the League's committee, the other being William Heaford, who was much associated with the East London Libertarian Sunday Schools after 1912. Jimmy declared that the aim of the school was:

"To break down national prejudices and that patriotic piffle which is inculcated into the children of our present-day schools." [46]

Later in the year he was to write that the school had been organised to:

"... break down prejudices which are set up in the weekday school. To teach a child to think and act for itself. To spread the idea of Internationalism. To point out to them that humility, patience and submission are no longer virtues, if ever they were; and that they must own themselves. So long as the nation to be really believes that Jesus Christ and his mortal apes, kings, MPs, priests, etc., are its divine shepherds and rulers the present state of serfdom is secure." [47]

This was a powerful indictment of the emergent national state system of education, and throughout its existence up to 1916, despite periods of closure, the Liverpool Anarchist-Communist Sunday School was to maintain and develop a comprehensive critique of the state education system.

Jimmy Dick had a considerable amount of influence on the school; it was very much his concern. He saw lectures as the most important medium and believed that it was the content that mattered most in learning; he was not so interested in pedagogy. And yet at the same time he vehemently argued for the capacity and ability of young people to organise their own lives and ideas.

Throughout the Spring of 1909 there was a series of lectures. Mat Kavanagh spoke on "The Paris Commune", Comrade Devas on "The Beginning of the World", Fred Bowers on "Fairies", Will Dumville on "Ye Gods", Comrade Fairbrother on "An Englishman's Home" and Comrade Kean on "The Whiteway Colony".[48] There was clearly some controversy about the nature of the subject matter. Some people involved with the Sunday School objected to the highly political nature of the lectures. Jimmy, though, defended the programme most vehemently, not out of a desire to build some sort of vanguard of politically conscious and active young people, but because he believed young people had a right to learn about politics, notwithstanding their ability to make up their own minds about what they thought:

"I fail to understand why some of our comrades disagree with us in this method of propaganda. Is it because they are not yet emancipated from the thraldom of superstition themselves? Or do they imagine a child to be another Peter Pan, the boy who never grew up? I would ask our comrades to remember that in five or six years these youngsters will be rubbing shoulders with the workers, and their ideas, whatever they may be, will be ventilated. The State and the Church capture the children for they know that the children of today are the citizens of tomorrow. I have come to the conclusion that many of us Anarchists and Socialists think that free ideas should be carefully meted out to a selected few, and not scattered broadcast amongst little people and big people of all classes.

The State carefully looks after the patriotic superstition that is nursed in school. We have only to listen to the poetry and songs the children repeat from time to time. Samples such as 'Our glorious standard launch on high to match another foe,' etc. and such hate-provoking rhymes as the 'Revenge' which undoubtedly leave the child with the notion that England is a paradise. Very few children are free from this patriotic superstition, and I think it is one of the finest methods of propaganda to let them know there are some who believe it is as bad as the religious superstition. We have suffered too long from that disease known as the 'swelled head', believing that a child does not think. A child will think if we teach it to do so; but leave it to the mercy of the present school method, and it will grow up in a spirit of subserviency." [49]

The lecture programme continued throughout the summer of 1909, but at the new premises, the ILP rooms at 1 Clarendon Terrace, Beaumont Street. On 24th May, Empire Day, children from the school distributed 2,000 leaflets in the city centre attacking the celebration of Empire Day in schools.[50] This is an illustration of the way in which children from the school began to take up political activity as a result of their experiences there.

When the school reconvened in September, that activity was to continue and develop. The lecture programme continued throughout the autumn and winter, but in the early autumn many of the children at the school became involved in the campaign to support of Francisco Ferrer. On 17th October 1909, after the execution of Ferrer, the children at the school decided to change its name to the International Modern School. A pamphlet was also published entitled *The Martyrdom of Francisco Ferrer*.[51]

By December 1909 there were forty-five children at the school and it split into two, as the age range of the children had become difficult to manage. Both Mat Kavanagh and Fred Bowers remained very involved in the school and, in the Spring of 1910, with the help of Mat Roche, launched an adult class as well. This was very similar to the kind of development that occurred at the Jubilee Street School in London.

During 1910 the school began to change. It had become extremely popular and, although funding was a problem, many donations were being received. During 1910, instead of there just being a programme of lectures, the school began to develop a more systematic approach. By the Summer of 1910 there were several classes in operation. Mat Kavanagh had responsibility for a class of older children, young people on the verge of looking for employment. In response to demand his classes focused on the theory of evolution. This was a very popular class, apparently because of the informal discussions which took place. Clearly the method of teaching had become less didactic.

There was also a class of children around the age of ten or eleven under the tutorship of Will Jones and, interestingly, there was one separate girls' class for any who wished to attend. There were two other classes: the adult education class, where there was a much greater focus on literacy and numeracy skills, although there was language teaching also, and a class for children under the age of ten, which was usually conducted by Jimmy Dick himself.

However, the winter of 1910-1911 was to bring disaster. With the numbers rising and the lecture programme and discussions becoming ever more diverse, and under increasing influence from the children in the school the aftermath of the Houndsditch Affair and Sidney Street Siege took their toll. For the last two weeks of December 1910, and throughout January and February 1911, the Liverpool papers were full of nothing else. The *Liverpool Weekly Mercury*, the *Weekly Post* and the *Daily Post and Mercury* carried article after article about the attempted burglary at the shop of Mr H. S. Harris, a gold and silversmith's at 118A Houndsditch, London, which ended with the deaths of five policemen and the Sidney Street Siege. Moreover the press linked these events to an international anarchist conspiracy which had its sights set on destabilising British society. Under the headline "Liverpool and the Anarchists - Is there a centre in the city?" the *Liverpool Daily Post and Mercury* carried a particularly disturbing article on 8th January 1911. It began:

> "In the provinces the most active centre is probably Liverpool. In some places anarchist Sunday schools have been opened where the children are told tales, practised in revolutionary songs and generally brought up in the ways of violence." [52]

The International Modern School now became the subject of speculation and concern in the media. Even the *Fortnightly Review* was to warn of the dangers of this pioneering school. Although the Houndsditch Affair had been used to smear the anarchist movement as bloodthirsty and murderous the *Review* was concerned about the danger of alternative schools. Jimmy Dick took some satisfaction from this:

> "We have it on the authority of the Fortnightly Review that our school is the pioneer school. This is news to me. 'If the schools do not increase in England,' it says, 'it will not be for the want of zeal on the part of the English anarchists.' It is well, comrades, that we have the 'zeal' to do things ... To increase these schools especially such as the one now established in America, would certainly be a great factor in realising that international solidarity for which we Anarchists are ever striving." [53]

However, the ILP were not altogether pleased at the publicity which the school had attracted and evicted the school from its buildings on the grounds that the children were a disruptive influence. Jimmy reported to *Freedom* thus:

> "There was a flutter in the dovecotes of the S.E. Branch of the I.L.P. But how were they to tell me without showing the 'trembling at the knees'? Ah, that was the question. So they trumped up a flimsy charge that my young comrades were naughty, they sang secular songs on a Sunday, they danced and ran about as children are wont to do, and I allowed them to do so.
>
> After the press had made calumniating statements against us, and told us what we did and did not do, they sent their representative to visit us; but the caretaker of the I.L.P. - anxious about the reputation, such as it is, of the I.L.P. - denied our existence. When I reproached him for it - oh my! What a dance and song he made about the 'reputation', about the 'electorate', and the voters - for you must know that their branch was graced with a City Councillor, and there's the rub. In two days I received notice to quit at once, and so all my party comrades are now turned out in the cold, cold world because we had no reputation." [54]

Quite clearly Jimmy's cynical and witty pen was not just reserved for the State education system!

However, the Modern School found a new home at Alexander Mall, Islington Square, and was determined to continue. By May 1911, though, it became clear that the school would have to close because the children could not travel easily to the new buildings.[55]

And yet that was not to be the end. In the Summer of 1911 the Modern School reconvened for a Summer outing and a search was undertaken for new premises. Furthermore Jimmy was invited by the Socialist Sunday School Union of Liverpool and District, to report to a conference on 30th July 1911. He did so and, whilst supporting the development of the Socialist Sunday School Movement, he took every opportunity to propagandise for his libertarian view of alternative education:

> "One thing that seems to mar the socialist Sunday Schools is the repetition of the silly platitudes and a declaration known as the 'Socialist Ten commandments'. Who had the audacity to draw up such a series of impositions, and dare to cram them down the child's throat, I do not know. The repetition of these moral musings does not tend to develop the mind, but rather to hinder the natural development of the child. It is a religious practice, form of priestcraft and cajolery, which will only result in developing a subservient, humble, meek and lowly spirit in the heart of the child. We have seen enough of the orthodox Sunday School morality. It is a 'virtue' that makes one vomit. Let us have done with this ceremonial business. Stereotyped characters are not for the new era. We want to make men and women not 'virtuous' automatons."[56]

Jimmy Dick left for London the following year. His dislike of "ceremonial business" and his distaste for "virtuous automatons" could stand as an epitaph to his work in Liverpool and to the significance of the International Modern School there. What is much more important is that his writings and activities display a fundamental respect for the dignity and independence of young people. Whilst the school did not necessarily pioneer any radical teaching methods, it illustrated the impoverished nature of the State system of education. He strove to build a form of education that was attuned to working class culture and which believed in the right of young people to make up their own minds about all issues.

Under the guidance of Mat Roche the school opened again in 1913 at the Communist Club. It continued until the Summer of 1914 in the same vein and occasionally convened up to 1916, but by then Jimmy had become very involved in the Modern School initiatives in London. He was never to return to Liverpool except for the occasional visit.

No Master High or Low

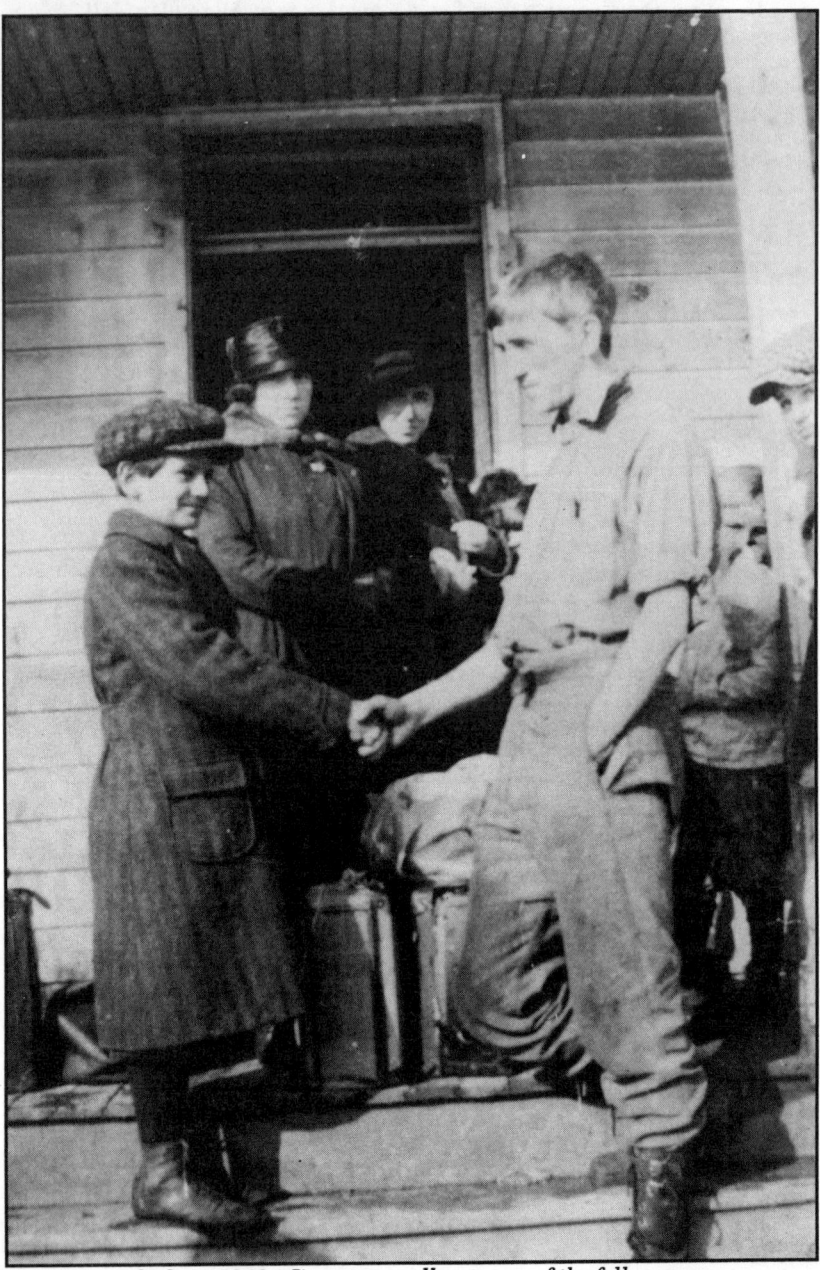

Stelton, 1918. Jim says goodbye to one of the followers.

6. THE TORCH OF LIBERTY

The Ferrer School, (New King's Hall, 135 Commercial Road East, London, 1912)

The Ferrer School which opened at King's Hall on 23rd June 1912 was a development from the Jubilee Street School. Quite why this development occurred is not certain, but it is more than likely due to space. When the school opened sixty children and thirty adults attended. It is probable that the club on Jubilee Street could not accommodate such numbers, especially as it was very often used by so many other people as well.

Mat Kavanagh opened the school and a speaker from the Central Labour College gave an address on mining. Thereafter the afternoon turned very much into a social event in celebration of the new venture. Throughout 1912 the school grew rapidly until, by the end of 1912, there were over one hundred children attending regularly. In March 1913 Nellie Dick reported to *Freedom* that the school was moving again, this time to 146 Stepney Green East. There were clearly more rooms that could be used at the new premises, and from now on the school was to be open every weekday evening.[57]

The school was now in great demand and became increasingly well organised. Nellie had met Jimmy at a May Day demonstration on 1st May 1913. He now became very involved in the school. Sunday afternoons were mostly given over to short lectures. The hand of Jimmy was much in evidence. However, children formed groups after the lectures, some by age, some by gender. Usually they wished to discuss the lecture topics, without the adults interfering, but frequently they began different discussions altogether. Sometimes children used the discussion groups to organise political activity. Nellie recalls that often many of the boys in the school would organise protection for Suffragettes:

> *"It was the time of the Suffragette Movement, when it was very rough, when they were chaining themselves up and speaking in Trafalgar Square. Our boys would organise to go out and make a circle around them and defend them from the police and from the soldiers and people who would try and disturb the campaigning. Our school was part of the movement that was struggling for freedom of thought."* [58]

Similarly Jimmy reported to *Freedom* that a discussion had taken place at one of these meetings to strike against the saluting of the flag in State Schools on Empire Day as was usually required. The children decided at first not to attend school, but many felt it cowardly not to face the issue head on. The children went to school and openly refused to salute the flag, thus making their own protest against British Imperialism.

Tuesday evenings were given over to a reading class. Whilst the teachers usually suggested books to read, any of the children's suggestions were accepted. A huge variety of books were read, including William Morris'

News from Nowhere. The school rapidly developed a large and wide-ranging library. Thursday evenings were given over to sports and dancing. The school had a cricket team, and Jimmy used to offer boxing lessons to any of the boys who expressed an interest

On Saturday afternoons the school also opened and began to develop a language section. Lessons were given in French and Spanish, but there was most demand for lessons in Esperanto. Mat Roche's daughter used to conduct this class.

During the Summer the school also organised many trips and social events, the latter being aimed at raising funds for the school. Jimmy described one trip for *Freedom* readers. It is worth quoting at length:

> "Saturday July 26th was a joy day for the rebels of this school. To journey straight from Whitechapel and be planted down in Shiplake-on-Thames was a contrast so vivid that it proved a fine lesson ... There we were right amongst the Vanderbilts and others of that ilk, enjoying the sunlight, blue skies, beautiful trees and the enchanting Thames, so long denied us. What a glorious time we had. And what children we all are when we are freely communing with nature. All thought of private property - if we have any - are left behind and the law and order of the old fogies passes away like a bad dream. Our revels are so free that the musts and must nots of which I for one am heartily sick, have no meaning in our joyous but too brief experience of an unchained existence. Let them call us savages if they will. We will accept the name, but we will prove to them that private owners do not even know how to enjoy the things they own. We are against the monopoly of enjoyment as of other things; and our fathers and mothers who have been good too long and so respectable must learn that the time is fast ripening when the 'bad uns' will play the devil with the fossilised notions of the past. Let us not worry about our "bad" behaviour; let us develop our rebellious nature; let us stick to our studies; and I venture to prophesy that in the near future we shall give a valuable object lesson to these suppressors of mirth and merriment. We have youth and 'savagery' on our side; in conjunction with knowledge there is hope." [59]

This report serves to remind us that the Ferrer School in East London, known by now usually as the International Modern School, was very much a school for working class children. Furthermore, in the stress it placed on dissent and knowledge we get some indication of how it had developed since 1907. Independence was encouraged and, more important, there was clearly a thirst for knowledge. It is interesting to speculate on the way in which this thirst for knowledge became synonymous with the anarchist movement at this time: knowledge and freedom went hand in hand.

As the school developed in size and organisation so too did the involvement of children in the running of the school. By January 1914 this was particularly evident in plans to publish a school paper called *The Modern School*. The first issue was written on cyclostyle and was published at the end of January 1914. The second issue was published in April and the third in July. Sadly none of these issues has survived, but they contained articles written by the children about the school and its activities. Issue number three apparently had an article entitled *What is Anarchy?* by Willie (aged 11), two letters from children in Canada and *Bits by the Bairns* (illustrated) by Henry (aged 7).[60] It was an eight page magazine with a frontispiece showing two children holding the torch of liberty on high with a copy of *Science and Truth* under their arms. The picture of a priest hurrying away with Bible in hand figured in the background.[61]

However, the issue over decision-making in the school became the subject of controversy at the end of 1914. In December 1914 Jimmy announced in *Freedom* that the International Modern School had moved yet again:

> "Be it known that the young rebels of the old school have taken up quarters at 24 Green Street, Cambridge Road East, where they will foregather every evening for conversation and merry-making. On Tuesday evenings at 8 o'clock a comrade has volunteered to teach French. Thursday evenings at 8 o'clock, discussion and reading class. Sunday afternoons at 3.30, our usual meetings." [62]

This seems innocent enough, but in the January 1915 edition of *Freedom* the following notice appeared:

> "The Modern School - we are requested to draw attention to the fact that only part of the school has shifted its quarters, the larger section remaining at 145 Whitechapel Road East. Those who may desire to become acquainted with us, please correspond with the Secretary of the Modern School, care of the 'Workers' Friend' 163 Jubilee Street, London, E." [63]

In the same issue of *Freedom*, a note written by Jimmy appeared. It said that the school had indeed divided into two parts with the "young bloods", as he called them breaking from the Jewish Anarchist Education League at the old school. Nellie Dick remembers this split and recalls that it was the older boys who wanted to leave. She and Jimmy decided to leave with them, and Rudolf Rocker's son, also called Rudolf, remained to continue with the other children. Jimmy seems to have made quite an issue of this at the time. In the *Voice of Labour*, in December 1915, he wrote of the split under the title *The School Children's Revolt*:

> "The East London Modern School has shifted into new quarters, at least a part of it - the rebel part. Realising their true position as Modern School children, this rebel part objects to the domination of elders, and like true Anarchists ... they have given a valuable lesson to their elders. 'We will not submit to what we consider to be an intolerable position,' they say, and straightaway, without reference to rules, regulations or precedent, they proceeded to find a meeting-place wherein they could meet and have their discussions, and run a school themselves. That they have succeeded goes without saying, for such a spirit, desirous of doing things, not dreaming them, is bound to succeed." [64]

Strong, libertarian polemic. But this seems to be what it was designed to be.

In the following issue of the *Voice of Labour*, the "rump" felt obliged to reply in an anonymous letter, but there is little doubt that the young Rudolf Rocker wrote it. He saw the issue differently, and presents a calmer picture. He wrote:

"It would appear from the note published last month about the Modern School that there is a section of children which is content to be 'dominated' and 'tyrannised' by its elders. We desire to protest against these expressions, for we are convinced that it is the writer's ignorance of our local affairs which causes him to use these words. Herewith our explanation to those that will hear us.

Some three years ago the present school was instituted by a group of Jewish comrades, known as the 'verband'; it was conducted under their guidance until about a month ago when the senior children, after discussion between themselves came to the conclusion that the school would prosper better if they themselves were concerned in the general management. On this point we all agreed. The division came because a part of the scholars (mainly the older boys) thought that the improvement could only be attained by a complete severing of the children from the 'verband' whereas we (mainly the older girls and smaller children) were of the opinion that the remedy was to be sought in co-operation between the adults and children ..." [65]

There the matter largely rested, although, despite the fact that the two schools went their separate ways, the issue did resurface from time to time, usually on Jimmy's initiative. What is important about this issue is that it ensures that we do not romanticise the history of the Modern School Movement in Britain; it was not without its ups and downs and personality clashes. More significantly, it is interesting to see controversy over such an important issue as decision-making. Apparently both schools benefited. A new "Education Group" was set up to run the school which remained at Whitechapel Road . It consisted mostly of children. At Green Street the older children set about developing their school on their own, with only minimal help from Nellie and Jimmy.

At Whitechapel Road Rudolf ran the school until he was interned. His half brother, Fermin, remembers some visits he made to the school whilst Rudolf was there and speaks affectionately about the way in which it was devoid of all forms of coercion:

"It was a unique school. Rudolf would have no rewards or punishments. Children learned as they wanted to learn." [66]

The school that Nellie Dick had begun as a young girl in 1907 had lasted for many years and, despite frequently changing premises, had maintained and developed a libertarian approach to education. Ferrer's ideas and approach took strong root amongst Jewish people in the East End, and they

The Torch of Liberty

constitute perhaps one of the most severe indictments of the London County Council Schools.

Nellie Dick, free school pioneer, photographed recently in the USA. A lifetime of dedication to liberty and freedom in education.

7. YOUNG REBELS

The Modern School, (24 Green Street, Cambridge Road, E. London, 1915)

The "breakaway" school did not stay too long on Green Street. By March it had moved to Ashburton House, Hertford Place, Globe Road, London.[67] Lectures still took place on a Sunday, but the school was also open on most evenings during the week. The school began to publish another magazine, this time entitled *Liberty*. Some copies have survived and they are full of information and articles written by the young people. They offer a most valuable insight into how people thought in the school, and what kind of an experience an alternative education offered.

Issue One, published in February 1915, contains a wide variety of articles. There are many on the war, condemning the British involvement, but also some written from a pacifist viewpoint. There are reports of activities in the school, and a marvellous piece about futurist art by "Barney". Perhaps the most interesting, though, is an article written by Ruben entitled *State Schools and the Workers*. It is worth quoting from:

> "The duty of the working classes is to take more interest in the education of the children in State Schools.
>
> They should protest against the teaching of religion and patriotism in schools."[68]

In Issue Two of *Liberty* there is an even wider range of articles, which gives some indication of the breadth of subjects and ideas considered at the school. There are features about evolution, votes for women and conscription. There is a review of Zola's *Germinal*. There are pieces of creative writing and poetry about truth and liberty. There is a report of a school strike at Ledbury:

> "The boys and girls of Ledbury played a lively part in the Herefordshire teachers' strike. They boycotted the strikebreaker headmistress by preventing her to open the school. When the children came into the schoolrooms they upset desks, threw inkpots, knocked down pictures etc.
>
> They have made use of direct action, which I think the grown-ups have never applied in their case and I hope they will take a lesson from the children."[69]

There is also a lively letters page, with one letter from The Modern School in Montreal, Canada, and another signed "Lily" about her reasons for liking the Modern School at Ashburton House:

Young Rebels

> "I must tell you my thoughts before I went to the Modern School and what my thoughts are now. Before I had friends from day school and they were very religious and as my parents were not so I could not make out which were right, my parents or my religious friends. At home we never keep up holidays (holy-days) but my friends always did so I felt very uncomfortable.
>
> Now I go to the Modern School and my new friends are just the same as I am. I feel much nicer because I see more children whose parents are like mine and wherever I go I am not ashamed to say what I think and that we of the Modern School are doing right." [70]

After the passing of the Military Service Act in 1916, "doing right" meant opposing the Act. Many of the boys in the school became involved in distributing anti-conscription leaflets. Nellie remembers this quite well:

> "And the war, our young boys of fourteen and fifteen were sometimes yanked up to the Tribunal because they were tall and they looked older. And once one of the boys was called up and he said that he belonged to this school, this Sunday school and he didn't think he had any war, and fighting to do with workers in Germany. And they said to him, 'How old are the children who attend that school? How young do they take them?' He says, 'As soon as they are able to think.'
>
> I want to say it was very tough on those youngsters because people, mothers who had sons, whose sons were going to war, would pin white feathers on them. They didn't know how old they were or not but if they were tall enough they would stick white feathers on them.
>
> We also had a serious matter happen one time when people had to go into hiding. They were getting older and they didn't want to be conscripted into the army and they were hiding out. Well soon after we had to close up at Ashburton House and Jim and I went to stay at Marsh House." [71]

Marsh House was at 1 Meckleburgh Street, an anarchist commune and meeting place for the London anarchists and the Anti-Conscription League. The Dicks lived there, and the school continued with them until they left for the USA in January 1917. However, the school was virtually at an end. In late 1915 and during 1916 it had its share of trouble with the authorities. The older boys were not the only ones under scrutiny. Nellie recollects:

> "Once we had a garden party which was raided by the police there was a spy in our group - who arrested everybody without a registration card. Also a Conservative paper in London, John Bull I believe, had a centre page article about our school which said that Jim was related to Lenin and I to Trotsky and that we dressed our children in little white aprons and were teaching them to make love and revolution.' [72]

In fact Jim and Nellie were legally married in 1916 so that Jim could avoid conscription, and when married men became eligible for the draft they

No Master High or Low

decided to go to the USA. With their departure the East London Modern School ended, but the Dicks were to become very involved in the International Modern School Movement in America, which became a strong alternative to the State system there. We can only speculate on how the movement in Britain would have fared had there not been such a sizeable emigration of Jewish anarchists to the USA. However, another Modern School was to appear in the 1920s.

8. FANNING THE FLAMES OF DISCONTENT

The International Modern School, (62 Fieldgate Street, Whitechapel, London, 1921)

On Sunday 6th March 1921 the last of the English International Modern Schools opened in Fieldgate Street. There was still a small group of Jewish anarchists living in London who had been associated with the Workers Friend Group, Louise Michel's International Modern School and the anarchist commune at Marsh House during the war. Some of these people, C. B. Warwick, Helena Applebaum, A. Gilbert, E. Michaels and H. and E. Samuels formed themselves into a group known as the Free Educational Group and announced in *Freedom*[73] in February 1921 that they were looking for teachers.

By June 1921, having started with thirty children, there were over one hundred at the school, and there was an average weekly attendance of eighty-five. The school declared its aim:

> "... to combat the anti-social environment of capitalist education as operating through the state schools and the religious institutions, and to bring up the child in the spirit of freedom."[74]

The school intended to entertain:

> "... such subjects that may develop the young mind towards the love of nature, beauty, self-expression and social outlook and activity."[75]

Further, the method was to attempt to:

> "... interest and instruct without the use of domination."[76]

These intentions illustrate the way in which the school was part of a continuing movement to build a libertarian school in the East End which would challenge the orthodox view of education; a school that was in the Ferrer tradition. A. Gilbert recognised the school's debt to Ferrer in October 1921:

> "... the present system of education which lays down hard and fast rules for children of all types is destroying their originality. The teachers and the Group, realising this, have one goal in view, the making of the individuality of each child, and to this end are following the rational methods as laid down by Francisco Ferrer."[77]

The school had classes in clay modelling, singing and story reading. These classes were aimed mostly at the younger children. There were other classes in freehand drawing, social science, free composition, hygiene, physiology and botany. There were also debating classes, where children would bring different topics for debate each week.

Lou Appleton was a pupil at the school for about two years. His mother, Helena Applebaum, (Lou changed his name to Appleton in the 1930s when he was having difficulty finding employment) was part of the New Education Group, and he remembers the delight of attending the school where, in the words of his mother, he felt part of a movement helping to:

"Fan the flames of discontent." [78]

However, Lou remembers the school even more as a rich cultural experience, where it was possible to learn in an atmosphere that was not straight-jacketed by rules and regulations, and where the teachers sought to offer a broad range of subjects. He remembers how often someone called Dr Salkind would come and hold everyone's attention for long periods with fascinating talks about evolution and science. He also recalls reading and singing the poetry of Morris Winchevsky. One poem in particular was recited time and time again. It was entitled *Yesterday, Today and Tomorrow*. It began:

"Our yesterday was very bitter

Our today is not sweet either.

Tomorrow only brings more rods for our backs

And chains for our hands and feet." [79]

Lou recalls that this poem must have been important to the Modern School because it focused everyone's attention on why they had to find an exciting form of education that would enrich people's experience rather than deaden them as the elementary schools did.

Lou also sheds even more light on the thirst for knowledge that existed amongst Jewish families, and the way in which libertarian views about education legitimised and helped quench this thirst:

"They had a terrific yearning to acquire more information. Many of them had come from little villages in the Ukraine where Jews had very little learning, or else what there was was tied up with religion. You have to remember that Jewish children in Russia could not go to school. Well about one in every hundred could go but that was all. Anarchism embraced knowledge. That was how it was in the Sunday school. All the time we were broadening our minds." [80]

Lou also recollects going on many trips, often in old high brakes to Epping Forest. *Freedom* records that the school often visited the Zoological Gardens. In the June 1922 issue of *Freedom* there is a detailed report about another trip entitled *May Day with the Modern School Children*:

"The children of the International Modern School took part in the demonstration in Hyde Park on lst May, the day on which worldwide Labour, young and old, registers its protest against Capitalism and exploitation. Starting from the Workers' Friend Club in a motor-charabanc, the children joined up with the East London contingent ... Through the minories and then Lower Thames Street and ... up Kingsway and along Oxford Street it went, the children singing waving their flags all the way full of pleasurable excitement." [82]

There is not any evidence that the children were involved in decision making in the school to any large extent, but the children produced three magazines entitled *The International Modern School Magazine*. Copies have survived and, as in the case of the earlier East London Modern Schools, they offer a valuable insight into the school.

In Issue One most of the writing is creative material with pieces about eclipses of the sun, ambition, domestic animals and a story entitled *The Boy in Rags*. There is also a revealing piece, *Why I attend the International Modern School*:

"In the present circumstances I am compelled by law to attend an elementary school which, unfortunately is not to my liking.

We find the discipline of the elementary schools very strict. It is not so in the International Modern School. Our discipline is self-respect, that is we do not run about like hooligans knowing that the teachers can do us no harm. By doing no harm I mean that they do not cane us.

Some of the subjects taught in the International Modern school are: clay modelling, astronomy, natural sciences, drawing in absolute freedom. In the council schools we are taught to be patriotic, but in the International Modern School, we are taught to be lovers of freedom." [83]

There is a similar range of issues covered in the second issue of the magazine. There is a piece by P. Rotbart about ancient village communities, an open letter to the Ferrer School at Stelton in America and short pieces about Russia, the Tate Gallery and India. Lou Appleton has a piece in the magazine about the life of Kropotkin. Perhaps the most interesting, though, is a satirical piece which is continued in Issue Three, attacking the State School system and offering the Modern School Method as a real alternative.[84]

Issue Three is in exactly the same vein, and is superbly produced. In addition to a wide range of articles there are some interesting notes about the school.[85] By December 1922 it was also open on Tuesday and Thursday evenings. On Tuesday, classes in Esperanto were held by N. Whycer, and on Thursday there were play rehearsals. All of this is indicative of a continuing Modern School tradition, which by this stage was nearly fifteen years old.

Lou Appleton eventually became a school teacher, spending most of his time in secondary modern schools. He believes that his time in the Modern School was very important to him, and feels that he took into the State

No Master High or Low

Schools a desire to relate to the children as human beings, and an intention to try to constantly encourage them to think for themselves and to question all issues.

The Fieldgate Street School continued until 1928, when it was forced to close because of a shortage of funds and difficulty in finding teachers. So drew to an end a twenty year history of International Modern Schooling in Britain, a history that has unjustifiably remained buried ever since.

9. THE COMMON THREADS

England and the Movement for Libertarian Education, 1890 - 1930.

There is clearly a rich history of libertarian education amongst working class people in England between 1890 and 1930. It does not amount to a mass movement, but a careful and detailed examination of the Libertarian Schools and Sunday Schools in London and Liverpool reveal that working class communities had a vision of the type of school they wished to see. They were perfectly aware of the aspects of the national state system that they did not like, and they proved perfectly capable of organising and funding their own schools, often for quite long periods of time.

The Modern Schools in England form part of the wider European movement for libertarian education in the period 1890 to 1920. The League for the Rational Education of Children was clearly an international organisation in the truest sense of the word, and the hand of Ferrer very apparent. By 1920 the influence of the League had spread as far as the Makhnovists in the Ukraine, and ultimately it was to play a significant role in the development of the Modern School movement in the USA.

The Schools also reveal a considerable amount about the nature of the anarchist movement in Britain before and during the First World War, admittedly mostly the Jewish anarchist movement. Many of the schools emerged in communities where anarcho-syndicalist ideas and activities were much in evidence, particularly in the East End. Perhaps more important was the thirst for information, for knowledge, for culture, which was an important factor in the attraction of many peoples and communities towards anarchist ideas. An examination of the history of the schools indicates a strong belief in direct action as a justifiable and liberating form of political activity. The active support for the Suffragettes, the refusal to submit to flag saluting on Empire Days, the leafleting against conscription and ultimately the "dodging of the draft", all illustrate that the Schools were not just places of study, but that they were part of the anarchist movement, almost a youth section.

As far as practice is concerned, the schools had their own individual characteristics, but there were many common threads. In the first place the schools expressed a fundamental belief in the autonomy of the individual. They sought to develop an approach to learning and teaching that was individualised, insofar as children were encouraged always to think for themselves in the way they desired.

There was no requirement that children should follow a particular programme of study. The range of subjects that were offered in the schools enabled children to make real choices about what they wanted to study. In fact the range of subjects in the schools made the State Elementary Schools appear boring and stifling by comparison. Clearly the children who attended the Modern Schools felt this to be the case. Children in the Modern Schools had power, they were able to exercise control over what they studied, with whom they studied and for how long, and to what end they studied.

In some of the schools they were also involved in the management and decision-making processes, although it would be misleading to exaggerate this. There is clearly little evidence, for example, to suggest that this was the case at the International School, the Liverpool Modern School or the Fieldgate Street School.

Secondly, the schools were united in their rejection of coercion and rewards and punishments. This was a reaction to the inhumane treatment of children in State Schools and an expression of belief in the dignity of youth. The schools were happy places, there was no compulsory attendance and yet the numbers of children who attended them were really quite considerable and in all the schools there was clearly a demand for them to be open "all hours".

The third area of uniformity of approach lies in the schools' united and comprehensive critique and rejection of state schooling, on the grounds that government sought passivity and docility amongst its young, and conformity to a particular moral, political and religious code. The awareness on the part of the school organisers, the teachers and the children of the apparently hidden purposes of a national State system of education are clear. All the Schools sought to develop a curriculum that was open-ended and that did not serve to merely reinforce the capitalist status quo.

Taken as a whole, the Modern Schools of the period 1890-1930 constitute a coherent and active critique of the national system of education. They are amongst the first educational initiatives in Britain which sought to place the child, and nobody else, at the forefront of the theory and practice of education. They pre-date Homer Lane and A. S. Neill and the later libertarian initiatives of the mid-1920s. Most important of all, they lay to rest the idea that libertarian ideas about education are the property of the middle class because only this class has had the money to afford an alternative education and the time and security to indulge in the luxury of free thought. The history of the Modern Schools belongs firmly alongside the work that Phil Gardner has pioneered on the lost Elementary Schools of Victorian Britain, and alongside the work that Stephen Humphries has done on working class opposition to State Schooling.[86]

However, it is not enough just to celebrate the existence of these schools. Their significance lies more in what they said, believed and represented, than in what they did. Whilst it is easy to castigate historians of education for their failure to look at these schools, there has to be a reason for this that goes beyond academic blindness. The schools failed to have more impact than they did because of their isolation. Although they were part of a broader political movement, there is little evidence to suggest that they looked to link up with other radical and progressive initiatives. Admittedly they were community projects, and served the immediate interests and concerns of their respective communities, but Louise Michel, Nellie and Jimmy Dick, and Helena Applebaum had a vision of education that they wished to see develop across society. The mystery and the mistake is that they did not take their message outside the confines of their own communities and political movements.

NOTES

1. Holmes, E., *What is and What might be.* Constable, London, 1911.

2. Holmes, E., *In defence of what might be.* Constable, London, 1914.

3. Holmes, E., op.cit., p315.

4. *Times Educational Supplement*, March 1916.

5. *The New Era*, Vol.1, No.1, January 1920.

6. For an excellent survey and analysis of the development of ideas concerning integral education see Smith, M.P., *The Libertarians and Education*. Allen and Unwin, London, 1983.

7. Goldman, E., *Anarchism and Other Essays*. Mother Earth Publishing, New York 1911, p149.

8. *Liberty*, Boston, October 1894.

9. Kennan, C., *A Libertarian School*. in *Freedom*. London, September 1897.

10. Goldman, E., op.cit., p35.

11. Turin, Yvonne., *L'Education et L'Ecole en Espagne de 1874 à 1902*. Paris 1959, p317. Quoted in Joll, J., *The Anarchists*. Eyre and Spottiswood, London, 1964, p234. (NOTE: I have drawn heavily on Paul Avrich's admirable book on *The Modern School Movement in America*, Princeton University Press, New Jersey, 1980, for much of the information about Ferrer.)

12. Ullman, J., *The Tragic Week: A Study of Anti-clericalism in Spain, 1875-1912*. Cambridge, Mass., 1968, p34. Quoted in Avrich, P., op.cit., p7.

13. Smith, M., op.cit., p47.

14. Ferrer, F., *The Origin and Ideals of the Modern School*. Watts and Co., London, 1913, p51.

15. *The Voice of Labour*. No.32., London, 24th August 1907.

16. *Freedom*. London, June 1908.

17. Ibid., August 1908.

18. Ibid., March 1910.

19. Ibid., February 1913.

20. *The Labour Annual*. London, 1900, p141.

21. *The Reformers' Year Book*. London, 1903, p101.

22. Thomas, E., *Louise Michel*. (Translated by Penelope Williams), Black Rose Books, Montreal, 1981.

23. Clemenceau, G., *La Melée Sociale*. Charpentier et Fasquelle, Paris, 1895, p138.

24. *Prospectus for the International School. Lib ED* Archive.

25. Ibid.

26. Ibid.

27. Ibid.

28. Thomas, E., op.cit., p318.

29. Fishman, W., *East End Jewish Radicals 1875-1914*. Duckworth, London, 1975, p30.

30. *Interview with Nellie Dick*, Miami, Florida. September 1986. *Lib ED* Archive.

31. Ibid.

32. Ibid.

33. Ibid.

34. Ibid.

35. Ibid.

36. This has been well documented by Avrich, P., *The Modern School Movement* op.cit.

37. *Interview with Nellie Dick*, op.cit.

38. *Voice of Labour*. London, 14th September 1907, p175.

39. *Interview with Nellie Dick*, op.cit.

40. Ibid.

41. *Freedom*. London, December 1908, p92.

42. *Freedom*. London, June 1912, p48.

43. *Freedom*. London, September 1912, p72.

44. Holton, B., *British Syndicalism 1900-1914*. London, 1977, pp59-60.

45. *Freedom*. London, August 1908, p59.

Notes

46. *Freedom.* London, February 1909, p16.

47. *Freedom.* London, May 1909, p39.

48. Ibid.

49. Ibid.

50. *Freedom.* London, June 1909, p47.

51. *Freedom.* London, November 1909, p87.

52. *Liverpool Daily Post and Mercury.* 5th January 1911, p7.

53. *Freedom.* London, April 1911, p31

54. *Freedom.* London, February 1911, p15.

55. *Freedom.* London, May 1911, p40.

56. *Freedom.* London, August 1911, p63.

57. *Freedom.* London, March 1913, p23.

58. *Interview with Nellie Dick*, op.cit.

59. *Freedom.* London, June 1913, p15.

60. *Freedom.* London, July 1914, p55.

61. *Voice of Labour.* London, 3rd July 1914, p3.

62. *Freedom.* London, December 1914, p90

63. *Freedom.* London, January 1915, p8.

64. *Voice of Labour.* London, December 1915, p3.

65. *Voice of Labour.* London, January 1915, p4.

66. *Interview with Fermin Rocker.* December 1987. *Lib ED* Archive.

67. *Freedom.* London, March 1915.

68. *Liberty.* Vol.1, No.1., *The Irresponsible kids of the Modern School*, London 1915, p5.

69. *Liberty.* Vol.1. No.2., London, 1915, p4.

70. *Liberty.* Vol.1. No.2., op.cit., p6.

71. *Interview with Nellie Dick*, op.cit.

72. Quoted in Avrich, P., op.cit., p242.

73. *Freedom.* London, February 1921, p14.

74. *Freedom.* London, June 1921, p32.

75. Ibid.

76. Ibid.

77. *Freedom.* London, October 1921, p63.

78. *Interview with Lou Appleton.* London, October 1987. *Lib ED* Archive.

79. Ibid.

80. Ibid.

81. *Freedom.* London, August 1922, p55.

82. *Freedom.* London, June 1922, p42.

83. *The International Modern School Magazine.* Vol.1. No.2., London, December 1921, p7.

84. *The International Modern School Magazine.* Vol.1. No.3., London, June 1922, pp3-4.

85. *The International Modern School Magazine.* Vol.1. No.3., London, December 1922, p5.

86. Gardner, P., op.cit., and Humphries, S., *Hooligans or Rebels?*, London, 1981.

PART TWO

Rural Retreats

THE LIBERTARIAN PRIVATE ADVENTURES IN EDUCATION

1890 - 1990

1. BEYOND THE CRANKS

Private debates for private adventures, 1890 - 1960

One of the most significant strands in the history of progressive, as opposed to libertarian, education in Britain is to be found in the private sector. Mention has already been made of the New Schools Movement, which emerged at the beginning of the twentieth century.[1] In 1934 a group of private schools collaborated in producing *The Modern Schools Handbook*, in which each contributing school gave an account of itself.[2] And in 1962, by way of a follow-up, H. A. T. Child edited *The Independent Progressive School*, which effectively updated the earlier guide.[3] These schools preached humanity, but generally they were not libertarian. A. S. Neill, given editorial space in the July 1920 issue of the *New Era*, suggested that, despite the progressivism apparent in the early wave of pioneering private schools, they still remained bastions of authority which sought to impose adult ideas and tastes on children. He labelled them "crank schools":

> "At our crank schools we find too many ideals. Children whose natural liking is for Charlie Chaplin are surrounded with art pictures, portraits of Walt Whitman and Blake; they hear music by Schumann and Beethoven ... while they prefer to listen to a foxtrot on a gramophone ... The psychoanalyst who treats children from a crank school early discovers that all the good taste has driven the more earthy part of the child's psyche underground ... The ideal of education is to allow a child to express all his soul, and Charlie Chaplin is just as necessary in the scheme as Shakespeare."[4]

These libertarian criticisms were directed at such places as Abbotsholme, Bedales and King Alfred's but, although they were made in 1920, they were still appropriate for many schools which were founded later and which were given glowing praise by T. Blewitt and H. A. T. Child.[5]

However, there were a number of private adventures in education which warrant consideration as libertarian initiatives.[6] The general purpose of this section is twofold. Firstly, it aims to rescue these schools from the progressive tradition, where in the main they have languished, being lumped together with highly authoritarian schools with a human face, and look closely at what made them distinctive. Secondly, within the overall structure of the book, it aims to emphasise that these initiatives are still only a small part of the history of libertarian education and schooling in Britain since 1890. Initially a survey of the debates and developments out of which these schools emerged is essential, in order to understand their direction, practice and significance.

For all A. S. Neill's criticisms of the schools associated with the New Schools Movement, this organisation was to be an important body in the history of libertarian education, if only because it provided the impetus for a debate about educational theory. The desire for such a debate was enormous as the outbreak of war approached. We have already seen how questions about the fundamentals of education were being asked by large sections of the working class in London and Liverpool, by a wide variety of socialist organisations, by School Inspectors like Edmond Holmes, and even by the *Times'* new *Education Supplement*.

Inspired essentially by the progress of the New Schools Movement, it was Edmond Holmes, in conjunction with Beatrice Ensor, another School Inspector, who sought to develop this debate and give it a focus. Sadly, when they established the New Ideals in Education Group, in 1914, they did not invite anyone from the anarchist or socialist movement. It may be, though, that they were unaware of the International Modern Schools and the important focus given to education in such journals as the *Reformers' Year Book*. Yet this is an indictment itself.

The New Ideals in Education Group was therefore a terribly middle class affair, concerned mainly with the private sector, and with a peer as its president. Nonetheless, when the first national conference of the Group was convened at Stratford in 1915 that very peer, Lord Lytton, said that the conference welcomed:

> "... all ideas which represent the substitution of the freedom and self-expression of the pupil for the imposed authority of the teacher." [7]

This was the spirit that Holmes brought to the group. In 1911 he had written:

> "The adult that exacts from a child blind faith and literal obedience, and having secured these, proceeds to tell the child in the fullest detail what he is to do, to think (or pretend to think), to feel (or to pretend to feel), is devitalising his whole personality ... Unless the child himself - his soul, his self, his ego, call it what you please - is behind his own actions, they are not really his." [8]

These were sentiments that Ferrer and the Dicks shared. They were sentiments that Neill shared as well, although ten years after they were written Neill was questioning how far the New Ideals Group remained true to such sentiments.

Holmes and Ensor were working in difficult times despite there being a receptive audience. Encouraged, though, by Holmes and Homer Lane,[9] who had both read papers at the Stratford conference, Ensor founded the Theosophical Fraternity in Education for teachers within the Theosophical Society. It was this group which was to launch the *New Era*. However, it was the embracement of Theosophy by the New Ideals Group which was to eventually play a major part in the alienation of the libertarians, largely led by Neill, something that was inevitable given the highly distinctive nature of the theory of libertarian education.

That was to come a little later, however. Earlier, the end of the war had brought great hope for the New Ideals Group. Norman MacMunn captured this when he wrote:

"Educational ideas which seemed startling in 1914 were hardly likely to perturb the world of 1920. Not only have men supped full with horrors, but through these horrors their vision has penetrated to primitive realities. Now is mankind ready to accept the failure of courses hitherto considered good and wise and safe ... and to examine more closely, and with less confidence, the foundations of their own judgements." [10]

Indeed, in the immediate aftermath of the war, many people were searching for ways to establish a new world; one rooted in co-operation and trust. The anarchists on Fieldgate Street sought such a world. So too, at the other end of the social spectrum, did Cambridge undergraduates:

"Most of us were pacifists of one sort or another, angry with the wicked old men that had stumbled into war and worse still had carried through a peace that mocked the ideals for which so many of our school friends had died." [11]

In response to an obvious need, the Theosophical Fraternity in Education held a national conference in 1920 but, more importantly, began publishing a journal. It was published from 11 Tavistock Square, London, and Beatrice Ensor was the editor. It was called *Education for the New Era: An International Quarterly Journal for the Promotion of Reconstruction in Education*. It has always been known as simply the *New Era*. Its opening editorial proclaimed that:

"Freedom, Tolerance and Understanding have burst the doors so carefully locked upon them in the secret chambers in the souls of men ... in all realms of thought and action they move: not least in education." [12]

However, as Ray Hemmings has perceptively noted, it is not a revolutionary or libertarian spirit that one catches from the pages of the early issues of the *New Era*. On the contrary the world was to be reformed by:

"... the teachers' greater respect for the child's feelings and opinions, through the medium of self-government, through an emphasis on humanistic values though by no means at the expense of religious values and by giving the child an environment infused with beauty." [13]

Such ideals were confirmed in the Theosophical principles of a new organisation that emerged out of the *New Era* in 1921, The New Education Fellowship. The first principle stated:

"The essential aim of all education is to prepare the child to seek and realise in his own life the supremacy of the spirit. Whatever other view the educator may take, education should aim at maintaining and increasing spiritual energy in the child." [14]

A. S. Neill could not stand the platitudes of the Theosophists, neither could he accept the reverence paid to Montessori, nor could he tolerate the lack of a perspective about authority and how to set about empowering children.

Having taught for a while at King Alfred's School, he was invited by Beatrice Ensor, who had been impressed with his *Dominie's Log* and *Dominie Dismissed*, to co-edit the *New Era* in July 1920. She was to regret this, but we should not. Libertarian education owes a huge debt to Neill, who captured magnificently the difference between it and its progressive shadow. The assault that he launched on the New Schools Movement, the Theosophists and the *New Era*, albeit a necessary one, ensured that The New Education Fellowship, which he never joined, became ever more liberal and safe. With the subsequent establishment of Summerhill and the emergence of an alliance between Neill, the Russells at Beacon Hill, and the Elmhirsts and Curry at Dartington Hall, Neill effectively created one of the main strands of libertarian education and schooling in Britain.

As has already been noted, in the third issue of *New Era*, in July 1920, Neill bore down on what he called the crank schools; schools where there were not many ideals. He had no time for the view held by the Theosophists about the supremacy of the spirit. He abhorred the way in which, at King Alfred's, Bedales and Abbotsholme, adults were constantly giving talks to children about what was and was not "good taste".

Although it was not included in his blast of 1920, Neill's rejection of Theosophy as a basis for educational freedom was underpinned by his rejection of the Montessorian method to which the Theosophists paid such attention.

Maria Montessori had been the first woman to qualify as a doctor in Italy. She worked initially with children who had mental disabilities, but also worked amongst poor working class children in Rome. She developed a strong belief in the ability of children to control their own activities and, at her school in the Via Giusti in Rome, she abolished all timetables. Children could choose their own activities and pursue them for however long they wished. Neill welcomed many of Montessori's ideas, in particular her belief that children should be freed from the dominance of adults. However, he was sceptical about her book *The Montessori Method*, which was translated into English in 1912, and found the devotion of Edmond Holmes' and the 1914 New Ideals conference to her ideas worrying in the extreme. This was because he found her method highly intellectual and sadly lacking in emotionalism. The Montessori world was:

"... *too scientific for him, too orderly, too didactic.*" [15]

This was essentially because Montessori had developed a range of "didactic apparatus" to assist children's work. For all her testified belief in freedom, this apparatus was, in her eyes, a necessary, even compulsory, tool.

From a libertarian viewpoint Neill's criticisms were well-founded for, whilst children could exercise choice and seek out adventure under the Montessori method, adults still controlled the environment. The system was authoritarian because it was dominated by adult guidance and "nourishment". For example, children were to work with the apparatus, they were definitely not to play with it.

Neill's dissatisfaction with the Montessori method moved him to the July 1920 "depth charge", as Ray Hemmings has described it.[16] It also moved him to begin a course of lectures in the Eustace Miles' Restaurant in London, and to engage on a speaking tour. In the main he spoke about anti-authoritarianism in education, self-government and the relevance of the New Psychology of Psychoanalysis. His life at the *New Era* was unlikely to last long.

However, he did speak out at the 1921 conference, organised by the *New Era* in Calais, where the theme was *The Creative Self- Expression of the Child*. Neill spoke on the vital corollary, *The abolition of authority*. Here he enlarged on one of his most essential convictions, arguing that the use of authority for instilling adult morality had the particularly damaging effect of stifling the natural morality of the child. He demanded that authority in schools be abandoned, and with it all forms of moral teaching. It frightened most people at the conference to death. His ideas were dangerous:

> *"... libertarian, anarchic ..."* [17]

Neill had shaken a few "high-lifers", as he liked to call them, and there can be no doubt that he enjoyed the mischief of turning heads, but his ideas were well-founded. He abhorred the way in which self-government was used in the 'crank schools'. For him it rarely went further than miniature Bow Street proceedings, where the children ended up becoming spies and policemen.

Beatrice Ensor began receiving a lot of mail about Neill, and as her son remembers:

> *"I vaguely recall my mother later in life referring to Neill as a person for whom she had an admiration but whom she could not accompany so far down the road of libertarianism."* [18]

Matters came to a head with the publication of the October 1922 issue of the *New Era*. Beatrice Ensor had been seduced by the fashionable ideas of Coue concerning suggestion and auto-suggestion. Norman McMunn had been invited by Ensor to review Coue's book on the subject for the *New Era,* which he accordingly did. The review was a sympathetic one. However, Neill could not resist adding a warning footnote to the review:

> *"Still, McMunn, I'm afraid of this suggestion business. It is not touching root causes."* [19]

Neill's main worry was that suggestion would work against the unconscious and undermined the whole point of psychoanalysis, which he had learned from Freud via Homer Lane. Ensor would have none of this, and in the January 1923 issue of the *New Era* she wrote:

> *"Mr Neill has very definite views on psychology and education, and it is probable that I print many opinions with which he would not agree. This has occurred in connection with my October editorial on suggestion and*

> *auto-suggestion and therefore in fairness to 'The Dominie' I think his name must be dropped from the magazine as co-editor."* [20]

Neill was little bothered about this because since August 1921 he had, in any case, been in Hellerau, Germany working in an international libertarian school. This school eventually came to Lyme Regis in 1924, and was named Summerhill. In 1927 it moved to Leiston, in Suffolk, where it has remained ever since. It is undoubtedly the oldest surviving libertarian school in the world.

However, Neill's relationship with the *New Era* and with The New Education Fellowship did not terminate there, and the developments in that relationship over the next five years reflect more light on the difference between progressivism and libertarianism. When Summerhill moved to Leiston, Neill very quickly found allies to his cause. In September 1927 Bertrand and Dora Russell opened Beacon Hill, a small school on the West Sussex Downs. Although Neill found himself at variance with Bertrand, he was attracted to the school and, when Bertrand left in 1931, Neill found that he and Dora had many common educational ideas.

Similarly Neill was excited about a school that opened in September 1926, near Totnes in Devon. It was called Dartington Hall, and was run by Leonard and Dorothy Elmhirst. In 1931 the Elmhirsts appointed Bill Curry to head the school.

It was this triumvirate of libertarians, Neill, Russell and Curry, that took a meeting of The New Education Fellowship by storm at Tavistock Square, London, in October 1932. Beatrice Ensor wanted to set up a new association of progressive schools to provide mutual help, advice, information and resources. She had to invite the three, but all were agreed that the Fellowship had to move towards developing libertarian ideals if they were to belong to it. Dora Russell recalled the meeting, which was chaired by Clifford Allen, in an interview with Jonathan Croall, shortly before she died:

> *"Allen was trying, as he always had done at the I.L.P. (Independent Labour Party) to reconcile opposing points of view. A. S. Neill and I were regarded as so far to the left, educationally speaking, as to be almost beyond the pale. It was said that we might be admitted to the organisation, though there were some members who would definitely not wish the names of their schools to be set beside Neill's and mine. I found this very funny and remarked that possibly Neill and I might return the compliment and refuse open association with them."* [21]

Neill, though, could stomach the high-lifers no more. After the meeting he wrote to Curry:

> *"I've told Mrs Ensor that I'm chucking those bloody meetings. You and I and Dora Russell talk a different language from them."* [22]

Exactly what that language was, and how united, remains to be seen, but it is a shame that the triumvirate did not seek out another contemporary initiative, the Forest School.

Beyond the Cranks

The end of the First World War also brought a revolutionary idealism to what could be called the Edwardian Green movement. Even before the war, libertarian groups had established co-operative colonies, the most famous of which was at Whiteway in the Cotswolds, where the emphasis was on creating an holistic ideology. Peter Kropotkin's *Fields, Factories and Workshops* and *Mutual Aid* were remarkably influential. The early 1920s saw a score of new movements emerge, many concerned specifically with young people. There was a group called the Woodcraft Folk, which sought to propagate the ideals of outdoor life. There was the green-shirted Douglas Social Credit Movement, and a pacifist band called the Hargreaves Group. Above all, there were the many hiking and camping movements which sought to open up the British countryside to greater numbers of young people. None of these movements could be considered libertarian, for many were organised hierarchically and were influenced by Baden Powell and the Scouting Movement. However, it was the dream of Ernest Westlake, the founder of the Order of Woodcraft Chivalry in Britain, to found a school. Westlake was an enigmatic character, and certainly no libertarian, but when he died in 1922, having bought forty acres of land in the New Forest for his project, Cuthbert Rutter began to develop the idea of creating a pioneering school there.

Rutter was not a high-lifer. He had taught in the East End of London, but was much attracted by the ideas of Kropotkin and by Westlake's emphasis on the rural environment. Most important of all, he was determinedly anti-authoritarian in his attitude to children, and a great believer in self-government. He became head of the Forest School, as it became known, in 1929, and remained there until the school closed in 1940, when the buildings were taken over for the war effort. As we shall see, the school was very different to Summerhill, Beacon Hill and Dartington Hall. But in one very important way it was much the same. Children held real power to control their own lives and learning.

If the outbreak of the Second World War was to see the closure of one pioneering private adventure in education, it also witnessed a minor wave of new ones. In 1940 John Aitkenhead opened Kilquhanity House in Kirkudbrightshire, Scotland. He was much inspired by Neill and described the school as:

"... a real war effort ... the answer of a number of men and women to the mass violence that broke across the world in 1939." [23]

In 1986 he recalled, in more detail, the circumstances in which the school was set up:

"What was it that was so attractive in Neill's idea of a school at that time? To answer this we have to remember that Europe was at war for the second time in a generation, and that Neill, along with so many others, had come out of World War One in 1919, a mere 20 years earlier, determined to do something about the madness that allowed the youth of Germany and France and Britain to be killing each other, with Americans coming in to help the war that was to end all wars. And here it was again! The babies of returning soldiers of 1919 and 1920 were being conscripted again for cannon-fodder. And moreover this was just

75

70 years after the introduction of compulsory 'education' right across Europe. So that men and women of Neill's age were thinking that if education, by way of schools, could do anything about such situations in the future, then there must be schools based on non-violence. We have to remember also, if we are to understand the appeal of Summerhill then, that the start of the war, as well as producing a flow of volunteers and conscripts for war, released a tremendous flood of idealism that was anti-war." [24]

Kilquhanity was built on the ever-surfacing tradition of libertarian principles. So was Burgess Hill, which opened in 1936 and prospered during the Second World War.

Another which opened in 1940 was Monkton Wyld School in Dorset. It was pioneered by Carl and Eleanor Urban, who had moved from Camden to escape the blitz. Neither of them could be described as libertarians, and in its early years the school belonged in the progressive camp of independent initiatives that Neill had rejected. In the late 1960s, however, the school began to undergo considerable change, including a decision not to have a head teacher. The only other school like this was Burgess Hill. In both institutions this audacious, anti-hierarchical measure was accompanied by an anti-authoritarian approach to teaching and learning. Burgess Hill and Monkton Wyld, together with Kilquhanity, constitute a second wave of libertarian private adventures in education.

Monkton Wyld underwent a minor libertarian revolution towards the end of the 1960s because of the arrival of a number of new staff who were involved in a resurgent debate about libertarian education. Michael Smith has provided an excellent survey of that theoretical debate, and has examined its relationship to the anarchist movement more generally.[25] That debate was to have most influence in Britain in the state sector, and the ground between the state and private sectors that was seized by the free school movement. For these reasons it warrants more detailed discussion later.[26] However, apart from the changes at Monkton Wyld, the debate had an impact on the private sector. It produced a small libertarian school in South London in 1965 called Kirkdale School.

In summary, there were effectively two waves of pioneering in the independent sector, in the 1920s and early 1940s, and a ripple in the 1960s. The schools were very much a product of their times and generally were the inspiration of individuals. Their organisation and orientation speak for themselves and it is to a closer examination of these that we can now turn.

2. MAKING MISTAKES WITHOUT FEELING STUPID

Summerhill School, (Lyme Regis, Dorset, 1924 - 1927; Leiston, Suffolk, 1927 - Date)

Summerhill is undoubtedly the most famous libertarian school in the world. It is an international residential school occupying a large Victorian mansion set in several acres of partly wooded grounds. There are currently about sixty children at Summerhill aged between six and sixteen. Half the children are British with the remainder from France, Germany and Japan. The international intake is a reflection of the effect of the publication of Neill's books abroad. The school receives no state subsidy or outside financial help and relies, therefore, on fees and the occasional gift.

Since 1924 there have been various significant changes not the least of which was Neill's death in 1973 after which Ena, Neill's second wife, became director until September 1985. Since then their daughter, Zoe Redhead, has assumed the role. The various changes, and the history of the school up to the early 1980s, have all been comprehensively documented, most notably by Neill himself and by Ray Hemmings and Jonathan Croall.[27] These include Neill's loss of conviction in the value of the New Psychology, his embracement of the ideas of Wilhelm Reich, the attitude of the school inspectorate and the decision not to take children over the age of eleven. It is not the intention to cover that ground again. Rather, in the context of this book, it is important to look at the issues of continuity, at the experiences of children currently at Summerhill, at the development of the school since the early 1980s, and to attempt some initial assessment of Summerhill's significance and an insight into its possible future.

Summerhill continues to run on the same libertarian principles which made it famous. The day-to-day running of the school is made by the whole community, staff and pupils in self-government meetings; the children are completely free to decide how they spend their time and there is a real freedom for children from adult morality.[28] These principles were central to Neill's thinking and the evidence of continuity spanning seven decades is remarkable.

Self-government in schools was first implemented by Homer Lane at the Little Commonwealth. Neill once called his visit there the turning point of his life, and used Lane's self-government model when he founded Summerhill. Self-government is represented in Summerhill today by four bodies: the Ombudsmen, the Tribunal, the Meeting and the Committees.

The Ombudsmen are volunteer arbitrators from amongst the children. They change once a fortnight and they try to settle any minor problems.

No Master High or Low

Should the problem persist or should one of the parties be dissatisfied with the Ombudsmen's suggested solution, anybody may bring this up at the Tribunal. Like the Meeting, this is a weekly gathering. Both the Tribunal and the Meeting are chaired by a volunteer, and decisions are made on a majority vote. The Tribunal meets on Fridays and acts as a judicial court, while the Saturday Meeting functions as a court of appeal and as the legislative assembly. The Meeting has complete jurisdiction over all areas of school life, except health, safety and finance which are reserved for the Director. It is also in the Meeting that any of the school's officers, Chairman, Ombudsmen and Committees may be voted out of office.

All of these posts carry no reward, privileges or authority. Social activities are co-ordinated by a variety of Committees, usually comprised of five members. When bedtimes get too rowdy, the Meeting may consider whether to introduce "beddies officers", volunteers who put the other children to bed and who can fine people, normally by depriving them of part of their lunch, for breaking the bedtime laws. The system is such that adults never need to fill a disciplinary role. Order is assumed by the whole community. Where the Meeting has decided that some behaviour merits a fine, anybody can fine anybody. Hence no small group of individuals has a monopoly on the maintenance of order. Fines, however, must be decided upon by the whole Tribunal, the only exception being the lunch fines levied by the beddies officers. Whilst fines seem to play a very important role, most sanctions voted by the community are trivial. A frequent response to anti-social behaviour is simply an expression of the community's disapproval, which is traditionally called a "strong warning". The name has no real significance. Other sanctions include tea biscuit or pudding fines, doing the washing-up, and entertaining the community at the end of term. Certainly there is no danger of a tyranny of public opinion, for the feeling of individual freedom goes too deep for the meeting to condemn anything except behaviour that infringes the freedom of others.

While other schools have taken up self-government, Summerhill is distinguished from all other schools, apart from Kirkdale and a few of the short-lived urban Free Schools of the 1960s, by its policy of voluntary attendance at lessons. As soon as voluntary lessons are mentioned, the sceptical authoritarian visitors to Summerhill retort that the children never go, that they cannot ever learn anything. They do not understand that when the element of compulsion is withdrawn education can be a joy. Lucy, a pupil at the school from 1983-1988, bears this out:

"You can relax at Summerhill when you have lessons and then and only then can you learn. How the hell can you learn something when you're tied to a chair in a classroom and daren't move. You can't think in classrooms, there's too much else to worry about." [29]

Summerhill teachers and students past and present believe that making lessons voluntary is fundamental to the institution. No amount of individual study plans, wide-ranging options or electronic gadgetry can, as far as they are concerned, disguise the fact that in state schools children are forced to learn, often with disastrous results. They have a point. Cramming knowledge that children do not want down their throats only leads to an

"Making Mistakes Without Feeling Stupid"

education allergy. Learning is compulsory, so it is hated, never to be returned to. At Summerhill voluntary attendance tries to ensure that people will never be put off self-education later in life if they were not interested in learning as a child. The emphasis is on giving children a taste of a subject if they want. They are free to go if they discover that at that stage in their life it is for them.

Learning is also seen in much broader terms at Summerhill than in most schools. Stephen, a student there during the 1980s, captures it all in a few sentences:

> *"Education should be about learning, not being taught. Here we've got all the academic stuff if we want it, but the school is not really about that. It's about learning with people and getting on with them and basically enjoying learning what you want."* [30]

The truth of the matter is that children do attend lessons and they do learn. Indeed they always have done. Very few choose to go to no lessons at all, and a good number go on to take GCSE examinations. I am particularly fond of one statement by Damian, a young German child, concerning learning and lessons:

> *"You learn here by asking questions. Summerhill lets you do that. I learnt a lot from making mistakes too. You can even do that here without feeling stupid."* [31]

Voluntary attendance at lessons also means that the teachers do not have to devote endless time trying to interest and control the bored and rebellious. In free classes the teacher no longer has to ensure order. Voluntary attendance can be the liberation of the teacher as well as of the child.

However, there is more to freeing the child than simply removing the compulsion in lessons. Too often children are made to swallow adult values. Too often adults pass on judgements and prejudices. If adult values are forced upon children they cannot be expected to grow up capable of making their own judgements, thinking for themselves. Neill refused to mould the child, Summerhill refuses to mould the child. The school does not have a picture of what children should grow up to be like.

When Neill died in 1973 many wondered if Summerhill could survive him. However, during Ena's time as Director, the school, if anything, became stronger. Zoe Redhead has a determination to see the school continue and remain true to her father's now well-established ideas. In 1986 she agreed to an interview with the magazine *Lib ED*. The interview reveals much about continuity but also about how the school is developing. The interview is worth quoting from at length:

> **"Lib Ed:** *How are you enjoying being director at the school?*
>
> **Zoe:** *Great. It's like wearing an old shoe for me. I don't particularly like office work, but I do it because it's a business. The best bit is that the school works, I am very inspired by what will happen in the future.*

Lib Ed: *Why has Summerhill been so successful?*

Zoe: *Neill was a very influential person and his early fight, and eventual success, was that he made Summerhill acceptable to school inspectors. He was a very dynamic personality. He wouldn't have liked to think that it was an accepted place, but it was. I think it's been here a long time because it works. Furthermore it doesn't compromise. Everything that Neill said about Summerhill is still so. His very basic 'freedom not licence' happens here. Freedom has always been absolute here.*

Lib Ed: *Do you think the residential aspect, which most other free schools haven't had, is important?*

Zoe: *I think we are lucky here that we have the kids all term and, in a traditional British way, they're away from their parental influence. If they're going home every night their parents are not absolutely committed to it.*

Lib Ed: *Could you tell us how staff are appointed?*

Zoe: *Well, they have to be nice people, but they have to be qualified to do the job. In the end appointments are down to me, because although all the staff meet everybody that comes and read the letters of application, I'm responsible for what happens. I know what I'm looking for. It isn't a big help if someone who has been here for a couple of years has a heavy say in who else is appointed. I can't really afford to appoint staff on a majority vote because I can't be sure that the other staff will get it right.*

Lib Ed: *Do you see yourself as the guardian of Neill's ideas?*

Zoe: *Yes, I do in a way. It's like when you make a cake. If you get the right recipe you stick with it. I don't want to change Summerhill, it works. I feel for the principles so strongly that when I make a major decision I know what Neill would have thought and would have approved of. I can just feel it all the time. I couldn't think of anyone else who could do it. I wouldn't pass the school on to anyone else, except my daughter Amy, she's 14 now. So in a way I am a bit of a guardian. Summerhill has to go on.*

Lib Ed: *Do boys and girls get the same out of school?*

Zoe: *Yes I think they do. Summerhill is very much an equal community, and whether male or female you'll get the same from it. But having said that I do think that boys and girls are different and we need to always remember that. I'm very interested in animal behaviour and basically the differences between male and female animals are not that different to human beings. I think we disinherit our animal beginnings because I think that's what we're all about still. You will find differences between boys and girls at Summerhill, but they are natural. For example, I think that adolescent boys are naturally much more aggressive than adolescent* *girls because it's natural for adolescent animal males to be more aggressive because that's part of their role in life.*

Lib Ed: *What about future developments of the school?*

Zoe: *It's only going to change structurally, basically practical issues, nothing to do with the philosophy. In fact there will probably be some pretty major changes in a fairly short time because I think the school needs it, physically, but it won't affect the way that the school runs."* [32]

There is little doubt that Summerhill is, and always has been, a great place for children but for many there are some problems. Firstly, the school believes that, as a free self-governing community, it is a panacea for all children's problems. Neill himself believed this. But the school is part of an unacknowledged wider community, and both staff and children have a history and relationships that predate and extend beyond their involvement in the school. Secondly, the day-to-day government may be in the hands of the children and staff, but the overall policy is, and always has been, predominantly decided by the head.

While Summerhill has stood out against, and implicitly challenged, the accepted form of education and continues to do so, it rarely challenges its pupils on an everyday basis. The children are surrounded by women employed in traditional female jobs, cooking and cleaning, which makes it likely that any inherent sexism is being confirmed. However, Neill's theory was that time spent at Summerhill would clear the mind. Many of the children at Summerhill today give voice to equal opportunities, but the structure of the institution does not necessarily confirm this.

Staff are not treated very sympathetically at Summerhill. They are paid very poorly, have no contract and work very long hours. This is not a new development. Under Neill, staff found themselves with few rights and were even occasionally fired. For the staff at Summerhill matters often fall between two stools. Their commitment is enormous, but they are not involved in many aspects of the school.

Lib Ed, and other commentators on Summerhill, have voiced these criticisms,[33] but overall Summerhill does work. For this reason Neill and Summerhill have made a massive contribution to the theory and practice of libertarian education.

3. GOING HOME TO SCHOOL

Dartington Hall School, (Totnes, Devon, 1920 - 1987)

Dartington Hall School, like Beacon Hill which followed it a year later, was started because its founders wanted a libertarian education for their own children. In September 1925 Leonard and Dorothy Elmhirst had bought the 820 acres that remained of an estate at Dartington, near Totnes in Devon, in order to begin a programme of rural rehabilitation through the provision of primary and secondary industries - farming, horticulture, forestry and saw-milling, textiles, cider-making and building. Leonard and Dorothy had met in the USA and Dorothy, whose children had attended an experimental school in New York, could not bear to think of their having to attend any form of conventional, authoritarian school. Hence the reason for opening the school in September 1926.

The Elmhirsts ran the school themselves for five years, but their primary commitment was really to the wider Dartington project. For this reason, in 1931, they appointed Bill Curry as head. He had recently retired from the well known American progressive school, Oak Lane Country Day School, in Philadelphia, and had taught briefly at Bedales. In many ways he became Dartington's Neill, and the development of a very distinctive libertarian theory and practice were in many ways due to him.

The history of Dartington Hall School up to the 1970s has been relatively well documented.[34] For this reason the detailed history of the school's development will not be covered here. Rather it is important to describe the school as it was experienced by children. This task is facilitated by the recent publication of a collection of reminiscences and reflections of former pupils edited by David Gribble,[35] a teacher at the school from 1962-87. It is also necessary to consider the later years of the school, looking at the reasons for its closure, and to assess the school's significance in the history of libertarian education and schooling.

Under Curry's headship the school evolved into a senior school at Foxhole for the 13-18 age group, a junior school at Aller Park for the 6-10 year old group and a middle school, also at Aller Park, providing a transition from junior to senior schooling. The first five years at Aller Park were "group" years. Attempts were made in every way possible to ensure that the classroom became a place of co-operation, rather than a centre of compulsion. The classroom was thought of as a natural part of an holistic environment providing for creative activity of every kind. This was part of the Dartington ethos.

Dougie Hart attended Dartington from 1929-33, having come from a strict Grammar School where he was beaten almost every day for being late for assembly. He remembers boarding, and recognises the important effect it had on him:

> "We all got a great deal out of the school. What I got out of it was becoming a bloody good human being. One may not come out tremendously highly academically qualified but a great many people survive and survive very well without qualifications. What Dartington did for you, particularly if you were there from the beginning to end of your education, was that it gave you a love and respect for the community in general, for each other, including the grown-ups. I don't want an old school tie, or anything like that, but I am bloody proud of my old school." [36]

Susanna Isaacs was at Dartington from 1930-9. She is lucid about what Dartington and Bill Curry meant to her:

> "I had one term at Dartington before Curry came to be headmaster and the first eight years of the twenty six that he was headmaster. My three siblings and I used to speak of 'going home to school' at the end of the holidays. Many years later I could understand from my own experience the young patient who said to me 'I only feel at home at school.' Curry believed that human personality is the foundation stone of society. Thus he took for granted that each child's personality was a foundation stone of the school as a social organisation. Curry's belief in our own individual and social importance gave us hope and strength." [37]

Sybil Crook, a pupil from 1929-41, captures Aller Park in two lines:

> "Aller Park memories are camps in Cornwall at Peartree Point and at Soar Mill Cove near Marlborough, enjoying school but never being clever at class." [38]

Under Curry's influence, then, Aller Park introduced children to the Dartington concept. It was a place where freedom was tasted by many for the first time. And it remained so to the end.

For the children of the middle school it offered a special freedom with enormous emphasis on co-operation. Nik Kenny a pupil from 1982-6 recognises this:

> "I went to Aller Park because my previous school was not giving me a good enough education ... Aller Park were the best days of my fourteen years that I've been alive. We were all too happy to get depressed. We were also full of energy we never slowed down. There was no bullying." [39]

Curry's ideas outlived his headship.

At Foxhole there was more structure, but although lessons were never officially voluntary, the ethos remained the same. Nobody had to do the subjects on offer. The day had a pattern, with a timetable, but the idea was to create as varied and exciting a range of activities that made choice and freedom real. In this sense Dartington was very different from Summerhill, with teachers making a large but varied contribution. Neill was always wary of teachers who were constantly setting up choices for children. And yet the experiences of pupils were generally positive ones. Prue Logie was at Dartington from 1946-51:

> "Moving up to Foxhole meant one's own room but also an hour of 'useful work' after breakfast each morning. I was happy so long as I could be in the book-binding room helping to mix paste, etc. ... Book-binding became my favourite hobby, whereas I eschewed 'art' ... we also had parties at Foxhole ... It was a caring community." [40]

Biddy Humphrey, who was at the school from 1961-66, sheds yet more light on what Foxhole was like and the effect it had:

> "So how did I react to all the opportunities that lay spread before me? Well the boys were obviously of considerable interest but their shortcomings were evident too, sharing the day with them evaporated the glamorous aura that surrounds the 'unknown' and is perpetuated by romantic magazines ... I absorbed the full timetable and expanded my academic quota but I also explored further afield and as more free periods came my way, I spent quite some time out and about ... What has stayed with me after all this? A desk draw still holds the exam passes I used to gain a diploma ... But I actually carry round with me a more jumbled reminder of school days. Joshua's exploits at Jericho mix with unconnected bits of Foxhole-made musicals ... More importantly I do not suffer the memories or nightmares of undone essays, distorted exams, pompous parent days or the necessity of carrot-luring prizes. I started to learn to work for myself ..." [41]

However, if children were in control of their learning at Dartington Hall they were also in control of the day-to-day operation of the "community". Self-government was central to the Dartington ethos, and it is this that places it within the libertarian, as opposed to the progressive, tradition.

The machinery for self-government differed at Aller Park and Foxhole. From the age of ten upwards the children at Aller Park elected group representatives to a council presided over by a teacher. The council met weekly and considered all day-to-day problems of behaviour which had affected others in the school, and made and remade simple rules appropriate to whatever situation had been brought before the meeting. The meetings are still remembered as crucial educational experiences by most ex-students. Jill Lance recalls:

> "Looking back I think that Bill Curry has been probably the greatest influence in my life. I remember so well the school meetings and the many other smaller meetings and lectures we had with him. His judgement seemed so reasonable and fair to me. He would often say in council meetings, when we wanted to make a rule to stop people doing something, 'If you make it, can you keep it? Have only a few laws and make sure that they are kept, and then appeal to peoples decency for the rest'." [42]

Curry took a leading role in the meetings, as did other staff. Indeed under Hubert and Lois Child's headship this tendency continued.

However, it is clear that the council served as a sort of introduction to self-government, for at Foxhole the system was very different. There was no representative principle at work in the Foxhole meetings. Attendance each fortnight was open to all staff and children, although the business was prepared by an elected Agenda Committee. Decisions were made by majority vote and the moot ran the school or it ran what it wanted of the school. Needless to say there was a range of uninteresting administrative business that was rarely discussed and remained in the hands of the staff.

However, it is important not to build up too romantic a picture of self-government at Dartington. The system was not flawless, and at a very basic level the difference between the system at Aller Park and Foxhole seems to display a lack of belief in the ability of younger children to play a direct part in the day-to-day running of a school. Two statements by ex-students are very revealing. Firstly, from Joe Hachett, who attended the school from 1958-64:

> *"The phoney democracy: I became an eager member of the Agenda Committee, an elected group whose business was to decide what was to be discussed in moot, a forum for the whole school. I've come to think that this committee was a legislative device to ensure that the really tricky issues never got an airing on the floor of the house ..."* [43]

And secondly, David Murricane, who was a pupil at Dartington from 1963-68:

> *"... the moot was the pupils' form of self-government, but there was no doubt about who were the real figures of authority. Housemothers were in charge, everyone knew that and much further down the scale came your tutor and him and Lois. If it was a hierarchy it worked, as in a school of 200 kids everyone had their say in an official way in moot, and in an unofficial way throughout their extensive school lives."* [44]

In April 1983 Lyn Blackshaw was appointed to the headship of the school which, by then, had 269 pupils. In the light of subsequent events it is difficult to see how on earth he was ever considered for the post, as he had no sympathy with libertarian educational ideas. One ex-member of staff had suggested that it was only because his curriculum vitae was bound in a book! Whatever the case, within six weeks of arrival Blackshaw launched a monumental assault on children and staff alike, and wrote a letter to parents about burglary, drugs, drink and under-age sex, which not surprisingly eventually reached the national press. This did untold damage to libertarian education in general, to say nothing of what it did to Dartington. For example, in September 1983 the *Times Educational Supplement*[45] ran an article linking the demise of Dartington, the closure of Monkton Wyld and the impending changes at Countesthorpe College, suggesting that libertarian practice in education in the 1980s was impossible.

No Master High or Low

By the Autumn term of 1983 the number of pupils at the school had fallen to 206. Roger Tilbury and Eric Adams were appointed as joint heads, but by 1985 numbers were down to 101. Brian Nicholson became headmaster at Easter the same year, but he and the trustees seemed to be losing faith in the prospect of Dartington continuing. This loss of faith became apparent in April 1986, when Nicholson and the trustees announced that the school would close in July 1987.

The closure revealed a fundamental weakness in Dartington's structure. The real power in the end rested with a group of people who were outside the institution, and who were easily convinced by the now powerful tabloid press. As David Gribble wrote:

"You cannot have a school based on respect for the individual if the ultimate governing system is authoritarian. A school must be run from within because when you go outside it you cannot see what is going on. To give people authority over an institution is to make them believe that they understand it. A school which allows children to find their own values cannot avoid providing ammunition for its critics. When part of the school's policy is to take some children with social problems then the image of the school is likely to suffer even more. Only people inside the school, seeing the many children who succeed without any problems, seeing the children with difficulties change and progress, can form any true picture of its merits." [46]

The last comment should rest with the pupils. Emma Fein who attended Dartington from 1975-83, wrote a poem for *That's All, Folks*. Rooted in a hostility to Blackshaw who, it turned out, had a rather dubious past, it captures not only the cause of the demise of Dartington Hall, but also the spirit of its expansion from 1926 onwards:

"Those eyes - why didn't we believe what we saw -

eyes of destruction

eyes of malice

eyes craving power, uncaring, unseeing -

searching and grabbing.

They were true to the last.

Believing in the good in humanity we stood as if naked.

Somewhere there is something good in everyone, people make mistakes but

if given a chance they will learn, they will grow and change.

Too innocent, too giving to beware of what is really there.

"Going Home to School"

Those eyes were too hard, too unfeeling to listen, to accommodate anything but that which their own gaze was after.

The mouth spoke.

Those that listened without truly seeing were taken in, clever words that squirmed and twisted.

The young have a clear sight - a way of seeing that some, many seem to lose with age.

We were open.

We were abused and were willing to forgive, many forgave without an apology.

Promises were broken again and again.

We saw the reality of the man behind those eyes, but we had no ultimate power -

Those that did listened without seeing.

I never realised how fragile the whole thing was. A community surviving on humane values was crushed by a liar - someone who craved power and projected his own hang-ups onto others.

Only someone who had dealings with pornography would see the world around him as a den of sex and vice -

If you live in a large family you learn to understand the true nature of love that exists there.

Much was learned, much has been lost.

One thing remains clear - look close and believe what you see in the eyes." [47]

4. A SCHOOL ON A HIGH HILL

Beacon Hill, (Telegraph House, Harling, 1927 - 34; Boyles Court, Warley, 1934 - 37; Kingswell Hall, Brickwell, 1937 - 40; Tresidder Mill, Porthcurno, 1940 - 43)

Founded in 1927 by Bertrand and Dora Russell, but run solely by Dora after 1931, Beacon Hill made up the trio of libertarian private adventures established in the 1920s. Just as Dartington differed from Summerhill, Beacon Hill had its own special characteristics. It was built on a philosophy that believed strongly in the independence and autonomy of youth and that rejected all forms of coercion and competition in learning. Probably more than either Summerhill or Dartington, it had a vision of fundamental social change. Bertrand and Dora were committed Socialists. Dora Russell has written two verses, composed in the later period of the school and sung to the music of a song of revolutionary youth, Shostakovitch's "Au Devant de la Vie", which express the aims and work of the school better than all the prospectuses and reports:

"A school on a high hill was founded

A school for you and for me;

By blue skies and green fields surrounded

A school in which we are free

All children shall be welcome here

Each girl and boy;

So let them come from far and near

To share our joy." [48]

Like Summerhill and Dartington Hall, the history of Beacon Hill has been well documented, particularly by Dora Russell.[49] However, a glance at the distinctive characteristics of the school, and how young people expressed themselves, is revealing, and useful as a means of understanding the diversity of this libertarian school.

At Beacon Hill Bertrand and Dora set out to educate whole people; for their own sake and for what they might achieve in human evolution. Their

A School on a High Hill

ambition was to influence government into turning away from power and war towards caring for people and fostering the creative sciences and arts. In this sense the Russells had been politicised by the war in a way in which neither Neill nor Curry were. They anticipated an era when constructive emotions would lead to a more rational world. The parental impulses of men and women would no longer be confined within their family, but would pervade all society. Dora, though, was not naive:

> "At the same time I also feared - and wrote - that large state organisations might prove too great a strain for human beings, and that industrialism might well put an end to the democratic way of life." [50]

Lessons and activities were not voluntary at Beacon Hill. Neill believed this to be a weakness, and illustrative of a lack of commitment to real freedom. Dora, on the other hand, was always at pains to point out to him the need to provide the broadest range of activities for children and young people to choose from, and to give them the scope to direct their own learning within a given structure. For Dora it was important that there was no system of competition or rivalry. As far as possible children worked at their own projects and at their own pace. There were also, naturally, projects undertaken co-operatively: play-writing and production, and a science society.

Beacon Hill had a strong system of self-government, which was effectively the heart of the school. Dora was a democrat. She believed in democracy fervently, but this was more due to a need to counter nationalism, chauvinism and autocracy. She was not aware that democracy needed to create an established authority, whose main concern was to keep its own citizens in order within the state and to fight enemies without. She hoped that, as socialism advanced, co-operation would increase. But she asked:

> "... was a child, subject in its earliest years to parental authority, rendered more powerful now that families were so much smaller, and next, forced to obey its teachers without question, over-disciplined in class, in games and even some military training ... , likely to develop into a self-reliant, independent democrat?" [51]

She thought not, and Beacon Hill's self-governing system was built with this in mind. It was never denied that children needed the background of adult protection, but it was held that this should express affection and a desire to help, not to inspire terror. Dora believed that relief from the pressure of adult authority could be found in a community in which children lived among their equals, meeting to discuss and settle together the problems of social living. The School Council that developed at Beacon Hill was not much concerned with crime and punishment. Instead it met to discuss what should be on the timetable, how the timetable could be organised to accommodate, for example, individualised learning, bedtime rotas, private versus public holding of toys and bullying. Anybody, child or adult, could bring a complaint or problem to a School Council meeting. It was important that freedom and self-government began as soon as children seemed able to take part in it, usually from the age of about five. This contrasted with Dartington Hall, and was contrary to the usual idea that progress should be a gradual emancipation from discipline to greater freedom. At Beacon Hill freedom could be exercised when a young person's destructive impulses could do relatively little harm. Children could therefore progress by experience to self-discipline, achieving a greater maturity than an individual suddenly released from restrictions.

In the summer of 1937, when the school had just moved to Kingswell Hall, there was a marvellous series of School Council meetings. An older pupil moved that all rules should be abolished, and the resolution was carried. Dora recalled that the younger pupils immediately rushed out shouting gleefully:

> "... 'bolish all rules, 'bolish all rules." [52]

It was not long before the Council restored "order", as most children discovered the unpleasantness of staying up all night, and having to eat uncooked food as the cook no longer felt obliged to cook.

Dora Russell felt that the children's work was the most illustrative expression of what Beacon Hill stood for. In her autobiography she included several plays and poems written in the 1930s. They make fascinating reading, and extracts from *Thinking in Front of Yourself*, which was performed in 1933-4, revealed much about the school's belief in personal autonomy, and the inequality that existed in society:

> **Youth:** *I must choose my work soon. I'm twenty already yet I can't seem to fit in anywhere. The world doesn't want me much, I reckon, but all the same I'm waiting to do something. Not just messing about, not just making money. I want to be of use and I want to have some fun out of it too. I've taken a fancy to some jobs but there's always been a snag somewhere. I can't make up my mind at all, it's absolutely hopeless.*
>
> **Chorus:** *Hopeless, hopeless, hopeless!! It's always hopeless.*
>
> **Priest:** *What's hopeless? I came to see if I could help you - your father said that you were rather doubtful about your future. If you'd only believe in God you could never be hopeless. You can rely on him. God cares for all, you know that.*
>
> **Youth:** *But I don't know. It's just like Father Christmas to me, all beliefs founded on the hopes of the ancients. Why should I believe in your God any more than in Buddha or Mohamet or Osiris? I've never noticed any of these gods helping me."* [53]

Dora concluded her autobiography with a question; "Was it all worthwhile?" Joy Corbett, who was chair of the School Council at the age of eleven and left in 1939, thought so:

> *"If there was one thing we learned it was the meaning of freedom. I learnt what freedom is by first hand experience. We had freedom in everything from self-government to self-expression. The school gave us a free rein. We had to learn moderation by trial and error. We both originated and*

enforced the rules. Once we did away with all rules. But it did not work out, so we made new ones." [54]

Beacon Hill was a pioneering initiative. With Summerhill and Dartington Hall it challenged the accepted practice that adults had to wield power over young people. The New Education Fellowship could never relinquish this view, which is why this trio are so significant in the history of libertarian education and schooling. It is unfortunate, though, that their significance may be largely historical, and that Beacon Hill, with a more politicised head, did little during the 1930s to spread its ideals. In this sense, like Summerhill and Dartington Hall, it was very much a "private" adventure.

5. THE WORLD THEY WANT

The Forest School, (Godshill, Fordingbridge, Hampshire, 1929 - 38; Whitwell Hall, Reedham, Norfolk, 1938 - 40)[55]

Founded in 1929, The Forest School was firmly rooted in the Order of Woodcraft Chivalry that had emerged during the First World War. When the school opened, though, its head, Cuthbert Rutter, had little time for any of the strict regimentation that the Order had become famous for. Central to his educational philosophy was the idea fostered by the Order that children should be educated in close contact with nature, and that entry into a highly sophisticated and technical world demanded an introduction to the natural resources of an enduring past.

These were ideas that stemmed from the co-operative and land-based colonies that prospered before the First World War which had re-emerged after the horrors that the war technology brought in 1917 and 1918. The Forest School came from a different inspiration than any of the three other private adventures considered thus far. And yet, different inspiration apart, it is clear that the Forest School expressed a belief in the independence and autonomy of youth that was otherwise to be found only at Summerhill, Dartington Hall and Beacon Hill. Ernest Westlake, founder of the school, who was tragically killed in a car crash before it could open, believed that the aim of the Order of Woodcraft Chivalry in founding a school should be to:

> "... give the children the world they want. The world a child wants is the one that most meets his powers at the moment, and for the most part the adult world does not." [56]

This view was not held by many in the Order, which is no doubt why Westlake went ahead on his own and founded the school, the prospectus of which stated:

> "... no child at the school is forced to learn anything unwillingly, but being free to explore the environment, and finding himself in the company of friendly and well informed elders, he begins his true education by asking endless questions." [57]

The school was sited in an idyllic spot. As a former member of staff recalls:

> "I was expecting to see a large school building but to my surprise it was just a small wooden bungalow in the middle of a pine wood." [58]

This was Woodcot, the kitchen, staffroom and sleeping quarters. The two-room school house was in a second wooden building called Sandemans.

Later another bungalow, Meerhay, was opened as a second dormitory and kitchen. Although nearly all the libertarian private adventures had rural sites, only the Forest School made it the basis of its educational philosophy.

Lessons at the school were voluntary until the age of twelve, but pupils invariably attended after a short period of adapting to such freedom. R. F. MacKenzie, a former teacher at the school, later to be head of Summerhill Academy, a state school with definite libertarian leanings, recalled an athletic young man of twelve who after tea on a Spring afternoon said:

"No, I won't be playing football tonight. I want to go 'round to the lab. I've got some botany drawings to make." [59]

In the free environment work and play were indistinguishable.

At Summerhill lessons were not compulsory at any age. The Forest School did not go this far, but the freedom that the children had already experienced, coupled with an explanation of the need to take exams if they wanted to go on to further education, meant that there was an awareness of the implications of examination work. As Rutter wrote:

"When children came to examination work they understood the necessity for it, tackled it with a will and achieved good results." [60]

There was no way that Rutter, with his East End background and an understanding of the need for access to higher education for working class people, could turn his back on the examination system. He seems to have successfully managed the problem of squaring freedom in education with that of a prescriptive examination system, a problem that was to face any State School with a libertarian ethos.

Ernest Westlake had believed that:

"All studies should start as far as possible from first hand experience." [61]

R. F. MacKenzie recalls an incident which highlights Westlake's point, and says a lot about the value of learning at the Forest School:

"One pupil, Pat, didn't attend lessons but was very keen on amateur wireless-making and improving sets with the help of the music teacher. The day came when the teacher said he could go no further without long division and multiplication and he wouldn't help Pat until he could do them. In two weeks of concentrated study Pat learnt more than most pupils do in much longer periods, mastering these skills and resuming his radio studies." [62]

However, it was the way in which self-government underpinned the whole community that places the school very firmly in the libertarian tradition. Self-government obviated the need for authoritarian adult intervention. There were regular School Courts which organised the day-to-day running of the school, made rules and dealt with transgressors. The very youngest always had a say, and each took it in turn to chair the meetings. There were few rules, but anti-social behaviour was strongly dealt with. The only real rules were the bedtime hours and the three "R"s' - Road, Roof and River - where the children were not allowed to go without adult permission. Although the rules were sensible and non-invasive, Margot Marland, a former pupil, recalls this complaint at a meeting:

> "... a little boy, Pat Woodruff, complained that this was not a free school because he suffered from endless rules: bedtime, having to wash his hands before meals, etc, etc. Cuthbert's eyes gleamed: 'Quite right, we have lots of rules and I would love to be without them. You Pat, have a lovely scout knife I long to own. I shall take it from you and you can't do anything about it as I am much stronger than you and there won't be a rule to protect the weak from the strong.' There followed a complete collapse of Pat and his supporters." [63]

This underlines the serious aspect of self-government. It provided a forum for discussion and rational explanation and removed the need for unreasoned diktats which only serve to alienate pupil from teacher.

In 1938 the school moved to the bigger premises of Whitwell Hall near Reedham in Norfolk. The move followed a dispute between the Order of Woodcraft Chivalry and the Forest School over nude bathing, of which the former disapproved. A new company, Forest School (1938) Ltd, was set up to run the school at Whitwell, with Anthony Ivins, Arthur Cobb and Cuthbert Rutter as directors. But two years after it opened the building was occupied by the Army and closed for the duration of the war. It never reopened, and so the "greenest" of the libertarian private adventures expired.

It is interesting to speculate on the reasons for the Forest School remaining hidden from history, even in the accounts of progressive education. It was probably even more peripheral to mainstream education than Summerhill, Dartington Hall and Beacon Hill, and in this sense it was an even more isolated initiative. It did little to campaign for its ideals outside the narrow circles of the Order of Woodcraft Chivalry. It was implicitly an inward looking initiative, and was never part of any educational movement. And yet its history is rich in libertarian practice and for this reason it warrants more attention than it has, to date, received.

6. A COLLECTIVE HEAD

Burgess Hill School, (Burgess Hill, Hampstead, 1936 - 39; Redhurst, Cranleigh, Surrey, 1939 - 45; Hampstead again, 1945 - 53; Boreham Wood, Hertfordshire, 1953 - 62)

As the adventure in the New Forest was drawing to a close, three new private adventures were emerging, at Burgess Hill in Hampstead, Monkton Wyld in Dorset and Kilquhanity in Kircudbrightshire. The latter was much inspired by A. S. Neill, and John Aitkenhead, its founder, was in the mould of Neill, Curry and the Russells. Burgess Hill and Monkton Wyld, on the other hand, began as relatively tame initiatives, in libertarian terms, which were radicalised during their development.

For this reason it is particularly difficult to generalise about Burgess Hill, and what has hitherto been written about the school seems to bear this out.[64] However, what is clear is that the school underwent a small revolution in 1940 when, for the first time, it was run by a staff collective. This made it the first school in Britain in the twentieth century to run without a headteacher, and there were also significant educational changes which warrant consideration.

Before 1940 Burgess Hill was little more than a preparatory day school, albeit one with a human face. Subsequently it challenged most concepts of traditional schooling. After 1947 there was a headteacher, but the school was still administered by a staff syndicate and continued to develop on libertarian lines. However, it was not until the 1950s that this development became complete, with the abolition of compulsory lessons, a practice which only really belonged to one other school, Summerhill. The late 1950s, though, also saw the emergence of considerable administrative and financial problems, which in the end contributed to the closure of the school in 1962.

In 1940 a majority of teachers at Burgess Hill wished to see the school develop a collective administrative structure and libertarian approach to learning. They felt that they were:

> "... partly reacting negatively to a regime that had become undesirable and ... wished to see that there was no post from which it was difficult to remove a person who had become at variance with the aims of the school ..."[65]

This gives some indication that, in the first four years of the school, the headmaster, who had been appointed by the Directors - themselves elected by members of the limited company who owned the school, including Herbert Read - in 1936 had been at odds with his staff. Peace emerged after 1940, when the Directors accepted an offer from a group of five staff to take joint responsibility for the school.

What this meant in practice was the development of a staff collective where teachers shared administration tasks such as accounts and appointments. In December 1942 the staff functions were defined as follows:

> "Full members of the staff shall be jointly responsible to the Directors for the running of the school. They shall propose to them the termly budget of income and expenditure. They shall be subject to a terms notice of leaving. They shall take turns in the chair at staff meetings. They shall be re-elected each year by an unanimous vote of the full members. In the event of a minority of one opposed to an election, the decision shall be reconsidered at the end of the following term. If there is still a minority the election shall not be made. New staff shall be appointed by a majority decision of the full members for a probationary period of a year. In particular cases, if it is thought desirable the probationary period may be reduced. Probationers shall not vote unless asked to do so by the full members. They shall be subject to half a term's notice. At the end of the probationary period a new staff shall either be admitted to full membership or retained as a specialist. A specialist shall be eligible for re-election as a full member at the end of another year." [66]

Then, in the Autumn of 1943, a School Advisory Council was formed, of which all staff and parents were automatically members. Anthony Weaver believed that this system of joint responsibility was liked by the children, and that it produced an efficient form of organisation. This seems to be borne out by an inspection by the Board of Education in 1943.

However, Weaver also casts light on the problems of collective organisation:

> "... one lesson to be learned by others interested in our experiment is that it is not sufficient for the staff to co-operate in their work but that they must also become legal owners of their enterprise. Mere co-operation is no guarantee against futility, and that people may establish excellent relationships between themselves does not necessarily show that their pursuits are valuable." [67]

There is an element of personal bitterness in this, for in 1946 the Directors of the school had decided to appoint a head teacher, Frank Lea followed later by H. A. T. Child and, in 1947, by Geoffrey Thorp. A lot of controversy surrounded these developments, but this has been documented elsewhere[68] and need not concern us here.

What is important is that, between 1940 and 1946, Burgess Hill developed a form of collective organisation, which led to significant educational developments. The most important of these were the removal of all forms of punishment and the creation of a weekly meeting for all pupils in the "senior school", those aged ten and above.

These developments continued after 1947, despite the appointment of a headteacher. Indeed, although it was the Directors of the school who had gone against the wishes of Weaver in 1946, by 1947 the school had been purchased from them by a new staff syndicate which elected Thorp headmaster. But the new office of headmaster was very different from that which had previously been instituted in the school. There were no pay differentials, and the day-to-day running of the school was in the hands of the staff meeting, which was attended by all staff and where the chair was rotated week by week. Tony Gibson claims that:

> "In practice the office of Headmaster which we got Geoffrey Thorp to fill did not bring any great complications. It is a tribute to him personally that he did his job in the climate of workers' control and did not interfere with other people doing theirs. Under the constitution the staff could remove the Headmaster or anyone else if they wished." [69]

This, and the continuation of libertarian educational development, seems to be borne out by Olive Markham, whose four children were all educated at Burgess Hill after 1947:

> "When we first saw Burgess Hill School, Geoffrey Thorp was the headmaster. He interviewed us, or we interviewed him - I think it was mutual - sitting on hard chairs in a big bare room heated by a very meagre gas-fire. Afterwards we went around the school and found it ugly, untidy, bare and comfortless. Only the walls, covered with paintings and drawings, showed signs of creative activity. At the back there was a sooty looking garden with huge leafless trees. But somewhere behind this unpretentious and forbidding exterior, we smelt a whiff of the freedom and non-conformity which we so wanted to incorporate in our children's education." [70]

Markham throws more light than anybody on what the school was actually like for children. There was no school uniform. Smoking and swearing were allowed, but a few simple rules existed too. Lessons were compulsory, though games were not. There were fixed hours for going to bed and getting up, the boarding section of the school having developed after the move to Surrey in 1939. Children who wanted to go out in the evening had to get permission, and say where they were going. There were also rotas for washing up and helping to clear away meals. The School Meeting developed into a forum where grievances and disputes were aired and settled. There were no marks, punishments or examinations, but if children wanted to take state examinations they could and did get all the help they wanted.

The school also developed an interesting reporting system. Markham believed this to be really innovatory:

> "It was in Geoffrey Thorp's time that the children were asked to write end of term reports on the teachers and these were sent to the parents together with the reports of the teachers on the children. In spite of some showing-off, the children were honest and were able to judge their own progress far better, in many ways, than the teachers. I still have one of these reports headed: Pupil's Own Report. It reads like this:

ENGLISH

I have nothing to say. Peter thinks I haven't been working but I think I have.

GEOGRAPHY

I don't think I take it quite seriously enough. I haven't done enough work on it.

SCIENCE

I like it very much and have worked quite hard. Mary is very helpful and cheerful.

FRENCH

I know a lot of vocabulary. But I'll have to do more essays.

ART

I have done some good things in clay and was just 'letting myself go' over a painting only it was burnt which is rather a waste.

GAMES AND SPORTS

Hockey I like. It would do John Rhodes good to play.

OTHER COMMENTS

School meetings are much better with John as Chairman and me as Secretary. I like expeditions. I would like very much to do cooking." [71]

Olive Markham has also documented some of the changes which occurred when Geoffrey Thorp retired in 1954 and was succeeded by Jimmy East. East had been at Summerhill, and faced a number of problems when he came to the school in Hampstead. Numbers were dropping - at one stage in the early 1950s there had been 120 children attending - and the London County Council was trying to shut the school, having condemned the building because of supposed bomb damage. East took the school to High Canons, a derelict mansion in Hertfordshire, and under his headship it became more libertarian. School Meetings continued, but carried more weight. The children became involved in more than the day-to-day running of the school, including staff appointments. Bedtime and getting-up time were left to the child's discretion. You could stay up all night if you wished. If you got up late you missed breakfast! At the beginning of each term children negotiated their own timetables with teachers. Reports were abolished as East believed that they were incongruous when the staff and children lived on such equal terms.

However, at High Canons problems became more acute. The move might have put some new life into the school, but it also killed it. A huge financial debt was incurred, and was never overcome, and this forced the school to close in 1962.

Burgess Hill warrants consideration as part of the tradition of libertarian education and schooling, albeit as a private adventure, because in the words of Olive Markham again:

> "... behind all the ambiguities and excuses, a real spirit of tolerance and freedom, unique in many of its expressions, existed to the end." [72]

The staff collective, the staff syndicate, the libertarian philosophy and the practice of education that derived from it, these were indeed unique. We also have to remember that the school survived for over twenty five years.

If history means anything other than the plain recording of "facts", then there are countless lessons to be learned from this initiative, one of the most important being the problem of collective organisation. Tony Gibson has shed light on the differences between a collective structure or constitution, and actual workers' control, the latter seeming to provide a more harmonious working model. There is more as well. When the school closed in 1962, it did so with few friends beyond the staff, students and parents, past and present. In many ways this represented a failure to build links with other initiatives which shared a common ethos. Many of the private adventures in libertarian schooling failed to have an impact on mainstream education because of their implicit isolated positions. That in the end also contributed to their demise. Burgess Hill is perhaps the saddest example of this.

7. URBAN TO RURAL RETREAT

Monkton Wyld School, (Charmouth, Dorset, 1940 - 82)

The original founders of Monkton Wyld School, Carl and Eleanor Urban, moved out of Camden to escape the bombing and bought Monkton Wyld in 1940 for £3,000. The school was created in what was originally the rectory of the local church. It was built in 1848, but by 1936 had become a hotel. A. S. Neill would have seen Carl and Eleanor as high-lifers had he known them in 1940. Indeed, on the only occasion he did visit the school much later, he is reported to have said:

> "There's something wrong here, everyone's working." [73]

From the little that either Carl or Eleanor wrote about the school it is clear that they were intent on developing a co-operative community which was co-educational and made full use of the beautiful and potentially productive farmland surrounding the school building. Emphasis was to be placed on working the land together, and academic learning was to be individualised.[74] Eleanor deplored competition in education, and Monkton Wyld was to offer a genuine alternative to parents seeking a non-competitive environment for their children. The effects of the outbreak of war in 1939 are apparent:

> "It is thought more realistic to compete with one's neighbour than to co-operate with him. Yet how essential co-operation is - in the home, in industry and in international affairs. Children whose whole school life is based on competition won't suddenly as grown-ups acquire the power to co-operate." [75]

When the school was inspected for the first time in 1949 the report, which was highly complimentary, was prefaced with a statement by Eleanor which sheds more light on the original intentions of the founders of the school, and where their ideas were rooted:

> "We had in common several things: a lack of interest in money making as a main motive for work, a dislike for dictatorship, power, politics and militarism ... we wanted to provide something of a microcosm with basic human activities such as farming and building going on ... the origin of the school certainly had something to do with war and peace ... destructive forces in European politics had stimulated us to attempt to be constructive." [76]

However, when the school opened it was very much part of the Independent Progressive School movement. It is apparent that Carl and Eleanor Urban ran the school autocratically, and feelings of hierarchy dominated staff and children. Rules were enforced that doubtless seemed ordinary at the time, but they made later pupils at the school shriek with laughter. For example, children (not adults) had to change their shoes when they came in, and only those on a privileged list could go up the main marble stairs; that meant those whose soles did not leave black smears! Bedrooms were strictly bedrooms not day rooms. Other cleanliness and health rules were as hard on the staff as on the children; nails and hair being inspected before breakfast implied that a member of staff was there to do the inspecting. The quarter hour of fresh air before morning lessons began meant that not only children were hurried out, in their outdoor shoes, of course, but that the teachers often had to amble around for fifteen minutes sheltering under an umbrella as well.

Under Urban rule life was ordered and orderly, but while the curriculum was traditional - arts, science, languages and sport - children had a lot of control over what subjects they studied and when they studied them.

The change from a fairly "normal" school, liberalised by mixing manual work and real life with learning, seems to have occurred in the middle period of the school's growth, some twenty years after its founding. The change in orientation was triggered by the replacement of the first wave of teacher founders.

The Urbans ran the place as they saw fit, and when Carl died in 1960 the geography teacher engaged to replace him, Peter Bide, was made to feel his junior status. But by 1965 Eleanor had also died, and all of the other original teachers had retired. Peter Bide found himself running the school as headmaster from 1965-7, but he was uncomfortable in this role and teachers appointed to the school between 1965-7, particularly Chris Fassnidge, the English teacher, wished to see the school develop on a co-operative and democratic basis.[77]

Initially this meant abolishing the post of headmaster and setting up a staff collective to share responsibility for the school. This immediately distinguished Monkton Wyld from most libertarian schools, with the exception of Burgess Hill and the urban Free Schools of the 1960s and 70s. But the establishment of the collective also coincided with more significant changes at the school.

What did the development of a staff collective mean? The clearest description of this is to be found in a document written, in 1982, for the School Inspectorate by the then languages teacher at the school, Steve Webster.[78] It captures the way in which the abolition of staff hierarchy produced a completely different form of organisation and changed the atmosphere in the school. From the document it is evident that responsibility for the day-to-day running and long-term management of the school came to lie jointly with the nine full-time teachers who formed the staff co-operative. The pupils were also encouraged to share responsibility in as many aspects as possible.

Because it is unusual for a co-operative to run a school, the staff were quite frequently faced with the problem of having to explain how the responsibility was shared in practice. People who asked for the headmaster could be directed fairly easily to the member of staff responsible for a

No Master High or Low

particular area of the administration. For instance, different tasks, such as finance, wages, salaries and examinations, were shared among the co-operative. Other people may have been interested in a particular pupil, and here again, as each teacher was responsible as tutor for a number of pupils, they could be directed to the particular person responsible. Other queries may have fallen outside these areas, and the staff that happened to be on duty had to sort them out, either taking them on personally or referring back to the full co-operative. Though there was always the danger of everybody being theoretically responsible, and nothing getting done, on the whole there were few evidently serious problems, although deliberations could often be more long-winded than in a hierarchical organisation because of the problems of wider consultation. The sort of difficulty that arose, for instance, was for duty staff at the weekend, faced with a disciplinary problem, having to choose between acting unilaterally, in order that a problem was dealt with at the correct moment, or waiting to consult the full co-operative - which might mean an awkward delay.

Why go to all the bother? Why not have one person quickening up the whole process, and taking quite a weight from the shoulders of all concerned? The staff at Monkton Wyld increasingly believed that this would deal a fundamental blow to many of the more subtle energies on which the school was coming to rely. It is hard, for instance, to imagine the degree of involvement which existed amongst the staff in the 1970s, if the staff had been instead subordinate to one person.

The school had become one which encouraged questioning. Yet continued acceptance of a headmaster after the Urbans' death would have implied more concern with seeking answers, dictated by somebody else as far as the new teachers were concerned.

The problem of authority, which many of the pupils and staff had, was also intimately bound up with this issue. Very often there was not one answer to a problem, but many. The recognition of this, the realisation that many people could contribute their own answers in the attempt to select the most suitable, led to a preparedness on the part of pupils to ask more questions of themselves, and to undertake more self-exploration, instead of being side-tracked into a rejection of (often arbitrary) authority.

Very often the process of group decision-making at Monkton Wyld reveals important facets of a situation which an individual would only partly understand. Often, for instance, it seems that it was the act of sharing opinions which enabled individuals to reinterpret their own information. The outcome was often far more creative as a result, and this was particularly obvious when dealing with transgressions against community regulations, when set punishments would have been completely inappropriate. The group was often able to reach a more caring and creative solution than an individual would normally be able to do.

There was therefore, by implication, an emphasis on the use of the imagination: avoiding the trap of being given one solution, or opposing it with another, but instead learning to see a spectrum of alternatives.

When the pupils were asked if they saw it as important not to have a headmaster, the reasons they gave for preferring a staff co-operative were interesting. It was good to avoid a headmaster, because the imposition of decisions breeds resentment, and without a head it is easier to tackle problems with authority. They stated outright that having a headmaster would greatly detract from the power of the School Meeting. Another reason put forward was that there was no jostling for positions of advancement, and any pupil could express their views to any member of staff and be represented by that teacher.

The development of a staff collective after 1967 was to be the basis for other more far reaching changes in the focus and orientation of the school. These changes were essentially concerned with instituting self-government and developing a clearly defined libertarian philosophy and practice. In this sense there is much to learn from Monkton Wyld about the relationship between staff and community organisation and learner's liberation.

Under the Urbans there had always been School Meetings but as Fiona Jenkyns, a pupil at the school in the 1950s, remembers:

"The meetings were mostly about work. We used to have to read our stories out or give talks. I hated it, it was embarrassing. Eleanor would always start off by saying, 'Now we've got a very interesting piece today.' Sometimes there were meetings about trouble or behaviour but not that often." [79]

After 1967 the School Meeting developed as a forum for discussion and decision-making. Issues of finance, the appointment of staff and admission of pupils remained staff decisions, but there was always lengthy consultation with pupils over these issues. Everything else came within the orbit of the Meeting. Both pupils and staff were free to contribute to the agenda and everyone had a vote. The Meeting was always chaired by a pupil and issues were decided by a simple majority.

What this meant was that pupils had a real say in the running of the school, and discussions had an air of reality about them. This highlighted how thinking had changed at Monkton Wyld, and how emphasis was placed on breaking down traditional patterns of imposed adult authority, with pupils being treated as individuals, to be respected and not patronised, threatened or indoctrinated.

A lot of what other schools would punish or seek to suppress - smoking, individual ways of dressing, bad language, strident and abusive ways of relating to people - became part of the educational process in which everybody shared. This was painful, untidy and noisy at times, but the School Meeting focused everybody's attention on what was happening in the school, which meant that it was a forum for heightening people's awareness of their rights and responsibilities towards each other.

During the Meeting pupils were often asked to account for their behaviour by other pupils, particularly if violence had been involved. Moral issues constantly cropped up, sometimes in relation to petty theft, but more often in terms of individual selfishness, thoughtlessness or carelessness. However, it was never so much the specific issues raised that mattered, so much as whether the atmosphere in which they were discussed made an honest, open and meaningful discussion possible.

That is not to say that there were transformations in attitudes or behaviour overnight. Rather people were constantly made aware of the fact

No Master High or Low

that, though they were individuals, they were also accountable to others for their attitudes and behaviour.

Because the power of the School Meeting became real, its decisions were usually respected. In fact as a democratic forum it represented a more genuine experience of democracy than existed in the outside world. It taught, also, the difficulties and frustrations of genuine democracy. People needed to turn up to the Meeting (they were never compulsory) if they wanted a say in decisions that affected them, and pupils, especially, were given the opportunity to share something of the real complexity of issues without feeling that the adults were hedging or about to go off and decide the matter for themselves.

The value of the School Meeting was considerable, covering a wide range of things. It encouraged people to speak their minds or give an opinion or air a point of view in front of a large group. It fostered a sense of accountability. It tackled a wide range of moral issues. It encouraged pupils to think about their environment and to suggest ways of improving it and it proved an experience of decision-making free from paternalism and help.

In many ways the more clearly defined libertarian philosophy and practice that developed in the school during the 1970s is illustrated by the changes that took place in the School Meeting. Equally illustrative are the experiences of the pupils who attended the school from 1967-82. Jonathan Lichfield came to the school in 1981, but his description of a day there gives a real indication of both how the school had changed since 1940, and also of what a day at the school was like:

> *"Every morning at about seven o'clock we get woken up by breakfast getters and left to crawl out of bed. If I'm lucky I might just make it by the time breakfast is cleared away at half eight. If not it's a case of CLANG, yes a bloody big bell which just happens to be outside my window tells me I really ought to get up. It's a quarter to nine and the daily School Meeting is about to start. They tell you it's not compulsory but if you're not there you still get invited to come. Invited that is by the heavy mob who storm into my room and tell me I ought to come because that's where decisions are made and blah, blah, blah. Well usually I don't feel like going so I don't. I generally manage to get up by half nine though and try to drag myself off to English. Lessons happen from half nine to one. Now usually I'm in English for about half an hour. What a bore, but I know I should do it. Anyway after that I go to woodwork. This is good. Break is at eleven by then I'm usually at the ropes outside hanging from a tree. I drift in and out of the workrooms between twelve and one. There's lots to do: languages, humanities, woodwork, art - you name it you can do it. I suppose I like to do a little bit of each when I feel like it. Then at one it's lunch. Only three dead this term. In the afternoons there's crafts and sports and stuff. I like the afternoons the best really. There's such a lot of choice. Afterwards, well nothing really. Well not nothing, you just hang around. There's always something that crops up. Tea is at seven and bed at ten. That's about it really."* [80]

Similarly illustrative are pupils reflections on the school after they had left. I have chosen to include two here, the first by Diane Jewess, who attended the school from 1977-80, the second by Patrick Oubridge, who was there from 1974-9:

> "I have been asked to write this as a former member of Monkton Wyld school. At the age of twelve I passed my eleven plus and went to a technical High School, after three years and much rebelling against the system, I was suspended from school and recommended for treatment with a child psychiatrist. His suggestion, considering the family problems at home, was boarding school. I went for one interview at a school in Derbyshire, they thought I would wreck their community and was turned down, even though I passed their entrance exam convincingly.
>
> About six months later when I had forgotten about boarding school, I was offered an interview at Monkton Wyld. I was amazed how informal and relaxed everything was. I was offered a place and arrived that September. The first thing I discovered was that I was no longer the exception coming from a broken home and to talk to people really helped me accept the fact. I spent my first term lazing around doing nothing, this new found freedom was too much. During my second term, when I realised that the teachers really were human contrary to what I had been led to believe from my last school, I started to work a little. The first brick from the staff/pupil wall was taken out by the fact that I was Diane and they were Dave or Pete not Mr Goodwin or Sir. By the end of my second term I looked upon them as friends, who were there to help and encourage me, not the dreadful enemy. After I found that nobody was standing behind me, watching over my shoulder threatening detention I began to get down to some serious work. This was much easier and nicer with such small classes and individual treatment. I took my Maths and Art 'O' levels when I was nearly fifteen, a year before I would have been allowed at a normal school, I passed both. Maths had always been my strong subject and I started my 'A' level at fifteen. I had been told at technical school it was silly me choosing Art as an 'O' level subject as I had no chance of passing.
>
> I came away from Monkton Wyld with five 'O' levels and an 'O' level pass in my Maths 'A' level. Monkton Wyld had much more to offer than academic exams. There was always all sorts of practical skills being taught, because some people really don't have a mind for academic work and excel much more in practical things, even though you're not led to believe this at a normal school. I may not have left Monkton Wyld with many exams but during my four years there I have learnt much more about life and people that I would ever have.
>
> I had a place at Bristol College when I left Monkton Wyld. But with no 'A' level, no place. I was unemployed for ten months but that really isn't unusual in these times of three million unemployed. I was at last offered a job with a firm of Chartered Accountants. I was taken on as an office junior in their personal tax department. After six months there I am now studying for my Intermediate Tax exam. I have shown my employers that I am worth training. My exam is done as a correspondence course and so

all the studying is from books with no teacher, the other girl that is doing the course with me finds it very difficult to work like this because she is used to having a teacher telling her everything to take notes on. But for me this type of studying is fine as I have been accustomed to taking the initiative when studying and doing it off my own back.

From a personal point of view, it is much more important that Monkton Wyld helps young people and gives them the attention and encouragement lacking in normal schools than whether the toilets and bedrooms are hygienic enough or whether the exam pass rate is higher than x%.

I think that there must always be schools like Monkton Wyld, because there will always be people like me who can't get on at a normal school, but have the potential. Just as there are always exceptions to every rule."

"Essentially for me being a pupil of Monkton Wyld meant that for five years I had some semblance of security and a focus for my social life. I didn't like going home at holiday time, and found it particularly frustrating that I had to. Now five years on all my pleasant memories are of incidents that occurred at the school. If a person is the sum total of his experience then without Monkton Wyld I'd be nothing.

At Monkton Wyld I had status that I've never had elsewhere, ambiguous it is true, but I had status and that is important. The environment I encountered when I came here was sufficiently flexible to accommodate me. Clearly any personal development is a process of learning and adapting or as I see it as a mathematician, programming and deprogramming. I came to Monkton Wyld with fixed ideas and it has been a long and strenuous exercise trying to integrate my fixed ideas with society's, fixed or otherwise. I think that the single most important aspect of the environment I found myself in is that I occasionally found peace of mind here and had a chance to relax. It is terrific getting away from the information barrage that one encounters in the outside world." [81]

Sadly in 1982 Monkton Wyld was forced to close after an Inspectors' report. We have to remember the context in which the inspection took place. The Conservative Party had been in power for exactly three years when the Inspectorate reported in May 1982, and the 1981 Education Act was just beginning to take its toll on Independent Schools that catered for children with any special educational needs. These children now had to be "statemented" and any schools that they attended had to be recognised and approved by the Secretary of State for Education. From about 1976 numbers had been falling at Monkton Wyld, and there had been an increase in the number of pupils on reduced fees. Financial stringency led the staff collective to accept an increased number of pupils referred by Local Education Authorities and Social Services. By 1982 fifteen of the forty seven pupils on roll were such cases. Although Monkton Wyld had always taken in such children, this constituted a significant increase even since 1979. Indeed, as many of these children were in their final years of compulsory schooling, an increased burden was placed on the school as a whole, but the Inspectorate chose to focus on this. Some staff felt that it was simply used as an exercise for what had become a problem for the Inspectorate. The school had had a new Inspector since 1979, Mr Woodhead, and he had made it clear on all his visits to the school between 1979 and 1982 that he had no sympathy with the ethos of the school. The conclusion to the Inspectorate report which he wrote read thus:

> *"The children at present in residence form a heterogenous group with a range of educational and personal needs so wide as to make the meeting of them an extremely difficult task. To attempt such a task in an unstructured and relatively unplanned situation makes unduly heavy demands on all concerned. Whatever the reasons the present position is that in a number of aspects of its daily life and academic work the school falls below acceptable standards. It cannot be said to be providing full-time education for its pupils or to be meeting the special needs of many of the children with adequate special provision. In the view of the HMI there is urgent need to reappraise the present arrangements for both education and core and to make significant changes in the regime if the school is to reach and maintain acceptable standards. This is particularly important if the school intends to seek approval under the terms of the 1981 Education Act. Most urgent of all is the taking of appropriate action to deal with those matters which in the panel's view threatened the health, moral welfare and safety of the pupils in the school."* [82]

When two staff visited the Department of Education and Science in the summer of 1982 it was made clear what the final lines of the report meant. Pupils needed structured timetables, there were to be no mixed corridors, the untreated milk available on the farm was not to be drunk by the pupils, the school needed a headteacher, the building needed to be put in better decorative order, the staff needed more contact with the mainstream of educational thinking. This was an attack that many staff felt unable to cope with. An attempt was made to begin a new school but, despite a brief parental and pupil occupation of the school in the late summer of 1982, the staff as governors of the school decided that it should close at the end of the summer of 1982. Only two of the nine full-time staff dissented from this view.

Monkton Wyld's significance in the history of libertarian education and schooling is considerable. For fifteen years it was collectively run, longer than Burgess Hill and almost all of the urban Free Schools of the 1960s and 1970s. Only Kirkdale and White Lion Free School existed as collectives for longer. Admittedly longevity should not necessarily be an indication of enormous success, but it was the development of collective organisation that gave the school a libertarian ethos and atmosphere, and it is difficult to find past pupil, parental or local authority criticism of it. People seem to remember Monkton Wyld since 1967 as a place of excitement, of learning, of autonomy or shared experience.

In the last analysis the respective paths of the forty seven children who were on the roll in the Summer of 1982 make interesting study. Eighteen of those have been on to further education, another seven on to higher education. At the time of writing only three are unemployed. No fewer than

No Master High or Low

fifteen are self-employed in the widest range of trades. Maybe the Inspectorate's fears and concerns were not all that well-founded and said much more about their views and attitudes towards education than about Monkton Wyld itself.

8. FREE AS A BIRD

Kilquhanity House School, (Castle Douglas, Kircudbrightshire, 1940 - date)

Kilquhanity House School (Killie) is one of the two surviving libertarian private school adventures. As has already been noted, it was the inspiration of John and Morag Aitkenhead, who in their turn speak affectionately of the influence of A. S. Neill. Like Monkton Wyld it was born in 1940, conceived of a spirit that was essentially non-violent. To emphasise this, Aitkenhead wrote in 1986:

> *"Similar ideas, similar idealism were motivating soldiers and pacifists alike only the soldiers had been proved so wrong, and so recently. At Kilquhanity we were agin the war but not agin the soldiers. We were agin the government too, and several of us went to jail for refusing to accept the conditions laid down by tribunals for conscientious objectors. An exciting, stimulating time! Our aim was simple: a school that would be international, coeducational and non-violent."* [83]

The same ideas have continued to motivate the Aitkenheads to this day, and Kilquhanity possesses all the features of a libertarian educational initiative; a belief in the autonomy of the individual child, an aversion to all forms of coercion and punishment and to institutionalised rewards and credits, a belief in self-government and a hostility to and awareness of the constraining tendencies of a national system of schooling. Its staff and pupils talked to the magazine *Lib ED* in 1988.

According to two pupils, Gillis and Aaron:

> *"Breakfast is out by 8.00am, and if you're not down for it by 8.30 you can kiss it goodbye."* [84]

Aaron added that you might want to do that anyway, but what is wrong with cold porridge?

For boarders like Gillis and Aaron, this is how the day begins. But really the whole community does not gather until after breakfast, when the "outsiders", day pupils, arrive. The split is about fifty-fifty, and all combine together on "useful work" after 8.30 am. This may mean helping to milk the cows, feeding the pigs and chickens, beginning the household chores, sweeping the dorms and preparing the vegetables for midday and evening meals. There is an emphasis on togetherness and co-operation, a lasting testament to the spiritual roots of the school in 1940.

At 9.30 am, compulsory lesson time begins, and continues until 11.00 am. It resumes again at 1.30 pm, finishing with the end of the official school day at 3.00 pm.

No Master High or Low

Waiting for lunch: Killie kids with the author.

However, we should beware of imagining some great authoritarian structure. John Aitkenhead has always wanted to have set lessons, but within the actual lesson time there is great freedom. In an English lesson, one girl may be reading a favourite author, another writing an article for the Killie magazine.

John has always talked of freedom in this way. "A person may be free to jump in the water or not to jump in the water. But if they jump they're not free to remain dry." At Kilquhanity, children can choose whether or not to do a particular lesson at the beginning of a term, but if they choose they must abide by the requirements of the teachers and the subject. They say:

> "... 'free as a bird in the air', but a bird has to obey the rules of aerodynamics." [85]

Set lessons provide the basic structure, and the important thing is that no lesson is compulsory. If you don't want to do Maths, then you don't have to, but you must choose something else.

Between 11.00 am and 1.00 pm there is free choice. This essentially means that pupils can do any activity. This might mean English or Drama, but it could also mean draining the meadow or repairing a fence. It may also mean doing nothing at all. Gillis told me that by 11.30 am he needed a rest, but others, including Tammy and Rachel, like the structured times and wished for far more.

After 3.00pm the outsiders begin to drift away but activity still abounds: around the pond, on the football field, in some of the workshops. For the boarders the last meal is in the early evening but, depending on your bedtime, there is also a hot milky drink available before lights out.

The Killie day is full of variety. The school is located in beautiful surroundings and is a haven of dens and secret places. There is a nice balance between "structured" activities and "free" choice. Further, the differing needs of a wide age range - from five to sixteen, boarders and day pupils - appear to be met.

Nothing epitomises Killie's sense of community more than the weekly meeting, which is built on the Summerhill model. The meeting is compulsory for everybody in the community. It takes place in a beautiful octagonal building called the Dome. People sit around the walls facing each other. Eye contact is possible with everybody. A student takes the chair and there are announcements and pieces of information given by teachers and pupils. Activities are also organised through the meeting. However, the main function of the meeting is to discuss the day-to-day running of the community, and any problems that arise out of it. The result is that it often acts as a tribunal. Disputes between children and between children and teachers are raised and discussed calmly and at length. There is a search for consensus.

What is unique is the close attention given to the business by the enormously wide age range. Children do not experience the meeting as a drudge or a bore, largely because it is about them, and as a result they fully participate in it. The meeting is also a safe arena. People are never put on trial, but the community often demands explanations. There are no official sanctions, but the meeting will always decide an appropriate course of action in relation to misdemeanours.

John Aitkenhead has described the meeting as:

"... like a primitive tribe. They can see justice being done and everybody can have a say, this is valuable. But think of the civics in this practical government. Real feelings enter into this, real lives are being affected, it's a thousand times better than mock debates. They learn patience and tolerance and charity." [86]

Indeed Kilquhanity is a tolerant community. It accommodates a wide range of opinion and has a commitment to a large degree of personal autonomy.

John Aitkenhead once wrote:

"Looking back over the years of the school's growth and at its present shape and form, I am reminded of a feature that has been constantly present; the building, the converting, the making that is always going on. I imagine that kids here for any length of time think they have built the school. As indeed they have - or helped to build it." [87]

This has happened, indeed is happening, in many different ways. Children build their own huts in trees, on the ground, even beneath the ground. Farm buildings have been converted for all kinds of purposes, but often retain the name of the original functions of the building. Amongst the bedrooms are the "henhouse" and the "duckhouse". "Printed and published in the bullock-shed" appears on the cover of each issue of the school's magazine.

The latest addition to the school's buildings is the Dome, which took seven years to build and now houses such activities as the weekly meeting and the theatre in the round.

John Aitkenhead articulates the meaning of this important area of school activity:

"Who could begin to measure the educational value to youngsters of being involved in such enterprises? The modern world is changing, and changing fast, we know, but it is society that is changing. The physical basis is still there, and the elements are the same as ever. Boys and girls have their feet on the ground, where we all live and move and have our being." [88]

Killie rambles. From farm to English room, from the pond up to the art and craft workshops, from the kindergarten to the kitchen. There is a staff room, endless bedrooms and a playing field. All is set within the most beautiful and unspoilt rolling countryside. Not surprisingly it is a peaceful place. Children can study English and Languages, Modern Studies, Maths, Woodwork, Art, Pottery, Crafts, a little Science but not very much, Cooking, Drama, Dancing. All this and more, and an endless range of outdoor activities which can begin on the farm and finish with a game of rounders.

John Aitkenhead once wrote a piece about rounders:

"Games, it has to be all ages together. Take playing rounders on half a football field. I suppose most schools wouldn't call it games at all, but the

charity - letting the little ones get to first base, no getting them out too soon - this is what games should be. I suppose a small school like this, for all ages, can be called inefficient these days, but only in the narrow sense, only in subject learning. It's not inefficient when it comes to the unmeasurable values that have been developed. Brains aren't everything. Human qualities like reliability, stickibility, integrity - these qualities grow here simply out of living together." [89]

The issue of compulsion has always attracted attention in any debate about Kilquhanity. Neill always felt that Summerhill was unique because there was no compulsory study. This was what made Summerhill free. Somehow any school that did not do the same could not be free - in Neill's eyes anyway.

But it is the experience of children that is important. At Kilquhanity there is a structure but it is not repressive. The children at the school do not experience compulsory lesson time as being authoritarian, and if they did they have the facility to change it.

"If you want to do something here you can. Anybody can use free choice how they like. It could be Latin, Greek or anything. But I get terribly confused at times. I know I like it here, it's a fantastic experience and a lot of the teachers and teaching are really good. I sometimes long to go to an ordinary school though because of the range of things that are immediately open to you. Here it all takes so much time and before you know where you are the motivation has gone. I worry about what I'm going to do with my life but on the other hand I know I'm happiest when I'm here." [90]

For too long John Aitkenhead, now in his eighties, has lived in A. S. Neill's shadow both as an educational thinker and as a practitioner. He has written very little, but his thoughts on schooling in general, and on child-rearing, the family, love experiments and playing the system in particular, are a gold mine of ideas, inspiration and advice. This interview he gave to *Lib ED* is worth quoting in full:

"Lib ED: *It must be fascinating, John, looking back to 1940 and the creation of Kilquhanity. How does 1990 look?*

J. A.: *Well, things have obviously changed tremendously. Look at the primary and junior schools, they've come so far. Of course, things are changing again, aren't they, but you'll never take some of the progress away. Most children can now go to school without fear of being beaten by teachers. You have to remember that. Mind you, if Killie was needed in 1940, it's as much needed today.*

Lib ED: *What makes you say that?*

J. A.: *Well, look at 1940. Similar ideas, similar idealism were motivating soldiers and pacifists alike, only the soldiers had been proved so wrong and so recently. At Kilquhanity we were agin the war, but not agin the* soldiers. We were agin the government too, and several of us went to jail for refusing to accept the conditions laid down by tribunals for conscientious objectors. An exciting, stimulating time! Our aim was simple; a school that would be international, co-educational and non-violent. Look around you, we're not at war, but education and schooling still needs such a model.

Lib ED: *If you had to capture the 'Killie spirit' in a few sentences, how would you do it?*

J. A.: *Well, Killie is about living together, sharing, loving. We don't get the grey-faced exam passers, those who can't enjoy school because of what they have to do to get to University. Killie is about the generation of happiness. That's really creative work, the work that must be done to enable happiness to grow and flower in a child.*

Lib ED: *In comparison to many other libertarian educational projects you seem to have managed to do something quite unique here by building a local school. There are a huge number of children from the surrounding villages.*

J. A.: *True. But remember that a lot of people have moved into this area in search of a different lifestyle. Killie just happened to be here.*

Lib ED: *Yes, but you have encouraged local attendance and involvement, haven't you?*

J. A.: *Of course. A lot of the libertarian schools have looked to overseas students to solve their financial problems. I could fill Killie with Japanese children tomorrow and improve our financial situation. I'd rather use the assisted places scheme and encourage local attendance. Boarding schools are not the solution. Uprooting a child out of their home - I'm not convinced they need it. And talk about uprooting a child from its country. Have you ever been to Japan? I was there just recently. It takes hours and jet lag is a reality you know. How could I demand six journeys to and from Japan per year of young people. I don't know how they handle it at Summerhill.*

Lib ED: *Well, Neill wouldn't agree with you, would he? What about the 'problem parent', the idea that children need to be away from their parents. That was part of the essence of Neill's philosophy, was it not.*

J. A.: *Well it was before he became a parent. I'm not sure afterwards. After all, Zoe was not too happy in Switzerland, was she. Children need loving. I'm not saying that in independent boarding schools they can't find love. I just think it's more difficult. We have boarders here, but they have to be very self-sufficient. The community helps them, but there can be no substitute for a caring, loving home.*

Lib ED: *Getting away from Kilquhanity and free schooling, John, what about education more generally? You've always maintained an interest in the politics of education. How do you see things?*

J. A.: Well, let's take Thatcher to start with. Educator, she could never be an educator. Look at her time as Minister of Education. Now we're reaping the consequences of all her prejudices that she never actually managed to turn into legislation. That's where all this testing nonsense comes from. But I'll tell you something, we have a chance here in Scotland to put something together. There's tremendous hostility up here you know to any threat from London about streamlining. We don't want it here and I have the feeling we won't have it.

Lib ED: *And the future, John?*

J. A.: Well, Kilquhanity will go on. If we can continue for another fifty years, then maybe a few more people will start to take notice. I just hope for more humanity in schooling and child rearing." [91]

The nearest pub to Kilquhanity is small and very local. Visitors are welcomed, but suspected. And if you mention John Aitkenhead's name there is even more cause for suspicion. Who wants to know? Are you journalists?

What lies behind this suspicion is an enormous respect for the man who has been a part of the local community for over fifty years. Locals in the pub identify with John Aitkenhead's passion for Scottish Nationalism. At the same time they respect his pacifism and belief in human virtue. And they admire Kilquhanity. This is an indication of Killie's success, survival and hope for the future.

Kilquhanity is popular in the local community. "Aye, he's wonderful with kids, old Aitkenhead - a marvel." But the difference between John Aitkenhead and the likes of A. S. Neill, Dora Russell and Bill Curry is that he has this huge identity with his local community. He loves Kirkcudbrightshire. He wants local people to understand his school. He sells his ideas in the shops, the pubs, the local press and on every line of the local grapevine.

The school is not without its problems both at a day-to-day practical level and also as a model.

Teachers get paid a very low salary, only about £1,000 per year. This inevitably restricts the field of applicants for any jobs and leads to a high turnover of staff. Despite this, several teachers in the school have been there for periods upwards of ten years. John and Morag Aitkenhead themselves live a frugal existence.

Similarly, resources are limited and some children do miss the learning opportunities they know to be available elsewhere - there is virtually no science on offer in the school, for instance.

The school is fee-paying and is, by implication, exclusive, but by clever use of the government's Assisted Places Scheme, Killie has a more or less comprehensive intake.

For over fifty years the school has asked some fundamental questions about the nature of freedom. "Freedom, not licence," was one of A. S. Neill's adages. Kilquhanity has faced many of the issues on the very narrow path between the two.

There is an atmosphere of family and parental concern about John and Morag Aitkenhead of which, one suspects, Neill was not very tolerant. But the belief that children cannot be left to themselves to explore all their desires, insecurities and day-to-day traumas underpins the whole approach to teaching and learning at Kilquhanity.

9. SUMMERHILL IN THE CITY

Kirkdale School, (186 Kirkdale, London, 1965 - 1990)

One could have expected that the resurfacing of a debate about libertarian education in the 1960s would have produced a host of new private adventures. In fact only one materialised, as the debate had more impact in the state sector, where libertarians had a huge influence in many of the progressive experiments, and on its periphery, where non-fee-paying free schools emerged in most cities. The new private school was Kirkdale School in London. It was established in 1965, by a group of parents, mostly teachers, who sought a libertarian education for their children. The school took over a Victorian house with a large garden, and opened its doors to children from the age of three-and-a-half to thirteen. Usually it had around thirty pupils, who were divided into three age groups: the Bees, aged between three-and-a-half and five; the Wasps, aged between five and eight; and the Hornets, aged between eight and eleven.

The basis of the school's philosophy was a firm belief and faith in children and in their capacity to organise their own learning. The founders of the school were much influenced by A. S. Neill and Bertrand and Dora Russell and believed that:

"... allowing children choice over what they do is the best way to emotional health, autonomy of thought and action, a developed sensibility and responsibility, and a greater adaptability." [92]

At Kirkdale teachers and parents believed that dividing children into rigid groups by age, and shutting them away in classrooms, limits rather than encourages learning. Although there were three groups at the school, children moved freely between them, taking part in any activities which interested them and working alongside children of different ages. There were no compulsory lessons and no grading, and there was a caring, family-like atmosphere which allowed children to flourish. Clare, who describes herself as a friend of the school, has written:

"In accepting children for what they are, as opposed to what an anxious parent or teacher might want them to be, it is important to understand exactly what children are. Of course every one of them is different, and every one of them is human, but in any group of which the majority are children, one must be able to accept noise, excitement and a messy environment. Children are not inhibited from expressing themselves by social etiquette and it is crucial to Kirkdale's beliefs that the school fits

the child rather than the child fitting what is the adult's conception of the school." [93]

Polly, a Hornet when she wrote this, bears out these sentiments:

"We dug up the Doctor's medicines, needles and found a book on doctor's stuff and found some bullets in the back garden. It was exciting and that was all." [94]

Like Burgess Hill and Monkton Wyld before it, Kirkdale had no headteacher. It was run as a parent/teacher co-operative, and the focus of the school was the weekly School Meeting. Although teachers and parents often met to discuss organisation and administration, this Meeting brought together teachers and pupils and was open to all members of the school. The Meeting discussed and makes decisions on the school's diary of events, aspects of the curriculum, behaviour problems and conflicts and any other matters raised. Everybody was encouraged to discuss their thoughts, feelings and motivations, and to think about their actions and their consequences. No punishments were used and decisions were reached by consensus.

Kirkdale was almost entirely financed by its members, either by the direct contributions of the parents or by the fund-raising efforts of the whole school. There was no fixed fee, but money was always a problem. Martin Summers, a teacher at the school, was always very aware of this:

"... the main source of money for the school has been parental contributions and they are still the life-blood of the enterprise ... To me the problem of money manifests itself in direct contradiction to the positive aspects of the school. For example the staff have to accept a level of earnings and a degree of commitment which limits their effectiveness through sheer exhaustion, and in fact which determines that only those who are young and without commitments can work here. Another problem is that although we do what we can to prevent it, we lose kids for financial reasons. I think this is terrible because the main challenge for Kirkdale would be to make what happens here available to a wider variety of kids. For me it's an exciting place to be, but I would hate to see the optimism of its beginnings in the 60s die in the harsh economic climate of the 80s." [95]

Kirkdale nearly died in the harsh economic climate of the 80s. A number of teachers left in 1986, and a group emerged to campaign for a state-funded Free School in Lewisham, but Kirkdale somehow struggled on, despite becoming even more dependent on parental contributions and had to move premises to New Cross.

It held to its original ethos, articulated in 1965 by Susie Powlesland, one of the co-founders, for twenty-five years:

"Most organisations appear to be self-regulating, (by which we mean in general that they have an inborn tendency to seek whatever conduces to good health and development). Mankind can be self-regulating as much as any other species, but the process is much more complicated and

consequently much more easily disturbed. To lead a satisfactory life it is necessary for human beings to enjoy some measure of acceptance, approval and affection from their fellows. Rejection and hatred lead to illness and even death. The adults in this school have the responsibility for trying to understand the behaviour and attitudes of the children. This means that anti-social conduct and non-cooperation is treated with tolerance and sympathetic consideration and that we use no punitive sanctions." [96]

However, faced with the problems and contradictions that have afflicted most of the private adventures, it closed in 1990.

10. DISTINCTIVE BUT EXCLUSIVE?

The Libertarian Private Adventures in Education, 1920 - 90

The schools described in this section were distinctive because of their libertarianism. They were all rooted in the belief that children have the capacity to direct and organise their own learning and in a conviction that schooling that was non-coercive and anti-authoritarian, devoid of punishment and institutionalised reward, was pedagogically superior. They all represented a challenge to orthodox schooling and were very different in organisation and orientation to the more respectable progressive private schools.

The political and social and economic circumstances, essentially the historical context, in which they emerge reveal much about their origin. Those of the 1920s were born out of the reaction to the barbarism of the First World War. Those of the 1940s sought to escape the vulgarity of the second. The revolution at Monkton Wyld and the creation of Kirkdale in the 1960s were rooted in the re-opening of the debate about libertarian education that accompanied a more widespread political awakening.

However, whilst these schools were bound together by their libertarian ethos, they had many differences as well, which suggests that there is no standard definition of a libertarian school. Summerhill and Kirkdale were the only ones where lessons were definitely non- compulsory. Some, like Dartington Hall, developed different forms of self-government according to the age of pupils. Each of the schools laid greater emphasis on certain areas of educational experience than others: Summerhill on total self-regulation; Dartington Hall and Beacon Hill on mutual co-operation; the Forest School on the environmental context; Burgess Hill and Kilquhanity, and eventually Monkton Wyld, on breadth of experience; Kirkdale on vertical age grouping. However, taken as a whole libertarians and educationalists have much to learn from them, for they are all schools which are rich in learning and co-operation.

And yet they were essentially isolated projects whose impact on educational thinking has been limited. Apart from Neill, whose books have had a great impact, as Ray Hemmings has demonstrated,[97] the inspirers of the initiatives were not propagandists. Whether they doubted the influence that they might have, or whether they just did not have the time to promote their ideas, is not clear. It is probable, though, that the middle class intake of most of the schools, and the inward-looking self-sufficiency, created an exclusive cosiness that made it all too easy to forget or even to ignore mainstream education.

It is important to remind ourselves that the libertarian private schools constitute only a small part of the tradition of libertarian education. The problem remains that, to date, they are the most well-known, except for some of the libertarian-influenced progressive state schools.

There are pedagogical and organisational lessons to be learnt from these libertarian private schools. As the experiences of children and young people at the schools indicate, it is possible to construct a curricular approach that is open, flexible, negotiable and non-authoritarian, that in the end can produce an educational experience to be valued emotionally and marketable in employment terms. Neill once said, quite simply, that freedom works. This account seems to bear him out.

Organisationally the lessons are unclear. As far as survival is concerned, the stability that figureheads like the Neills and the Aitkenheads have given to Summerhill and Kilquhanity suggests that there are virtues to headship. But the collective and co-operative experiences that were developed at Burgess Hill, Monkton Wyld, and at Kirkdale, suggest that libertarian practice in education will often only develop out of a sense of non-hierarchical organisation. Tony Weaver and David Gribble's suggestions about the ownership of initiatives are of particular relevance here.[98]

Little has been said about accountability. At Monkton Wyld in 1982 the teachers definitely believed that they could take on the inspectorate and win. They justified and defended the school on libertarian grounds and ignored the power that the inspectorate held. In the end this proved their undoing.

Libertarian education must, or at least must appear to, produce the goods that the government's inspectorate desires. This is not to say that it should produce docile, subservient young people. It means that it has to be efficient, well-organised and able to demonstrate the superiority and success of its pedagogical and organisational approach. Neill, on the other hand, wooed the inspectorate, which could be his most lasting bequest to libertarian educators.

Perhaps the most important lesson that should be learned from the history of the libertarian private adventures is from something they did not have, or at least rarely had. Gatherings of the clans were all too few and far between and the private adventures all too rarely looked outside their own four walls. Workers and pupils from Summerhill, Dartington Hall, Kilquhanity, Monkton Wyld and Kirkdale could have met and organised with the many workers and pupils from the twenty or so urban Free Schools and state progressives like Summerhill Academy, William Tyndale, Countesthorpe College and the Sutton Centre in the early 1970s.

And yet, on the other hand, maybe this is a naive dream, for libertarians are a diverse breed. Perhaps that explains why there is a strong libertarian educational tradition, but no tangible movement.

NOTES

1. See Introduction.

2. Blewitt, T., (ed), *The Modern Schools Handbook*. Gollancz, London, 1934.

3. Child, H.A.T., (ed), *The Independent Progressive School*. Hutchinson, London, 1962.

4. *New Era*. Vol.1, No.3, July 1920.

5. Blewitt, T., op.cit., and Child, H.A.T., op.cit.

6. I do not claim to be the first to do this. In his book *Neill of Summerhill*, Routledge and Kegan Paul, London, 1983, Jonathan Croall argued strongly that a number of schools including Summerhill warrant specific consideration as libertarian and not progressive initiatives.

7. Quoted in Croall, J., op.cit., p101.

8. Holmes, E., *What is and What Might Be*. Constable, London, 1911, p47.

9. Homer Lane was at this time running the Little Commonwealth in Dorset, a libertarian school for the unschoolable. The school is considered in Part Three.

10. Macmunn, N., *A Path to Freedom in the School*. Bell, London, 1921, p1.

11. Martin, K., *Father Figures*. Hutchinson, London, 1966, p103.

12. *New Era*. Vol.1. No.1., January, 1920.

13. Hemmings, R., *Fifty Years of Freedom*. Allen and Unwin, London, 1972, p34.

14. *New Era*. Vol.1. No.7., October, 1921.

15. Quoted in Croall, J., op.cit., p105.

16. Hemmings, R., op.cit., p34.

17. Boyd, W., and Rawson, W., *The Story of the New Education*. Heinemann, London, 1965, p69.

18. Quoted in Croall, J., op.cit., p108.

19. Ibid.

20. *New Era*. Vol.4, No.13.

21. Quoted in Croall, J., op.cit., p165.

Notes

22. Ibid.

23. Child, H.A.T., (ed), *The Independent Progressive School*. Hutchinson, London, 1962, p76.

24. Aitkenhead, J., *That Dreadful School,* in *Resurgence*, Devon, Sept-October 1986, p6.

25. Smith, M.P., op.cit., pp114-52.

26. See Parts 4 and 5.

27. Neill, A.S., *That Dreadful School*, Herbert Jenkins, London, 1937; *Summerhill; A Radical Approach to Education*, Gollancz, London, 1962; *Talking of Summerhill*, Gollancz, London, 1967. Hemmings. R., and Croall, J., op.cit.

28. Much of the rest of this section is based on two articles by David Stephens a teacher at Summerhill from 1984-7, and the *Lib ED* Collective who visited the school in 1986, published respectively in *Freedom*, London, June 1985, pp8-11; and *Lib ED*, Leicester, 1986 Vol.2. No.3., pp9-12.

29. *Interview with Summerhill students*, Leiston, Suffolk, June 1986. *Lib ED* archive.

30. Ibid.

31. Ibid.

32. *Lib ED*, Leicester 1986, Vol.2, No.3., p12.

33. For a particularly strong criticism of this type see Lister, I., *Deschooling, Revisited.* in Illich, I., *After Deschooling What?* Writers and Readers, London, 1974, pp4-28.

34. In particular see Bonham Carter, V., *Dartington Hall*. Phoenix, London, 1958. Child, H.A.T. and Child, L.A., *Dartington Hall*. in Child H.A.T., (ed) *The Independent Progressive School*. Hutchinson, London, 1962. pp42-55, and Punch, M., *Progressive Retreat*. Cambridge University Press, London, 1977.

35. Gribble, D., (ed), *That's All Folks*. West Aish Publishing, Devon, 1987.

36. Gribble, D., (ed), op.cit., p17.

37. Gribble, D., (ed), op.cit., pp18-19.

38. Gribble, D., (ed), op.cit., p39.

39. Gribble, D., (ed), op.cit., p182.

40. Gribble, D., (ed), op.cit., pp61-2.

41. Gribble, D., (ed), op.cit., pp118-9.

42. Gribble, D., (ed), op.cit., p63.

43. Gribble, D., (ed), op.cit., p107.

44. Gribble, D., (ed), op.cit., p120.

45. *Times Educational Supplement*, 16th September 1983, p7.

46. Gribble, D., *Dartington Closes*, in *Lib ED*, Vol.2, No.3., Leicester, 1986, p6.

47. Gribble, D., (ed), op.cit., pp166-7.

48. Quoted in Russell, D., *The Tamarisk Tree 2*. Virago, London, 1980, p196.

49. See especially Russell, D., *The Tamarisk Tree*. op.cit., and Russell, D., *What Beacon Hill Stood For*. in *Anarchy 71*, Vol.7., No.1., London, 1967, pp11-16.

50. Russell, D., *What Beacon Hill Stood For*. op.cit., p16.

51. Russell, D., op.cit., p12.

52. Russell, D., *The Tamarisk Tree 2*. op.cit., p76.

53. Russell, D., op.cit., pp119-20.

54. Russell, D., op.cit., p197.

55. I am indebted to Daniel Simon who kindly donated a copy of his unpublished dissertation, *Forest School Camps - An Image of Childhood Over Sixty Years*. to the *Lib ED* archive. I have drawn heavily on his work and any research evident in this section is his.

56. Westlake, E., *The Forest School*. Order of Woodcraft Chivalry Publishing, London, 1930, p24.

57. *Prospectus for the Forest School at Sandy Balls*, Godshill, Hampshire, University of Warwick Library.

58. Brand, N., *Early Days in the Forest School*. Holloway Publications, London 1986, p14.

59. MacKenzie, R.F. *State School*. Penguin, London, 1970, p8.

60. Rutter, C.K. *Forest School Hampshire and Norfolk*. 1968, p3.

61. Westlake, E., op.cit., p26.

62. MacKenzie, R.F., op.cit., p10.

63. Marland, M., *Correspondence*. University of Warwick Library.

64. Gibson, T., *Youth For Freedom*. Freedom, London, 1951, pp12-13; *Workers' Control at Burgess Hill School*. in *Anarchy*, Vol.9., No.11., London, 1969, pp350-2; *Burgess Hill School: A Personal Account*. in the *Raven*, No.3., London, 1987, pp201-18; Markham, O., *Progressive Experience*. in *Anarchy*, Vol.4., No.9., London, 1964. pp264-7; Weaver, A., *A School Without A Head*. in *Anarchy*, Vol.9., No.9., London, 1969. pp274-8.

Notes

65. Weaver, A., op.cit., p274.

66. Weaver, A., op.cit., p276.

67. Weaver, A., op.cit., p278.

68. See Gibson, T., *Workers' Control at Burgess Hill.* op.cit., pp350-1.

69. Ibid.

70. Markham, O., op.cit., p264.

71. Ibid.

72. Markham, O., op.cit., p267.

73. Croall, J., op.cit., p214

74. For the only account of the early development of the school see Urban, E., *Monkton Wyld School.* in Child, H.A.T., (ed), *The Independent Progressive School.* Hutchinson, London, 1962, pp108-23.

75. Urban, E., op.cit., p111.

76. *HMI Report*, 1949. *Lib ED* Archive.

77. *Internal Document*, 1967. *Lib ED* Archive.

78. *Internal Document*, 1982. *Lib ED* Archive.

79. *Interview with Monkton Wyld ex-students*, June-December 1986. *Lib ED* Archive.

80. Ibid.

81. Ibid.

82. *HMI Report*, May 1982. *Lib ED* Archive.

83. Aitkenhead, J., op.cit., p8.

84. *Interview with Kilquhanity Students*, October 1988. *Lib ED* Archive.

85. Aitkenhead, J., *Kilquhanity House School.* in *Anarchy*, Vol.8. No.10., London, 1968, p323.

86. Aitkenhead, J., *That Dreadful School.* op.cit., p8.

87. Ibid.

88. Ibid.

89. Ibid.

No Master High or Low

90. *Interview with Kilquhanity Students*, op.cit.

91. *Interview with John Aitkenhead,* October 1988. *Lib ED* Archive.

92. Davidson, C., *Alternative Ways.* in *Resurgence,* Devon, September-October 1986, p17.

93. *No Ordinary School. Kirkdale - a living alternative. Lib ED* Archive.

94. Ibid.

95. Ibid.

96. Ibid.

97. In the first appendix to his book *Fifty Years of Freedom.* op.cit., Ray Hemmings includes the details of responses to a questionnaire he circulated to 102 selected head teachers about the influences of A. S. Neill.

98. See the chapters on Dartington Hall and Burgess Hill.

Put your right hand in: A Summerhill meeting.

PART THREE

On the Edge

LIBERTARIAN SCHOOLS FOR THE UNSCHOOLABLE

1910 - 1990

1. SCHOOLING THE UNSCHOOLABLE

Libertarian Ideas on Special Education, 1910 - 1990

In our society children experience great stress. This is not altogether surprising given the deference that is expected of them by government, its institutions, and adults in general. Government though, has chosen to categorise some children as being under more stress than others. It has created a terminology which has seen some children described as disturbed, maladjusted and, more recently, as in special need.

Such forms of classification are not helpful, nor are other attempts to remove the responsibility for the burden of children's stress from society, its institutions and adults onto the children. However, amidst the institutions that have been created for so-called disturbed, maladjusted and special needs children, there are, and have been, several which have been influenced by libertarian ideas. Homer Lane's Little Commonwealth (1913) was amongst the first in Britain, while Rowen House (1979) affords a contemporary example.

It is interesting that those involved in libertarian education have been able, often with governmental approval, to develop and sustain initiatives by virtue of the nature of "special" clientele. Indeed it would be fair to say that educational officialdom has often proved much more amenable to the development of radical and experimental projects for children in special need, probably because of the complexity and sometimes apparent impossibility of discovering appropriate forms of schooling.

The cynical have no problem in understanding this. For them it is a response of those in despair who are, in reality, aware of the inadequacy of orthodox views of education and schooling in meeting the needs of a section of society considered to be "on the edge". Others choose to regard it more positively. Father Owen, for example, was ordained in 1932 after working with the Ragged School Union in Lambeth, South London, and joined the Franciscan Order in 1936. Thereafter he worked in a variety of projects for the unschoolable, including a community for young "wayfarers" at Cerne Abbas, in the buildings previously occupied by the Little Commonwealth. He believed that notions of school conformity were often destructive to valuable individuality.

> "I always thank God that there are many maladjusted - there are far too many people who are well adjusted to a society that should not be adjusted to. The so-called maladjusted are far better 'material' because they question everything and, in my opinion, are more thoughtful than many of their age." [1]

In the early years of the twentieth century an enlightened debate was taking place about freedom and education. We have already seen how many of the private libertarian schools emerged as a result of that debate. A similar body to Edmond Holmes' Ideals in Education Group met regularly in the years immediately preceding the First World War, to give consideration to work with destitute and delinquent young people. The group included William Hunt, Leila Rendel, Homer Lane and Russell Hoare. All of them were occasional attenders at Holmes' group too. However, they saw themselves as being more radical than the early *New Era* Group, and were often ignored by Holmes and Beatrice Ensor. They were much closer to A. S. Neill, Dora Russell and Bill Curry in their thinking, and it is interesting that Neill considers the lives of Lane and Rendel to have had more influence on him than Holmes and Ensor.[2]

Hunt was an interesting character, but he never actually worked in a school. He spent most of his working life as superintendent of Wallingford Farm Training Colony which housed about 250 rejects of the Poor Law System. David Wills, though, has suggested that his ideas had great influence on Rendel and Lane. He records something that Hunt once said to him:

"People are always saying to me, 'What do you do to these boys?' and I say 'We don't do anything to them.'"[3]

Hunt was no advocate of laissez-faire, but the respect that he had for any individual young person was shared by Rendel, Lane and Hoare. These three individuals, who came from very different backgrounds, were to be behind the creation of the first three libertarian schools for the unschoolable, in 1911, 1913 and 1914 respectively.

Leila Rendel's origins were in nineteenth century liberal philanthropy, Homer Lane came from vigorous New England Puritan stock, and Russell Hoare had anarchist roots. However, they shared a fundamental belief, and that was a total respect for the autonomy of the individual. They came together as a result of a shared desire to completely challenge the then orthodox view that the only type of education which befitted the "unschoolable", whether non-attender, criminal, retarded or disabled, was an authoritarian and punitive one. In the almost progressive era of Edwardian Britain they were able to do so almost without interference, and often with governmental approval.

Of the three, most is known of Lane, due largely to Wills' exhaustive biography.[4] However, it is clear that when they met, Rendel, Lane and Hoare focused on three general issues around which they discussed and developed strategies for dealing with the unschoolable. These were personal autonomy, the law of love, freedom and responsibility and decision-making processes. The initiatives that the three worked in, the Caldecott Community, the Little Commonwealth and Sysonby House respectively, were all different, but they were underpinned by libertarian values which placed control for learning, living and loving in the hands of the learner. One cannot detach their idealism from the era in which it emerged. Indeed when we consider the work of thinkers like Nellie Dick, Neill and Lane, we learn as much about the era in which they developed their ideas as we do about the individuals themselves. It is no coincidence that the International Modern School Movement, Summerhill and Caldecott Community, the Little Commonwealth and Sysonby House were created in much the same era, despite their different focuses and clientele.

Much the same is true of a later period, the late 1930s and early 1940s. We have already seen how this period produced a second wave of libertarian private schools. The same period saw an expansion in the number of libertarian schools for the unschoolable: Red Hill School (1934), Hawkspur Camp (1936) and the Barns Experiment (1940).

W. A. C. Stewart has suggested that this expansion can be linked directly to the effects of the wave of the New Psychology in the late 1920s and 1930s.[5] Certainly Otto Shaw and Dave Wills, who were instrumental in the expansion, were much influenced by Neill's embracement of the New Psychology. There is evidence to suggest that their schools were built on many of the principles that Percy Nunn had elucidated in *Education: Its Data and First Principles*,[6] one of the most influential studies of the era. Nunn wrote as a liberal thinker who wished to enable each child to realise its potential more completely, and he called upon studies of human psychology and educational practice for this purpose. While the schools in his book were chosen from both the maintained system and the independent sector, including public and progressive schools, there can be no mistake that his prescriptions advised emancipation, the chance to experiment, to play, to create. He acknowledged the place and necessity of routine and ritual, but as a secure starting point from which independence could grow. These were principles that became close to the heart of Otto Shaw. For Wills they were already there after his discovery of Lane.

Similarly it was these ideas that were at the heart of the late 1960s and 1970s wave of libertarian schools for the unschoolable. Rowen House, founded by Bryn and Meg Purdy in 1979, is perhaps the most interesting. Bryn Purdy spoke to the magazine *Lib ED* in 1987, and the influence of Lane, Neill and the New Psychology are all evident:

> "I believe in a balance between freedom and authority. When I visited Summerhill I really believed in freedom but experience taught me that there was a limit, not a boundary to freedom. Somewhere beyond freedom there is permissivism, what Neill called 'licence'. I positively am a responsibilitarian who embraces authority but who rejects authoritarianism and permissivism. Concerning authority we have to remember that the word 'authority' is cognate with 'author', one who originates, creates. In educational terms authority may be used to create equal relationships between adult and child. Adults have a responsibility to create relationships with children, not to establish a control over them."[7]

Why was it that the period immediately before the First World War, the late 1930s and early 1940s, and 1970s saw the development of libertarian schools for the unschoolable? Essentially for the same reason that similar periods saw other libertarian experimentation. In each of the three eras a significant debate was taking place, not only about educational provision, but about the nature of that provision. Each era saw the development of ideas about personal rights and autonomy, about non-coercive pedagogies and about self-government. The schools included in this section were all built on these principles.

2. THE WHOLE CHILD

The Caldecott Community, (26, Cartwright Gardens, London, 1911 - 17; Charlton Court, East Sutton, Kent, 1917 - 25; Cuffley, Hertfordshire, 1925 - 41; Egdon Heath, London, 1941 - 5; New House, Mershan Le Hatch, 1945 - Date)

In her early twenties Lelia Rendel had been greatly interested in Margaret MacMillan's pioneering nursery work. This has been well-documented by Maurice Bridgeland.[8] The Caldecott Community was to evolve out of a working girls' club and day nursery run by her Aunt Edith. In the nursery and girls' club the emphasis was on the "whole child", and the Rendels wanted to develop as free an environment as possible in which education could flourish. In the first Annual Report of the Community in 1911 the principle aim was enunciated:

> *"To awaken in children that independence of spirit and joyousness of life which will alone give them the power of realising to the fullest extent the possibilities of development within their reach."*[9]

The children who attended the Community in its early years were working class, but neither "in care" nor convicted by the courts. Their paths to the Community were varied. Alice Woods has given a very illuminating account of the Community's early years.[10] It is clear from her account that the emphasis was on individual development and corporate consciousness.

In 1925, when the Community moved to Cuffley in Hertfordshire, it was decided that it would no longer admit only the socially deprived, and numbers rose considerably. However, by 1934 many local authorities were asking the Community to accept, as its special concern, the disturbed and difficult children of broken homes. In 1938 Caldecott became one of the first schools to be recognised by the Board of Education, under section 80 of the 1921 Education Act, as an appropriate establishment for those children whose behaviour had led to their exclusion from normal schools. By 1962 the proportion of such children in the Community had grown to almost two thirds of the pupil population.

It is worth considering what the government was recognising. Caldecott was a self-governing Community. There was no set timetable or formal classes. The emphasis was on learning by experience and discovery. But it is clear that Caldecott became an environment that was warm and stable. George was a pupil there for six years in the 1930s:

"It was the first home I had. To me it seemed perfectly natural to do what you liked, so long as it didn't interfere with anybody else that is. I had a big shock when I left. I found a job but it was all rules and regimentation. She was a brick was Miss Rendel." [11]

This is not to imply that there was no structure. Children were often placed in groups for particular activities; Rendel did not hold to the view that things would just happen. Her belief in freedom was a belief in human dignity: everybody had the right to choose, everybody had the right to make decisions, everybody had the right to say yes or no.

It is difficult to give a glimpse of what life was like at Caldecott in such a short space, especially as the Community has lasted for such a long time. However, up to 1969, when Rendel died, many things remained constant. The most important of these was the control which pupils exercised over what they did. Activities were constantly set up, but every pupil had the right of refusal and the right to pursue an activity of their own.

The strength of the Community lay largely, perhaps, in its continuity, which was maintained by a nucleus of loyal, poorly-paid staff. When Rendel died in March 1969, her co-director since 1931, Ethel Davies, remained in charge. She had originally come to Caldecott in 1928 as an assistant housekeeper for a salary of £50 a year. But Maurice Bridgeland should have the last word:

"Caldecott fulfilled many needs and will doubtless continue to act as a 'forerunner' in social-educational care in accord with the spirit of its founder whom no change of scene, financial crisis, world disaster or advancing age could frighten into a static security." [12]

3. FREE TO WORK OR LOAF

The Little Commonwealth, (Flowers Farm, Evershot, Dorset, 1913 - 1918)

Homer Lane came to England in 1913 at the invitation of George Montagu, later Ninth Earl of Sandwich, who was anxious to start a self-governing colony for young delinquents. He had heard of Lane's work at the Ford Republic, just outside Detroit, USA, and saw him as a likely director. Lane certainly impressed Montagu, and by July 1913 he was running the Little Commonwealth in Dorset.

Lane's story and that of the Little Commonwealth have been told by many.[13] Yet it is still difficult to build up a clear picture of what life was actually like at the Commonwealth. Much of the writing has focused on Lane's ideas and the various scandals which accompanied him. However, what is clear is that the Little Commonwealth was built on four principles, love, freedom, self-government and co-education. The structure through which these principles were expressed is most simply stated in a lecture given by Lane in 1918:

> *"The Little Commonwealth is a co-educational community inhabited by children ranging in age from a few months to nineteen years, those of more than thirteen years of age having been committed for a term of years for crime - as to a reformatory ... The younger children are those who would in any case be subject to institutional care in asylums and orphanages ... The population of the Commonwealth is five adults, four of whom are women, forty-two boys and girls of fourteen to nineteen years of age and nine younger children. This population is distributed among three 'families' grouped by congeniality ... Boys and girls live in the same families, sharing equally in the responsibility for the welfare of the younger children. The chief point of difference between the Commonwealth and other reformatories and schools is that in the Commonwealth there are no rules and regulations except those made by the boys and girls themselves. All those who are fourteen or over are citizens having joint responsibility for the regulation of their lives by the laws and judicial machinery organised and developed by themselves. The adult element studiously avoid any assumption of authority in the community except in connection with their respective departmental duties as teachers or as supervisors of labour within the economic scheme."* [14]

The "economic scheme" was considered to be the basis of public morality since the basic punishment was to be unemployed and to become a burden on one's family. A member of the Commonwealth described the economic scheme in 1914. It is a fascinating view from the inside:

> *"We are free to work or loaf as we choose. Our work is paid for in a currency of our own, equal in value to the coin of the realm, at the rate of three pence an hour. The diligent citizen earns something over 10s a week, this pays for his board, food, lodgings and clothing and leaves him a little sum over which he either spends on luxuries or banks against his return to the outdoor world ... If the free citizen slacks or refuses to work at all he gets no wages and so he cannot pay his way. But, as he is still supplied with the necessaries of life, somebody has to pay, and in this case the somebody is everybody. He is supported, like the unemployed without, by the rates and taxes. But not for long. The rest of the community who are milked of their spare earnings to pay his weekly bill, soon let him know that he is not behaving as a citizen should, and in the short history of the Commonwealth the pressure of public opinion has never yet failed to produce the desired effect."* [15]

If this economic scheme was the basis of living and existence in the Little Commonwealth, the Citizen's Court was the basis for decision making and self-government:

> *"It is in the Citizen's Court that one may get into closer touch with the spirit of the Commonwealth than in any other community function and it is here that I look for the spiritual expressions of our boys and girls."* [16]

The Court had an elected judge and officials. Its main function was to hear complaints about work or conduct, to discuss some aspects of policy and to award punishment. For Lane, though, it was also one of the main agencies of therapy in the community.

Also important at the Little Commonwealth was the family unit, the three cottages in which the pupils lived: Bramble, Veronica and Heather. A real family life was built in these dwellings, and Bazeley[17] attributed the vitality of public opinion which was the life-blood of the Citizen's Court to this family unit. Lane believed in building a loving community as well as one which was self-governing and respectful of personal autonomy.

Most of the citizens of the Commonwealth were deprived and delinquent, but Lane managed to create an environment that recognised individual rights as well as being committed to developing a sense of shared responsibility. He was keenly aware of the need to place potential adventures and learning experiences in the paths of pupils, and held a view of freedom that was constrained by a rejection of licence. Lane was no advocate of an unstructured world where some sort of natural order could be established. He knew that his clientele were at the Little Commonwealth as a result of emotional and psychological problems that were socially constructed. What he built was a therapeutic community that strove to undo that destructive experience using libertarian methods. The sad thing is that the value of the Little Commonwealth, as an example of libertarian practice, was largely undermined by the scandal that accompanied its closure in 1918, when the Home Office withdrew recognition from the Commonwealth after Lane was accused of seducing two young women there. The charges were never substantiated, but the damage was done both to the experiment itself and to its potential influence. And yet there are many who believe Homer Lane and the Little Commonwealth to have had a long lasting influence on the nature of educational provision both inside and outside the state system.[18]

4. THE RESIDIUM

Sysonby House, (Riverside Village, Melton Mowbray, 1914 - 19)

Established in 1914, with Russell Hoare as superintendent, Sysonby House was for:

> "... those who for some reason or other nobody else will touch ... the residium left when the crafts, educational, reformatory, ecclesiastical, social and charitable have sifted their clientele and can attract or will admit no more!" [19]

Before the war Hoare had been involved in relief and club work in East London. He was an anarchist, and known to many involved in the International Modern School Movement. He had attended several meetings at the Jubilee Street Club in Whitechapel and was in regular communication with both Lorenzo Portet and William Heaford, who were on the committee of the International League for the Rational Education of Children.

Hoare held a very different perspective to Rendel and Lane, although he was closely associated with both. For him the Caldecott Community and the Little Commonwealth were conformist and essentially wedded to a capitalist ethic. He saw them as reformatory institutions, with a view as to how their citizens should develop. He had no such vision, only a belief in the dignity that he felt accompanied personal freedom. He was in many ways a complete individualist, much more so than Lane, who has carried that mantel.

So at Sysonby there was no elaborate superstructure of self-government. Hoare believed that such systems were a sham, a means through which adults could impose indirect authority or the community could distort the individual's development by a display of adult forms and adult stability. Radical self-government by young people he saw as fluctuating:

> "... between the three extremes that make up the triangle of adolescent polity: tyranny, anarchy and the golden rule ... it being both too realistic and too idealistic to be capable of that continuous process we call development, evolution, progress ..." [20]

Sysonby was thus stripped of all authority other than that of Hoare's personality. There were few defined or structured activities. Young people worked on the building and the grounds. They cooked and cleaned, but it seems that there were no timetables or rotas. Sadly very few records have survived either personal or official, and in consequence it is difficult to build up a detailed picture of Sysonby.

Sysonby is interesting, though, because of the questions that Hoare posed about the relationship between adults and children. How far his methods worked is virtually impossible to gauge, but the way that he wrote about adults' responsibilities in relation to children is moving to say the least. He believed in the value of adult participation in the community at Sysonby, but only if the adult was capable of remaining an individual with experience and with more mature spiritual values without assuming any rights of authority. In the same talk to the Conference of Educational Associations he said that:

> *"It seems to me that boys and girls need real live grown-ups living among them, need their help and guidance, need them to be real and alive, and above all to be themselves, if they are in any way the right people to live among them. And so I would say, find a person who is a real person, a personality, and let him be himself, as big as his personality, as strong as his personality, but do not let him try to be artificially bigger or stronger, to rely for discipline or control on external aids, on the prerogatives of seniority, or its physical or emotional strength, or its worldly wisdom, or an assumed character, or an institution's machinery or penal systems. Let him meet the boys and girls frankly on their own ground, where they can cope with him, understand him, trust and love him."* [21]

With this in mind, Hoare and Sysonby leave a considerable legacy to the libertarian tradition of education and schooling. He had a clear belief and desire to establish as equal a relationship as possible between adults and children, recognising their rights, their differing needs and their individual experiences.

5. THE TESTING GROUND FOR PROGRESS

Red Hill School, 1934 - Date, (East Sutton, Nr. Maidstone, Kent)

Otto Shaw was born in 1908 into a fairly conventional family. He began his working life as neither teacher nor analyst, but as a petroleum technologist. He worked in an oil refinery. On his own admittance it was reading a book by A. S. Neill which changed his whole life.[22]

After being psychoanalysed, and making an intensive study of delinquency, he began Red Hill as a residential school for intelligent maladjusted boys and girls of secondary school age. However, after the school was supported by the Local Education Authority in 1941, and recognised by the Ministry of Education as a Grammar School after the 1944 Education Act, its clientele was all male.

Shaw was outraged by the idea that education in any form should be based on moral persuasion, coercion or punishment. Although he chose to work with young people who were supposedly highly intelligent, he was still working with the unschoolable, and the methods and approach he developed were essentially libertarian.

Red Hill was a self-governing community where the emphasis was placed on shared responsibility developed through a School Meeting. In the early days the School Meeting was run as a kind of enlarged family council, the main object of which was to demonstrate that the adults were not an alien, aggressive, and dangerous group, but prepared to respect the opinions of the pupils.

As the school developed so did self-government. By the 1940s any complaints and accusations that were raised in the School Meeting were referred to a School Court run by a group of pupils known as Bench Members, a Red Hill equivalent to Summerhill's Ombudsmen. The School Meeting also began to delegate responsibility to a number of committees, elected twice a year, concerned with food and hygiene, sports, social events, maintenance and resources like the library.

Unlike Lane, Shaw did not see self-government through the School Meeting as psychotherapeutic. He saw it in much more personal terms, as a vehicle for building closer relations between adults and young people. In the appendix to Shaw's *Maladjusted Boys*, Ivor Holland explained it thus:

> "Difficult parents have set up in the child's mind images which stand in the way of mutual confidence even when the teacher is not made a direct substitute for parents ... But unless such barriers are broken not only will the staff of the school be unable to give any adequate guidance, but also the insecurity which lies at the roots of the child's maladjustment will be perpetuated. The object of self-government is to place adults in a new and

different relationship to pupils which will make it harder for them to be set down, ex-hypothesi, as members of a different group with alien aims and intentions." [23]

For Shaw self-government was all about equality. It created an environment and atmosphere in which learning and progress could take place. In many ways he did not see the School Meeting as such an educative force, as did Neill or Lane, but even so his commitment to it was total.

Shaw was as much psychotherapist as teacher, and it is important to look at the kind of approach he adopted. Red Hill was created as the wave of interest in the New Psychology developed, and all of the libertarian initiatives for the unschoolable that emerged in the late 1930s were committed in some form to psychotherapeutic approaches. We also have to remember that so was Neill, and much of this was due to the influence of Lane, whose methods had an impact on the whole application of psychotherapy to education in the period up to the outbreak of the Second World War.

In *Maladjusted Boys*, Shaw outlines many case histories which reveal a simplicity of principle and boldness in approach.[24] In an article for the magazine *Anarchy*, Anthony Weaver chose one particular case study to illustrate Shaw's approach:[25]

"*Cecil's mother was a prostitute; he was daily in the company of her men and became involved in their quarrels. One afternoon, when he was eleven, his mother returned home, and from her almost demented conversation, he discovered she had gone to the river and drowned the baby she had borne a few weeks previously, and her manic comments seemed to suggest that she would soon kill herself. She left the house and presently he followed what he believed to be her path, to discover, by the side of the river about an hour later, some men and some policemen standing over her drowned body in the same part of the river in which earlier that day she had drowned her baby.*

He was now put into the care of the local children's committee but aggressive, truculent and dishonest behaviour caused his quick passage from altogether six Homes one after another.

'Quite obviously,' says Shaw 'the challenge of a child who had no reason to believe in other people's trustworthiness was very deep and if we were to succeed we had to withstand whatever reactive test he inflicted upon us ... It is insufficient to be patient; it is insufficient to give affection, but both have a promise of success if the boy is continually told why he is doing the thing that not only hurts others but bars the affection of others and therefore hurts him as well. The path was long, but after five months he began to smile; he had taken to asking for instead of demanding things, but at no time had any moral advice been offered as clearly such would be highly suspect.'

His first Christmas came, and as it was undesirable for him to return to his own home area, he was asked if he would like to accept an invitation, if such were offered, from a staff member ...

> He chose, and 'shaw enough' the invitation was forthcoming. Along with the Shaw family Cecil had his own pile of presents which, in his case, included a bicycle. When he had received it on that Christmas morning, so it is reported, a real sense of gratitude glowed.
>
> After this fortnight his return to school was marked by a relapse to his unhappy truculence and it was noticed that he was wearing a watch, the result, it later transpired, of a kind of forced loan. To have asked the obvious question would have denied the trust hitherto shown to him. Shaw took off his own watch before meeting him, seemingly by chance, in the corridor, and lifting his wrist called:
>
> 'Oh damn, I've left my watch somewhere. Do you know the time, Cecil?' Two days later, on hearing that the watch had been returned to the other boy, Shaw ordered Cecil sharply: 'Come to my house at 7.45 tomorrow morning.' Despite protests, he came, had breakfast and accompanied Shaw to a shop in the village where it had been previously arranged that the most expensive watch stocked should cost three guineas. Shaw then asked him to choose the one he liked, and when he had done so said, 'Right. That is yours.' Immediately he demurred, 'Oh I can't take that, it's too valuable.' A few seconds later he was crying. Shaw explains that the point of this story is that it anticipated theft: 'It is little good to pardon theft after it has occurred by making up or not making up to the thief by some gift what he has symbolically stolen.'
>
> Somewhat later the English teachers reported an inexplicable deterioration in Cecil's spelling. Words involving a, e, i, d, and s, he could not get right. He brought the matter up in private session.
>
> Shaw asked him to write the five offending letters on cards and arrange them in any way his imagination suggested. After some hesitation the word SADIE appeared at which Cecil blushed and began to sob. 'That's my mother's name. She was called Sadie' - over and over again he muttered. At the time of the curious impairment of his spelling he had realised it was the second anniversary of his mother's death: the discussion was later shown to have completely remedied the misspelling.
>
> Needless to say his relationship with adults and with the boys gradually improved. He left for a university and shortly afterwards was to get married."

Shaw used this kind of approach in order to "free" his pupils to learn. The classrooms at Red Hill were a kind of testing ground for progress in psychotherapy as well as being of innate value. At Red Hill there was no emphasis on simply increasing knowledge or passing exams. The pupils' work was, in the first instance, initiated by themselves. Shaw, however, wished to place all options in front of his pupils, and it would be misleading to suggest that he placed no importance on academic progress. On the contrary he employed a highly qualified and professional staff and, as Maurice Bridgeland has illustrated, many of his pupils achieved considerable academic success.[26]

6. THE HORRORS OF PERSONAL SELF-DISCIPLINE

Hawkspur Camp, 1936 - 1940, (Hawkspur Green, Great Bardfield)

The Hawkspur experiment was very much the inspired initiative of David Wills. He had been a brother in W. H. Hunt's Wallingford Farm Training Colony in 1922 but, after a Social Study Diploma Course at Birmingham University, he began to develop an interest in planning a therapeutic community for problem children and young offenders in particular.

Wills published his plan, which was clearly much influenced by Lane's ideas, and it attracted the attention of Marjorie Franklin, the inspiration behind the Q Camps Committee, which was formed in 1934 to put into practice the principles of the Grith Pioneers with groups of deprived young people. The Grith Pioneers were an outdoor organisation which promoted pioneering and self-government as an educational experience.[27]

The chairman of the Q Camps Committee was Cuthbert Rutter and he felt that, instead of having a series of camps in different places, one permanent camp would be easier to run and could be a more lasting and stable educational experiment. A site was found in Hawkspur Green and Franklin suggested that Wills be offered the responsibility for co-ordinating the project. Wills was only too pleased to accept and the project began in the Summer of 1936. The Q Camps Committee retained an important administrative and advisory role, but Wills was very much the man on the ground.

Hawkspur was aimed at:

"Young men ... who seem likely to respond to an unconventional but carefully thought-out open-air life ... but who never the less are not sufficiently advanced in citizenship to fit as ordinary members into an unmodified environment." [28]

In fact most of the young men who came to Hawkspur did so after all else had failed.

Nevertheless the camp was built on libertarian principles. In the first instance Wills was determined that there should be an atmosphere of shared responsibility, within which self-government could operate. As practised at Hawkspur, and in subsequent institutions with which Wills was associated, shared responsibility differed from the concept of self-government considered thus far. Wills was very honest about the difficulties of building a system of self-government where all had equal rights. He tried to develop a system which recognised that in any democratic structure some would hold more power than others, often by virtue of personality and experience. As he once said of meetings at Hawkspur:

> "... if I really press a point hard the decision never goes against me." [29]

He believed that the occasions when such pressure was used were rare, but adults, especially, were aware of this, and its possibilities and advantages. He impressed the need for all of the staff to be conscious of their power in a democratic forum and to be able to divest themselves of all authority as required. This, for him, was genuinely shared responsibility, relying, not on a structure to build equality, but on individuals addressing their own personal power, actual or potential.

These ideas extended and applied to all at Hawkspur as far as Wills was concerned. He sought to make young people aware of their positions in a structure; collective decision-making only had meaning if individuals were aware of what they were doing within a given process, and this was the reason why shared responsibility and self-government were therapeutic. He put it succinctly in his writing about Hawkspur:

> "Having to discipline oneself instead of being disciplined by others is a burden ... So now we can see self-government in a new light. It is not merely a privilege that is bestowed on them because we superior mortals think the experience might be useful for them. It is absolute necessity to enable them to set a term to the horrors of personal self-discipline which we have thrust upon them by refusing to be authoritarian." [30]

What this meant in practice was that the decision-making body, known as the Council, grew spontaneously, and its authority was limited to the domestic affairs of the camp. It combined both legislative and judicial functions, but its chief importance was as a vehicle for the expression of public opinion.

Council Meetings occupied a lot of time at Hawkspur and, while individual therapy sessions were run by Wills and other staff, it was the Meetings and the work that grew out of them that were important at Hawkspur. Work which was fully shared was seen as having value as inspiration, encouragement, adventure, education and discipline. A. T. Baron, a member of staff, wrote:

> "It would have saved us some real hardship, and have sometimes been cheaper to buy doors, windows, and other joinery ready-made or ready-milled. We did not do so, even though this meant our working in the midst of winter covered only by a roof in a shelter with neither walls or a solid floor which it was impossible to warm, because we worked to build the camp as nearly unaided as we could. We also avoided using metal bolts and other sundries for the making of which we had not yet the equipment. This meant the invention of gadgets which would serve the same purpose, or a reversion to the methods of craftsmen of the days before machinery." [31]

Thus, at Hawkspur, work was thought to develop not only skills but also self-respect. It was achieved without compulsion and was organised by the Council through the exercise of shared responsibility.

The experiment lasted for only four years, closing in 1940 as funds ran out, and as the Home Office equivocated over recognition. The Q Camps Committee withdrew and Wills accepted an offer to become the warden of another experiment, the Barns Hostel. However, we should not judge Hawkspur by its short life for, in many ways, Wills broke new ground within the libertarian tradition. He addressed an issue of fundamental importance in his attempts to construct a self-governing process that understood the need for individuals to assess their own personal power within an apparently democratic structure. The system was not enough for him and the personal had to be political at Hawkspur.

7. FROM TRUANTS TO CITIZENS

The Barns Experiment, 1940 - 1944, (Peebles, Scotland)

The Barns experiment was a War School for unschoolable and unbilletable evacuees. It is only known through David Wills' own writings.[32] Its relevance is the anti-punitive and non-coercive ethos that Wills strove to develop there in its short life.

Wills was determined that he would try to develop the kind of work he had begun at Hawkspur. He was dealing with a very difficult group of young boys, aged from nine to fourteen, who had refused to attend school, were impossible to billet and who were frighteningly aggressive. Wills was advised to be firm, but set about creating a rule-free environment where the experiment would become a product of the clientele and staff. Wills was adamant; there was to be no punishment system, no set lessons, no defined activities.

During the first four months of the experiment Wills readily admits there was chaos, surging unrest and destruction:

"The chief game seemed to consist of charging wildly through the house howling madly and slamming all the doors on the way. Any kind of organised activity was impossible. Crockery would be dashed onto stone floors, games destroyed, furniture broken, stones hurled through windows. Meal times were an indescribable battle and there was mass truanting." [33]

For Wills this process was a search on the part of the boys for the only security that most of them knew; imposed discipline. Wills refused to give in. After four months, on the suggestion of two of the boys, a decision-making body was created, known as the Citizens Association, a kind of voluntary organisation of all those willing to work for Barns. This body and principle was fully accepted by all the boys in attendance at the end of 1940, and the induction of boys into the experiment entailed an explanation of and eventual commitment to the Association.

The whole of the experiment was built around the Association, which organised and controlled the Barns' day: bedtimes, meals, lessons, anti-social behaviour and so on.

In many ways there is a need to put Wills' work in Peebles alongside his work at Hawkspur. Together they manifest, perhaps more than any other initiative, a belief in personal autonomy and non-coercive educational practice that William Godwin had demanded 150 years before.

8. CONTINUING THE LINE

New Barns School, 1965 - Date, (Church Lane, Toddington, Gloucester)

New Barns School was established as an independent school in 1965 by the Homer Lane Trust. It grew out of a small group of people who were living together as a community in London. They found the educational climate in the mid 1960s repressive, but at the same time it provoked some questions. The Homer Lane Trust had been established to further Lane's ideas, and it made a considerable contribution to the debate about freedom in education in the 1960s.

David Wills became the Chairman of Governors of the New Barns, and the school started by making provision for children who displayed evidence of serious emotional and psychological disturbance, expanding later to include those whose difficulties could be presumed to have a basis in psychotic or organic disorders.[34]

The school caters for an age range of eight to thirteen, and the age of admission is in most cases between eight and eleven. In some circumstances children may be admitted at seven, and the child might remain at the school past the age of thirteen where there are very positive therapeutic reasons to justify this.

New Barns is concerned to make provision for children with a particular form of special need through environmental therapy. It seeks to provide a community recognising, and tolerant of, the need of children to work through their symptomatic behaviours. This can be expected to take negative forms, including degrees of withdrawal and aggression.

The influence of Lane and Wills is very apparent. Any visitor to New Barns will quickly become aware of "The Meeting", a name given to the collective activity of the community. There is a Meeting after each meal, which discusses proposals covering almost every aspect of community life. It hears complaints by and against both children and adults, usually dealt with by restitution. There are also Meeting officers, similar, as at Red Hill, to the Summerhill Ombudsmen.

New Barns is a community where children can experience and respond to innumerable relationships and situations on many levels, as their needs and development demand. The emphasis is on the kind of shared responsibility that Wills developed at Hawkspur and Barns. The community recognises that shared responsibility cannot be a panacea for all ills, and there is a lot of importance attached to individual relationships between children and adults, which provide some kind of protection from what can be overwhelming group pressure.

The range of activities on offer at New Barns, and the specialist teaching available, is impressive. Of all the libertarian schools for the unschoolable it has probably given more thought, time and capital to this. Teaching groups are very small and there is a completely informal and individual approach.

Organised group work is considered undesirable, and is virtually impossible anyway. The morning session of the school is usually devoted to the individual and basic work of the children. There is no formal curriculum and a wide range of work is available.

During the afternoons, with almost every member of the staff participating, a programme of creative activity is on offer. There are opportunities, again in very small groups, to participate in pottery, painting, basket-work, woodwork, games, building, bicycle maintenance and gardening. Much of this work also relates to the needs of the community and one is struck by the integration of academic learning, therapeutic care and community work.

In many ways New Barns School stands at the end of a line of development that began at the Little Commonwealth and went through Hawkspur and Barns. It is a lasting testament to the libertarian idealism of Homer Lane and to the thoughtful and practical application of such ideals by David Wills.

9. CHILDREN UNDER STRESS

Rowen House School, 1979 - 1992, (Holbrook Road, Belper, Derbyshire)

Rowen House School, named after the nineteenth century innovator, Robert Owen, was opened in 1979. It is the inspired initiative of Bryn and Meg Purdy, and Neil Redfern, who joined them in 1981, and offers a residential community education to girls, ranging in age from nine to sixteen. Most of the girls who attend the school, twelve in all, are referred and funded by Local Authorities. They are deemed to have a variety of educational and emotional problems.

"Children under stress" is how the staff at Rowen House (five full-time and three part-time) choose to regard the girls. This is as distinct from being disturbed or maladjusted or in special need, which often implies an irremediable category of handicap. The stress is seen as being quite discrete from the child. Rowen House seeks to create an environment which can help the child become aware of the phenomenology of her stress, its causes, its symptoms and, above all, its remediability by positive and practical steps. The aim is to create as relaxed a community as possible, consistent with the needs of the individual child and the stability of the group.

The school itself is situated on the edge of a council estate on the outskirts of a small industrial and market town. Its frontage is part of an ordinary residential road. Its rear overlooks rolling Derbyshire hill country. The child is, therefore, not separated from society and contact with the community is encouraged. Friends are met and invited into the school. The girls attend local youth activities, join the Public Library and occasionally attend local schools and Colleges of Further Education. Furthermore, they do not stay at the school at weekends. They go home, or to "befrienders", local families who invite them into their homes.

The school offers a highly individualised programme of education and communal education in personal relationships. Most of the girls are deeply antipathetic to schools and schooling. "Formal" lessons operate in the mornings, with "option" times in the afternoon. However, there is no compulsion upon the girls to attend lessons or options. As far as their formal education is concerned, everything is developed co-operatively and collaboratively between teacher and student.

"Therapy" is not so much practised "on" the pupils, but is experienced among the girls and teachers themselves. A "Moot", open to all people in the school, but again not compulsory, is held at the beginning of each day. It is an hour-long forum where points of principle are discussed and established, and where particular day-to-day issues raised by members of the community are talked out. Occasionally decisions are taken to restrict cases of persistent anti-social behaviour. Even in such cases the community aims at consensus.

The gate opens for those at Rowen House

This method of discussion is in evidence during much of the school day, between individual staff and a girl or girls, and between the girls themselves, who fulfil a mutual counselling role. In many ways it is their experiences of, and attitudes towards, the school that are the most illuminating. Several of the girls talked to the magazine *Lib ED* in 1987 about this.[35]

Firstly Julie spoke about her general feelings about the school:

> "In this school everything's out in the open. You don't get staff going and talking behind our backs. Like when I was in the other schools teachers were always doing that, you know, finding out what you'd been doing, coming back and telling you off about it. Here it's different. The Moot is important. That's where everything gets talked out. Anybody can talk, you know, say what they like. It helps people to get to know each other. The teachers are dead different. They treat you like people. You don't have to go to lessons either. I go to lessons when I feel like it. I suppose it's important to go to lessons, but there aren't any set lessons. That makes it different. You just go to a room and do different things when you want to. You do Maths and English and stuff but it's different. I can't explain it but it doesn't feel like a lesson in a normal school. I suppose it's me who decides when I'm going to work. It's my choice. You know, Meg doesn't make you go to a class. Anyway why should she? It's not for her benefit. It's for me. It's up to me isn't it? People who come here have got a lot of freedom. They're not always told what to do. They don't have to go to lessons. They can talk to people about their problems. There are rules here but it's different to most schools. We have a say in what goes on. Say if Bryn wanted to build a new bedroom. He'd talk to people about it and it would get talked about in the Moot. And also when there is any trouble it's talked about in the Moot as well. That sort of thing never happens in other schools. It can be hard in the Moot because it's like grassing on your mates but somehow it is different. I still think I'm grassing on my mates if I talk about them in the Moot but I suppose I'm not really."

Dawn also spoke about the Moot:

> "The Moot is there to talk. We talk mostly about other people and try to sort out their problems and any problems that might be going on in running the school. Some people think it's grassing but grassing is talking about people behind their backs. In the Moot the people are there and you don't really talk to them, you talk to the Moot but you're in front of them. The Moot makes it possible to be in the open with people and to share things with people. I think it's a very good thing because you can't sort things out with one or two people. If two people aren't getting on it's not just their problem, it's everyone's. It's the same with the school. We all belong here, we live here, we are involved in helping the school work. Mind you, don't get the wrong impression. Some people really don't like the Moot and if you're being talked about in the Moot it's horrible. I actually can't stand it. If I'm talked about sometimes I walk out or just shut off. But in the end the Moot makes you think about whatever problem it is. It won't go away until you've faced up to the problem. The

> big difference between the way in which problems are sorted out here and most schools is that here everybody is involved and people get to the bottom of problems. By problems I don't just mean school problems, but people's problems too. The Moot is about helping people as well as the school."

Nikki said what she felt about being in a girls-only school:

> "It's strange being in a school where there are all girls, but it's better. You don't have all these problems about who's going out with who. But the big thing is there's more privacy. At the school I was at before boys were always dominating. The girls used to look up at them all the time. Well not all the time. And not all the girls. But lots of girls show off to boys. It's much easier for girls to be themselves here. Also we get to do what we want to. This place could work if boys were here but they'd have to be different. I wouldn't disagree with boys being here, in fact, it would be quite nice. But I just think it would stop us from being close together. We really do get to do what we want."

Then when pressed she offered her thoughts on "maladjustment":

> "I just hate the word maladjusted. The other day Bryn said to someone who was visiting, 'We're a special school'. I was really annoyed with him. We're not special either. Alright we're here because we've had problems. It's not necessarily our fault you know. I think if there's anyone who's special it's the teachers in the schools. What a bunch. All they could say about me was, 'There's something wrong with you'. Maybe there was but what did they try to do about it? I can't stand labels. Backward, I don't like that either. It doesn't explain anything. I'm not any different to anyone else, except that I used to find it difficult to talk to people about what I was feeling and certain things that had happened to me. Yeah, I know they called me maladjusted. I tell you what that means to teachers: stick stroppy kids in a corner, put a label on them, don't give a toss and forget they're real people. Like they call handicapped people special, don't they? It depends which way you use it, I know, but these people are not special, well they shouldn't be anyway. It's like when people use the word nigger for black people. They are not niggers, they're black people. Labels stop us from thinking. They're a form of prejudice. It's like calling somebody big tabs because they've got big ears or big nose or big head, small, short. Labels, they make me sick. I'll tell you what, right. Nobody's perfect. I used to label people. Sympathy for people was inside me but it couldn't come out. It was like there was barbed wire round it. But when I came here, right, I could tell people what I felt, I expressed my feelings. I told people what had happened to me. People used to listen. I realised I was alright you know. I wasn't thick, I wasn't a problem, I'd just had a hard time. Now I can see what all sorts of people feel. Labels, you can stick them, they don't tell you anything."

These descriptions and assessments are very revealing, offering a real insight into how the unschoolable feel about their situation and the

Children Under Stress

libertarian approach that has been "used" on them. The girls appear to experience the school as a caring community where no attempt is made to force them to adjust. The emphasis is on coming to terms with themselves and making an attempt to understand the roots of their stress. There is not a "norm" to aim for and there is clearly a respect for young people at Rowen House, a respect that features in all of the initiatives in this section.

"It's much easier for girls to be themselves here"

10. A CONTRADICTION IN TERMS?

Libertarian Schooling for the Unschoolable, 1910 - 1990

The libertarian schools for the unschoolable offer interesting comparisons with the other schools that have been considered. Firstly, the waves of experimentation are virtually identical, the period immediately before and after the First World War, the mid to late 1930s and the late 1960s and 1970s. This is hardly surprising as these were years of more general experimentation and cultural progressivism.

Secondly, the schools considered in this section have been pulled out of a much more general progressive tradition of pioneering work with those young people considered to be in special educational need. Maurice Bridgeland's much referred to study *Pioneer Work with Maladjusted Children* thoroughly examines this tradition in the same way as Trevor Blewitt and H. A. T. Child have examined the wider independent progressive school tradition.[36]

Thirdly, many of the schools were in effect "private adventures". They warrant separate consideration only because they were set up with a very different clientele from Summerhill, Dartington Hall and Beacon Hill.

There is a last comparison and this is more to do with the nature of the educational provision in the schools. What unites the Little Commonwealth, The Hawkspur Experiment and Rowen House, to name but three, is the importance attached to personal autonomy, the aversion to systems of reward and punishment, hostility to coercive pedagogy and the fundamental and central belief in self-government.

However, it would be an oversight not to consider the particular and specific contribution to the libertarian tradition. Lane was a true pioneer. In many ways it was he and the Little Commonwealth who legitimised an approach that had some sort of therapeutic credibility. In many ways Wills was even more interesting. One senses in him a nagging doubt about what many see as a simplicity inherent in the Neillian concept of freedom which focuses essentially on the removal of constraints, be they family, adult or dictums. At Hawkspur, in particular, there was a struggle to find an appropriate form of self-government that was pertinent to the needs of a particular community. It was an open struggle and one about which Wills himself is honest. The lesson would appear to be that there can never be a blueprint for any libertarian practice in schools, only a generalised method or overall approach.

A close examination of the schools reveals as much about the nature of schooling as it does about a particular type of child. The young women at Rowen House capture the very essence of this. It is not so much that they are unschoolable or that they do not want to attend a school. They demand

A Contradiction in Terms?

respect and desire a secure and stable environment where they know that their views will be considered and acted upon, not just tolerated and ignored.

However, whether we like it or not, the pupils of these schools are casualties and rejects of a particular kind of society. While the schools are clearly child-centred, there is still inevitably an overbearing stigma that is attached to being set apart. The important point, however, is that the experience of the libertarian approach shows that it may be applied generally and is not solely appropriate to the unschoolable.

NOTES

1. Quoted in Bridgeland, M., *Pioneer Work with Maladjusted Children*. Staples Press, London, 1971, p236.

2. Neill, A. S., *Neill! Neill! Orange Peel*. Quartet, London, 1972.

3. Wills, W. D., *Throw away thy Rod*. Gollancz, London, 1960, p18.

4. Wills, W. D., *Homer Lane*. Allen and Unwin, London, 1964.

5. Stewart, W. A. C., *Progressives and Radicals in English Education 1750-1970*. Augustus Kelley, New Jersey, 1972, p246.

6. Nunn, T. P., *Education: Its Data and First Principles*. London, 1920.

7. *Lib ED* Leicester 1987. Vol.2, No.6., p12.

8. Bridgeland, M, op.cit.,

9. *The Caldecott Community. First Annual Report*, p3.

10. Woods, A., *Educational Experiments in England*. Methuen, London, 1920, pp82-9 and 121-4.

11. *The Caldecott Community. Annual Report 1946*, p8.

12. Bridgeland, M., op.cit., p89.

13. Bazeley, E. T., *Homer Lane and the Little Commonwealth*. Allen and Unwin, London 1928; Wills, W. D., *Homer Lane*. Allen and Unwin, London, 1907; Perry L.R.(ed) *Four Progressive Educators*. Collier-MacMillan, London, 1967; Lane, Homer, *Talks to parents and teachers*. Allen and Unwin, London, 1928.

14. Lane, H., op.cit., pp 188-9.

15. *The Times Educational Supplement*. 6th January 1914, p6.

16. Lane, H., op.cit., p192.

17. Bazeley, E. T., op.cit., p121.

18. See Part 4.

19. Hoare, R. F., *Principles of Discipline and Self-Government. An experiment at Riverside Village*, published in *Report of the Sixth Annual Conference of Educational Associations*, London, 1918, p231.

20. Hoare, R. F., op.cit, p237.

Notes

21. Hoare, R. F., op.cit., pp241-2.

22. Shaw, O. L., *Maladjusted Boys*. Allen and Unwin, London, 1965, pp62-4.

23. Shaw, O. L., op.cit., Appendix 1.

24. Shaw, O. L., op.cit.

25. Weaver, A., *A One-Man Show: The Story of Red Hill School*. in *Anarchy*, Vol 7., No.1., London, 1967. pp22-3.

26. Bridgeland, M., op.cit., p171-8.

27. Franklin, M. E., (ed) *Q Camp*. London, 1966, p10.

28. Bridgeland, M., op.cit., p184.

29. Wills, W. D., *Throw away thy Rod*. Gollancz, London, 1960, p77.

30. Wills, W. D., *The Hawkspur Experiment*. Allen and Unwin, London, 1941, p52.

31. Barron, A. T., in Franklin, M. E., (ed) op.cit., pp33-4.

32. Wills, W. D., *The Barns Experiment*. Allen and Unwin, London, 1945.

33. Wills, W. D., op.cit., p11.

34. *New Barns*. Homer Lane Trust, 1975, p7.

35. *Lib ED*, op.cit.

36. Bridgland, M., op. cit.; Blewitt, T., (ed), *The Modern Schools Handbook*. Gollanz, London, 1934; and Child, H.A.T., (ed), *The Independent Progressive School*. Hutchinson, London, 1962.

PART FOUR

Inside the State

LIBERTARIAN EDUCATION AND STATE SCHOOLING

1918 - 1990

1. EFFECTING CHANGE

Libertarianism and the debate about education, 1918 - 1990

The previous two sections could easily lead to a conclusion that libertarian approaches to education have had most impact in private residential education. Whilst continuity and longevity have been features of such schools, most libertarian experimentation and development has actually taken place in State Schools and urban Free Schools.

We have already seen how the earliest influence of libertarian educational theory was felt in working class communities in London and Liverpool, with a wave of International Modern Schools being established immediately before and after the First World War. Similarly the 1960s and 1970s saw a wave of Free Schools established in working class areas of major cities in Britain. However, this section examines the nature and impact of libertarianism within the national state education system.

State Schools have always been sites of conflict for teachers and students alike. Predictably most attention is paid to the former, due to the professional status that is afforded them. Consequently we are able to read quite easily of the attempts by teachers to obtain higher pay and better conditions of service.[1] It is more difficult to find out about the attitudes and experiences of children in State Schools. There is a popular stereotype and academic orthodoxy that portrays school pupils as disciplined, conformist and submissive to school authority. Only scant attention is paid to non-attendance, to disruption and to the organised campaigns of children in schools.

In recent years the government has launched a series of enquiries, the most significant of which was headed by Lord Elton, investigating the behaviour of children in schools, but this has been largely in response to demands made by the teacher unions and professional associations. There has been little effort made to examine children's experience of state schooling or to understand the nature and impact of state schooling on them.

Only Stephen Humphries in his excellent book *Hooligans and Rebels* has done this.[2] He has argued that the insubordination, impertinence, defiance, wilfulness, obstinacy, conceit, irregularity, ill-manners, ignorance, inattention, laziness, dishonesty and foul language that children have been accused of in State Schools for decades are, in reality, legitimate forms of opposition on the part of the young and disempowered. He argues that children's disruptive behaviour in school, a constant feature since attendance became compulsory, is the largest single indictment of authoritarian schooling, and suggests that the twenty-five per cent of young people who have regularly absented themselves from school constitute a significant body of opinion voting with their feet.

It is such a perspective, which demands a change in schools for the young, that provides the background for a general consideration of the way in which libertarian ideas and libertarian educators have tried to effect change inside State Schools since 1918.

Government has never quite had its own way with schools and schooling. Britain has always had a huge variety of State Schools and differences abound from county to county, city to city, town to town and village to village.

How unified the system will now become, with the advent of a National Curriculum, standardised testing, the decline in importance of Local Education Authorities and the consequent development of local financial management, only the twenty-first century will tell. But if history is anything to go by, it seems unlikely that the dissenting tradition is at an end.

There is a rich vein of progressive experimentation in British State Schools that runs through this century. For example, as Brian Simon has written:

> "The English primary school - or at least its most advanced section - is probably unique in the world and is certainly arousing widespread interest ... Its main features include flexible grouping systems, especially the rapid shift towards non-streaming, together with in many cases vertical grouping; a new approach to the curriculum, or rather, to the content of pupils' activities, based on enhancing the child's activity in variously structured learning situations; the promotion of artistic, aesthetic and musical activity with the emphasis on creativity and many other features." [3]

Similarly Clive Harber and Roland Meighan have recorded a host of progressive tendencies inside secondary schools in their book *The Democratic School*.[4] However, we are not centrally concerned with progressivism.

After 1918, as English primary education became more humane and began some progressive experimentation, Edward O'Neill was going many steps further in Prestolee Elementary School near Farnworth in Lancashire. Influenced by A. S. Neill and the libertarians in the New Ideals in Education Group, he had abolished the timetable and facilitated the development of a curriculum where children could initiate their own work programmes to a degree hitherto unknown in a State School. Prestolee was probably the first libertarian influenced State School.

Similarly, in 1945, Alex Bloom was appointed to the headship of St. George-in-the-East Secondary School in Cable Street, Stepney, and as the early hostility to the new tripartite system began to develop Bloom sought genuine libertarian practices in his school. The keystone of his educational beliefs was co-operation, and as a consequence of this came his rejection of punishments and rewards and his institution of a Council of Pupils to discuss the year's projects and to choose their own curriculum.

However, it was the 1960s and early 1970s that saw libertarian ideas about education making a significant impact inside the state system particularly in five schools: two in Scotland, at Braehead School and Summerhill Academy, and three in England at Countesthorpe College, the Sutton Centre and William Tyndale School. It is interesting that this period saw libertarianism having more impact inside State Schools than in private residential education, where only the changes at Monkton Wyld and the creation of Kirkdale have warranted attention. This was in part due to the emergence of the deschooling movement, but also a consequence of the widespread interest in libertarian approaches to education that accompanied a more general revived interest in anarchist ideas at this time.

The word "deschooling" was first used by Ivan Illich, initially in articles he wrote for the *New York Review of Books*, but then in his book *Deschooling Society*.[5] The message implicit in the term "deschooling" accorded well with the libertarian currents of the time and Illich's work found an audience amongst the active European student movement. Illich's thesis was that society dominated by schooling was becoming a schooled society. This was not an educated society, but rather a society conditioned into a set of attitudes, beliefs and values which accompanied any mass education system. This was the result, not of education, but of the institutionalisation of education, which led to the assumption by most people that school was the only important place where learning occurred, that only school knowledge counted, that learning was the result of teaching, and that teaching required professionals to do it.

Illich counterposed that education could be liberating. He argued that education held the key to personal liberation and, ultimately, to social revolution. He believed that a liberation movement starting in school could help to change society through a radical programme of deschooling.

Such a prospect was utopian in the extreme, but Illich's programme of creating learning networks which provided access to resources, skill exchanges and peer matching had a great effect on educational thinking at the time. He was not alone in arguing for such educational reform, but it is his ideas that are important in order to understand the context in which schools like Countesthorpe College and the Sutton Centre emerged. They, like Prestolee and St. George-in-the-East before them, were very much a product of a particular set of historical circumstances.

2. OUT WITH THE 3 Rs

Prestolee Elementary School, (Farnworth, Lancashire, 1918 - 51)

E. F. O'Neill was born in Salford in 1890. He developed a thirst for education from a very young age but found school stifling and repressive, with its rote learning and regimentation. By the time he was sixteen he was a pupil teacher, with his heart set on becoming a qualified teacher and a determination to right the educational wrongs he had felt as a school pupil.

Eventually he went to Crewe Training College, where he qualified as a teacher, and after spells at Saint Luke's School and Saint Oswald's School, both in Salford, he was discovered by Edmond Holmes who recommended him for the headship of Prestolee School in Farnworth.

Holmes had been impressed by O'Neill after he had become involved in the New Ideals in Education Group. He was familiar with O'Neill's work at St. Oswald's, where children were encouraged to work at projects at their own pace and the need for a set timetable was played down. Indeed, O'Neill spoke to the New Ideals conference in 1917 and 1918 on this very issue.

O'Neill was one of the few of the core of the New Ideals Group who worked in the state system. It was probably for this reason that Holmes admired him. For Holmes, the priority was to effect change in State Schools, and he found it difficult to relate to many of the private sector interests in the New Ideals Group. O'Neill had similar difficulties, and others that were more based more in educational differences rather than class ones. In 1917 he delivered a talk to the New Ideals conference entitled "Developments on self-activity in an Elementary school". The talk provoked considerable controversy, and many of the audience questioned the degree of personal autonomy O'Neill was prepared to afford to children. After he took up his post at Prestolee he had little further contact with the New Ideals Group, which prevented an interesting potential alliance with Neill, Russell and Curry once they had emerged as a grouping by the late 1920s.

At Prestolee, O'Neill set about organising a small revolution. He proposed to flush out the old three Rs of rote, regimentation and regurgitation and to do this O'Neill had, as John Watts had noted, to:

> "... leap decades, beyond the practice of streaming, beyond mixed-ability grouping, to the logical conclusion that today is still a needle of hope in a haystack of conformity, namely, the integrated day with individualised timetables." [6]

Implicitly, O'Neill abandoned the "banking" system of education years before Paulo Freire had even identified it. He refused to accept that children had to have knowledge deposited in them, and he also recognised the very limited extent to which children will work for indefinite and delayed goals. Education had to foster individual growth.

O'Neill was able to tolerate the old regime for only twenty-four hours. His first day at the school began with orderly queues in the playground, a devout morning assembly, strict Scripture and Arithmetic lessons and constant harassment from the school caretaker, a rigid disciplinarian. On Day Two O'Neill told the caretaker to keep out of his and the children's way, and the morning assembly became a sit-down story. Teachers' blackboards were turned into tables, teachers' scheme books dispensed with and the timetable, usually displayed glazed in a handsome frame, eclipsed by a colour print of the Laughing Cavalier in the same frame. Playtimes were abolished, tea was available all day long for staff and pupils alike.

O'Neill then set about creating a new order. Children were allowed to work on whatever subject they liked, for as long as they wished and with whom they chose. Everybody was encouraged to go and get, and later put away, anything needed. The monitorial system was completely dispensed with. As far as possible children were allowed to become property owners, each being supplied with pen, pencil, ink and paints.

For O'Neill it was all or nothing, but these early days were turbulent times as far as relations with the rest of the staff were concerned. In many ways, this was the sign of things to come. Most of the staff were irritated, muddled, hurt and made to imagine they were valueless. However, O'Neill's reforms met with immediate approval from the children and, more important in terms of the survival of the school, from the relevant authorities.

Edmond Holmes was very important, because as an ex-School Inspector he wielded a lot of influence with the authorities. He reported on Prestolee thus:

"Mr O'Neill has had effective charge of his new school for only eight months. What he has accomplished in those few months borders on the miraculous ... If I were to characterise in a few words the change that has been effected I would say that learning by doing has taken the place of learning by swallowing ... The child who is learning by swallowing is at best learning the one thing he is required to learn ... The child who is learning by doing is learning many things besides the one thing he is supposed to be learning. He is learning to desire, to purpose, to place, to initiate, to execute. He is learning to profit by experience, to think, to reason, to judge ..." [7]

O'Neill remained the Head of Prestolee for over thirty years, and whilst he had many conflicts with other staff and with groups outside the school, he survived every inspection and the closest of scrutinies by the Local Authority and School Governors. He was able to do this because he demonstrated that his approach worked. He refused to coerce children, he did not obstruct them and he recoiled from the use of extraneous incentives; either rewards or punishments. There were difficulties and abuses without end - stealing, smoking in closets, rowdyism - but O'Neill exacted every bit of education that he could from any situation. Further, he was able to articulate his philosophy openly and lucidly.

How important was Prestolee? For the libertarian tradition it was critically important. It was the first State School influenced by a libertarian approach to education. Its intake was predominantly working class. It survived for over thirty years. It was able to demonstrate the superiority of a libertarian pedagogy. John Watts captures the school's importance:

> "Don't let us be told that it can't be done. O'Neill did it within a local authority, with scanty material resources, with ordinary children and with the wholehearted support of ordinary parents, who saw that even the humblest home could expect its children to be taught with love, respect and pleasure."[8]

3. A KEYSTONE OF CO-OPERATION

St. George-in-the-East School, (Cable Street, Stepney, London, 1945 - 55)

Alex Bloom was appointed to the Headship of St. George-in-the-East Secondary Modern School in Cable Street, Stepney, in October 1945. The School had been closed during the War and by 1945 was virtually derelict. When the School re-opened Bloom was given 260 boys and girls from local Primary Schools and ten teachers, most of them unknown to each other and hardly any of whom he knew. In a tribute to Bloom after he died, though, *The Times* reported of Bloom and the School:

> "What he did know was Stepney, with its bomb ruins and overcrowded medley of tongues and peoples. He saw no point in starting an ordinary school in that particular place and year. Instead he designed one in great detail to meet the social and emotional needs of his particular adolescents. He did not believe that gradualness or a piecemeal reform would meet those needs and he himself laid down to his staff the School aim; the establishment of a community to which each child should contribute from his own growing confidence and competence, and in which his contribution would be spontaneous, not the by-product of regimentation, punishment, reward or competition." [9]

What did this mean in practice? Tony Gibson has provided some insight in one of the very few records of the history of the School.[10] Bloom had an integrated approach to both the use of space and learning. He had huge open-plan areas, no rigid timetable and teaching based around project work. The keystone of his educational beliefs was co-operation, and consequently he rejected all forms of punishment and reward. He instituted a Council of Pupils, open to anybody to discuss projects for each school year and to choose their own curriculum.

Bloom wrote very little, but in 1951, in a letter to *The Times Educational Supplement*, he captured the essence of his approach in his own words. The letter is worth quoting from at length:

> "Let me assure you first that our purpose in removing the normal incentives to effort is not to hide from the child his weakness. So many children enter the Secondary Modern School trailing dark clouds of failure. These mists and the inhibiting effect of the fear of failure have been dispelled. The positive compulsions of streaming, marks, prizes, competition and the negative compulsion of imposed punishment - the teachers' artful aids - these cannot help to restore the child's self-esteem. By removing them we enable and encourage him to adventure, and if he

> *fails, he fails with impunity and with a smile but with every social inducement to improve his skills.*
>
> *You feel that the rather sophisticated satisfaction of work well done is an inadequate reward. But what if that satisfaction alone is adequate? What if by their fourth year the children no longer seek carrots? Would you deny them the joy of disinterested achievement?*
>
> *Further, you suggest that because of its ubiquity competition is both right and inevitable. True it is, that from the cradle man is subjected to the conditioning of an unceasingly competitive environment and has to face innumerable competitive situations. But this does not prove that competition is right and must continue. Perhaps something should be done about the conditioning. Industry today is learning that the old incentives, for various reasons, have failed and is looking to the social motive to replace them. And a glance at the troubled state of our competitive world is hardly an argument for their continuance.*
>
> *Collaboration with and competition against are mutually exclusive concepts. Competition and rivalry impede the free flow of friendly communication and stunt the growth of group consciousness and co-operation. We have therefore discarded them."* [11]

Bloom died in September 1955 and the school slowly reverted to more 'normal' practices. In an obituary to him and the school in *Freedom*, October 1955, Colin Ward speculated on Bloom's significance:

> *"And now that Bloom is gone, whatever happens to his School, isn't it a real and precious achievement in these last ten years, to have given to some a happier and more adventurous adolescence and to send them into the world with a little less of the spirit of our competitive and acquisitive society, and a little more of the spirit of social co-operation, of spontaneity and freedom?"* [12]

Indeed Bloom's significance and the importance of his School go further than this. Like Prestolee before it, St. George-in-the-East was a state school influenced enormously by libertarian ideals. Placed alongside the International Modern Schools of the earlier decades of the century we can see a libertarian approach to education extending well beyond its traditional place in education history, the private or unschoolable sector. We can also identify a tradition held together by common ideals rather than by common influences. A detailed examination of later libertarian initiatives provides further evidence of this tradition within the state system.

4. IN JOHN KNOX COUNTRY

Braehead School, (Buckhaven, Fife, Scotland, 1957 - 67)

R. F. Mackenzie was appointed to the headship of Braehead Secondary Modern School in the summer of 1957. He brought with him a libertarian education, spirit and ethos that was the product of a varied and interesting background and that seemed at odds with the puritanical culture rooted in Buckhaven where Braehead was to be found.

And yet this clash had a kind of honesty and reality about it. As Paul Foot commented when the school was amalgamated with others in 1967, after ten years of libertarian-influenced experimentation:

> "A. S. Neill was forced to practise his theories with the children of middle class parents who could afford his fees. Most other reformers of modern times - Curry of Dartington Hall is the most obvious example - have taught children who have been properly brought up. By contrast, the children of Braehead come from tough, rough backgrounds where every penny must be counted. The Headmaster has no right to pick and choose pupils and parents. He has to take them as they come, unsoftened by the veneer of good manners and liberal generosity. Nor is there any of the tolerance of permissive ideas which can be found in the south. Buckhaven lies near to the heart of John Knox country where one of the most puritanical, disciplinarian movements took root and prospered." [13]

Mackenzie developed many of his ideas about education from a year's teaching at the Forest School, soon after leaving University. Mackenzie recalls:

> "It was an exhilarating mixture of Freud and the Red Indians. A lot of it was quite mad, of course, and the children were entirely unrepresentative, since their parents had to pay fees. We were all reading and discussing A. S. Neill at the time, and the place proved to be the accuracy of his basic theme - that people who are free grow up happy, that if children are not happy, it is because they are not free." [14]

These ideas were partially submerged by the Second World War, during which Mackenzie became a navigator in the RAF. He went back to teaching after the War, but resolved not to experiment on the peripheral, almost exclusive, terrain of the middle class any longer. He maintained that educational experiment and reform had to be pioneered in the state system. For this reason, his work at Braehead, and later at Summerhill Academy, are significant within the history of libertarian education and schooling in Britain.

The problems that Mackenzie faced were considerable. When he took up his post as Headmaster, the Convenor of the Staffing Committee of Fife

No Master High or Low

Education Committee made the standard speech of welcome. The words of the speech encouraged experiment and reform, but Mackenzie felt that this was only as long as they made no real impact on the school or on the community.

So there was no immediate revolution when Mackenzie took over Braehead. He was not the kind of person to impose his terms and views. An older member of staff admitted his astonishment at discovering, in one of Mackenzie's books, that:

> "... the Headmaster really thought all that." [15]

Normal curricula, routines and techniques dominated the early years at Braehead. Mackenzie's ideas were put into effect more by omission than by intervention. School uniform was a good example. When asked whether the School should have a uniform, Mackenzie, who hated uniforms, shrugged his shoulders and said the children could decide. There were no uniforms!

To begin with, the two main departures from ordinary Junior Secondary routine were in the teaching of Art and the extra-curricular activities. The Art teacher at Braehead during Mackenzie's time was Hamish Rodger, who saw Mackenzie's appointment as the perfect opportunity to teach Art in the liveliest way. Art lessons saw pupils ranged across the barren Artroom, drawing and painting as they chose with individual instruction. The results were staggering. The School was decorated from top to bottom with magnificent pieces of Art, and displays were hung at exhibitions in Aberdeen, Dundee and Glasgow.

In late 1960, a young mountaineer, Hamish Brown, called in at the School and asked if he could fill in three spare months teaching English. Before long, he was organising expeditions into the Highland mountains and moors of Inverness and Argyll. He also began canoe building and offered gliding lessons.

Most of the Art experimentation and outdoor education was greeted by Buckhaven and by Fife Education Committee with great suspicion. Braehead parents saw the education being offered as second-rate. Grumblings reached the Press, especially as Mackenzie started offering pupils choice over what subjects they studied.

Suddenly, as attention was focused on Braehead in the press, in Colleges of Education and in other schools, the Fife Education Committee became worried. Mackenzie was having an impact, but it was not an egalitarian message that he was preaching. As the fight for comprehensive education was beginning, his was an anti-authoritarian message, one which frightened most people, even the Left, to death.

By 1965 the Fife Education Committee had decided that it wanted Braehead to amalgamate with other local schools, to make a viable large comprehensive school. Mackenzie was not against this in principle, but felt that it was a way of stopping libertarian educational practice from developing any further in Fife. Mackenzie was billed as being against comprehensive education. The wife of a Scottish left-wing M.P. put it thus:

"That man Mackenzie, he patronises his kids. He sees them not as good enough to learn, and all he can do is just keep them happy. He's against the comprehensives." [16]

This was an appalling smear. Mackenzie made his views on the relationship between the campaign for comprehensive education and libertarian practice quite clear:

"There is something seriously wrong with an education system that ruthlessly destroys parents' hopes for a child when he is eleven or twelve and as a consequence decreases the child's confidence in himself. The comprehensive school in its present form is assuredly not the answer. The comprehensive school is an administrative not an educational change. The same treadmill is in operation in comprehensive as in Junior Secondary schools. The trouble goes much deeper than administrative change can effect. It needs reassessment of the whole content and method of school work. It needs a new kind of education." [17]

However, Mackenzie was not able to continue the development of libertarian-influenced schooling at Braehead after 1967. The School closed as a result of amalgamation and he found himself without a job.

The story was to continue, though, but at another school. Mackenzie would not be kept down and neither would his ideas. Braehead was important. Situated in a working class area, where interest in the educational process was not obvious, it drew enormous support. Mackenzie aroused suspicion, but as Foot has demonstrated, he became a popular figure.[18] Mackenzie was the first since Bloom to give libertarian ideas a chance in a State School. His bravery warrants recognition but what was to follow at Summerhill Academy was even more significant.

5. THE REBEL HEAD
Summerhill Academy, (Aberdeen, 1968 - 1974)

R. F. Mackenzie was appointed to the headship of Summerhill Academy, a comprehensive school for twelve to eighteen-year-old young people in Aberdeen, in 1968. The *Aberdeen Evening Express* greeted the appointment with an article whose headline read:

"Rebel Head's 'Scrap Exam System' Demand." [19]

Mackenzie was quickly branded as a hot head, and in possession of a mission to:

"... take education out of the middle ages." [20]

The reality was that Mackenzie was determined to build on his experiences at Braehead and to develop a libertarian school where the consumers would be directly responsible for their experience of education.

The academy had been built as a showpiece Junior Secondary School in a predominant working class area of Aberdeen and opened in 1962 to accommodate about 1000 pupils from twelve to fifteen-years-old. Six years later it was restyled as a comprehensive school catering for twelve to eighteen-year-olds. From the outset in 1962 examination work took first priority. The first head at Summerhill had set a tone of cheerful briskness for the school with catch phrases like:

"... proud of its academic achievements ..."

and

"... a sense of discipline tempered with kindness." [21]

The Labour-controlled Aberdeen Education Committee had the job of running the school when it became comprehensive, and it was they who chose the name "Academy". This meant that the aura of a grammar school was handed to the school. For Mackenzie this was an omen:

"It revealed the failure of Aberdeen Council to understand what comprehensive education is all about and to appreciate the nature of the promise it contained. The same old examinations, the same old wielding of the belt, the same authoritarian attitudes, the same neglect of working class children; these were things forecast by this choice of name ... No sooner was the battle for comprehensive education won that it was lost." [22]

However, Mackenzie set about his task with an almost carefree enthusiasm. After all, his views were well-known, he had been given the job, and when William Ross, an ex-Secretary of State opened the Academy he drew reference to the Summerhill of A. S. Neill and concluded with the hope that:

> "Summerhill Academy will be as well known in the future for the pioneering work, for the successful work of furthering worthy ideas in Scottish education." [23]

Mackenzie made clear his determination to do without the tawse, he introduced an open pupils' council to meet weekly to discuss the curriculum and general school policy; he proposed a school newspaper to be run by the pupils; he stressed the need for a less authoritarian approach to discipline; he argued for the integration of academic and pastoral learning; he introduced choice into all subject areas and looked to vary the school curriculum giving it breadth and diversity. He was not against examinations but indicated his desire to take education beyond traditional schooling as represented by examinations. He brought a libertarian spirit to the Academy and introduced several changes that were clearly libertarian-influenced.

However, Mackenzie found it difficult to introduce these changes. The school had more than 1000 pupils and an established staff accustomed to a policy which ensured their privileges and prestige. Every proposed innovation caused staff controversy and eventually Mackenzie was sacked. How that happened reveals much about the philosophy that Mackenzie brought to Summerhill Academy, and even more about the problems facing those who seek to develop libertarian practice in state schools.

The incident which triggered the succession of events that led to Mackenzie's sacking concerned a pupil who told a teacher that he would knife him. It transpired that the pupil's mother was in hospital and he was living at home, worrying about her. His dog had been ill and although the boy had sat up with it all night the dog had died. The following morning the boy had quarrelled with another boy in his class. A teacher spoke sharply to him. An angry exchange followed which culminated in the pupil making the knife threat. Mackenzie tried to understand and explain the offence. For many teachers this was an abdication of his real responsibility. Mackenzie was accused of siding with the pupil. It was an accusation that was to surface time and time again.

In 1972, as media attention focused on the school's "liberal ethos", Mackenzie convened a series of staff meetings. He opened the first with a short talk on school policy referring to the lack of consistency in attitudes amongst staff and he laid stress upon confused thinking about discipline. He asked his teachers to be much more involved in working out policies, making enquiries into new ideas and new kinds of curricula. He encouraged staff who were unhappy with his ideas to leave. In many ways this was a mistake because it precipitated a showdown. Mackenzie recognised this much later.[24]

A month later half of the staff signed a document drawing the Director of Education's attention to their concern about the school. They claimed that most teachers, parents, pupils, institutions and other agencies, local and outside the district, felt that the policies of the school were likely to perpetuate the:

"... continued and rapidly deteriorating situation presently existing in many areas of the school's functioning."[25]

What is revealing is that the signatories identified the central problem as one of authority:

"... so-called anti-authoritarianism is fashionable ... the collapse of secular and learned authority in our society has inevitably affected our schools ... It is the basic premise of this document that authority must exist because it is necessary for the maintenance of any form of pluralistic society and this is particularly relevant to the specialised society of a school."[26]

Mackenzie was in trouble. He supported pupils against teachers, he was concerned about recalcitrants and he discouraged the use of sanctions. His days were numbered for he had too few friends. He had succeeded in increasing the attendance rate at the school, he had significantly improved the experience of schooling for a sizeable number of children, but he had increasingly done so in a maverick, almost isolationist manner. Unlike E. F. O'Neill he had failed to take his staff with him, possibly trying to achieve too much too quickly.

A sizeable number of staff organised the campaign against him, eventually drawing up a condemning document. Mackenzie was completely opposed to the document because of its stress on the need for Godliness and good learning, as epitomised in the tawse and examinations. His suspension was recommended by the Local Authority Staffing Committee, and by March 1974 he was out of a job.

There are many lessons to be learned from the Summerhill Academy experience about how libertarian ideas and approaches to education are possible and can survive in a state school. Staff at Countesthorpe College and at the Sutton Centre were to learn many of these same lessons, the biggest of which is an educational and a pedagogical one. Mackenzie deserves to be remembered for it in his own words:

"It all comes back to this: you can't have an enduring political change unless it is supported by a cultural change; you can't have cultural change unless you set the schools free from their present function of being indoctrinators of the status-quo. Change begins in the school, or as Attlee said, in the minds of men."[27]

6. A TEAM APPROACH

Countesthorpe College, (Winchester Road, Blaby, Leicester, 1970 - Date)

Countesthorpe College opened amidst a blaze of publicity in 1970. It was one of three new purpose-built community colleges in Leicestershire which constituted a third stage of development in what was, in the 1960s and early 1970s, a radical Local Authority. Its history is probably the most important of all the State Schools influenced by libertarian ideas. For this reason it warrants detailed and close examination.

In 1957 the then Director of Education for Leicestershire, Stewart Mason, signalled the introduction of the first two stages of a development programme, the establishment initially of "High Schools", accommodating students from the ages of eleven to fourteen, and "Upper Schools", for the fourteen to eighteen age bracket. The third stage of development attracted attention because of the intention to give certain schools "community status", and also because these schools were to be given scope to develop their own methods of administration and their own approaches to teaching. Mason did not prescribe the kind of things which he expected to see in the new community colleges, rather he encouraged the appointment of staff who were seeking developments in education which went beyond the abolition of the eleven-plus examination and the advocation of equality of opportunity.

Tim McMullen was appointed head of Countesthorpe in 1969 and was given six months to plan the new school, which was scheduled to open in 1970 with an intake of fourteen to eighteen-year-old students. His intentions were fairly clear:

> "If you really believe as I do that the development of the next fifty years will be to mix a central elective democracy such as we've got at the moment with a great increase in the rate of grass roots participatory democracy ... then you've got to start it in school,"

and:

> "Three main differences will, I think, mark any school I have the fortune to control in the future: the whole academic emphasis will be on the individual learning, not the teachers teaching; the intrinsic motivation rising out of the child's curiosity, desire and achievement and creative desire will be stressed equally with the extrinsic motivation; and the school and community will be one unit." [28]

McMullen made it clear that Countesthorpe College would encourage students and staff to be active and not passive, and that in consequence a hierarchic, authoritarian management system, dominated by a head, would be an impossible framework for such development.

The commitment to individualised learning took shape rapidly, with the development of a common core curriculum of four basic subjects: Maths, Science, Languages and Physical Education, and three interdisciplinary subjects, CW (Creative and Expressive Words, Music and Drama), 2D and 3D (Creative and Expressive two- and three-dimensional Arts and Crafts), and IG (Study of the Individual and Group). All students would have periods of independent study. The commitment to individualised learning was a commitment to human freedom; students were to be encouraged to study in areas of their choice albeit within a confined space; staff and students were to call each other by first names; there was to be a "Moot", a weekly meeting of all staff without a fixed chairperson or formal agenda.

McMullen's relationship to the Moot was important as it was to be this body which was charged with making decisions in the College and about its future. He was, in effect, a chief executive and looked upon himself as the executive agent of the Moot responsible for efficiently implementing the decisions made collectively by the staff. On many occasions the decisions taken by the Moot were different from the personal view of McMullen.

By 1972 the Moot had taken some significant steps, making decisions on the nature of sanctions within the school and student dress. More important, the Moot had overall responsibility for the appointment of new staff and the distribution of additional salary allowances. The Moot decided whether any appointment was to be advertised, and delegated power to a committee of staff to act as the appointing body. The committee was made up of those with a special interest in the appointment. Needless to say, the local press was not exactly supportive. "New school is a monstrosity" read the *Leicester Mercury* headline on 22nd May 1970.[29] This was a sign of things to come.

By early 1972 the College was facing significant problems. McMullen's health was not good and the College had quickly built up a reputation for being too casual, largely as a result of the reporting of the vitriolic *Leicester Mercury*. McMullen left the College in 1972 and was replaced by John Watts, who made it clear at his interview that he supported McMullen's conception of the school. He encouraged dialogue amongst the staff about future development. Watts felt that the basic organisation of the College was sound, although like many of the staff he was concerned about the organisation of the curriculum. Some wanted to retain the basic organisation but to increase the options to cater for "non-academic" students. Some wanted to abandon the core curriculum altogether. Others wanted a total change whereby the school was broken up into "mini-schools", with teams of teachers having responsibility for groups of 120-150 students.

"We have neither sufficiently demonstrated to students the strength of our own commitments, values and interests, nor have we shown sufficient regard for theirs," [30]

wrote the group who wanted to place the pastoral system at the centre of the College's learning system. The proposals were discussed first in the spring term of 1972. From then onwards a team approach evolved. Mini-schools were introduced, based on core subjects but allowing pupils to negotiate completely individual timetables. Further, students were able to control when and for how long they worked on particular subjects. This reorganisation helped the College to settle down from the beginning of the third year. With the already established democratic framework this was to constitute the basic organisation and direction of the College for the next ten years.

In 1975 Watts was the editor of a book about Countesthorpe's first five years.[31] It quickly found its way into most university education departments and Countesthorpe College soon built for itself an international reputation for progressivism in learning and organisation in education. In many ways it was held up as some sort of educational beacon. Here lay a huge problem which was to eventually prove one of the reasons for the College's decline in the 1980s. Countesthorpe College became an island of enlightenment. Little attempt was made to forge links with other community colleges in Leicestershire trying to adopt similar methods; no attempt was made to build "alliances". Further, there was no real national perspective. At the time of the Tyndale enquiry the College's union group sent a letter of support to Terry Ellis and Brian Haddow, teachers at William Tyndale School, but the College had failed to forge real links with other progressive schools. Admittedly the College had its own problems, but this failing was an inevitable consequence of the College's island mentality. Visitors were encouraged, but the emphasis was on observation and duplication rather than on building a national movement.

These failings exposed cracks in an apparently flawless philosophy. There were others too. There is no doubt that the mini-schools, or teams as they became known, were places of great comfort for students.[32] They were very exciting places to be and public examination results, especially English and Social Studies, were very good - a clear indicator that students can achieve success in examinations when they control the syllabus, a testament to the success of C.S.E. Mode 3. However, the teams were very precious. Many specialist subject teachers resented the priority given to teams, but within the teams there were also problems. The emphasis was always on negotiation and contract; students had to negotiate a curricular contract with their tutor and were monitored accordingly. The degree to which the monitoring was pursued varied enormously. Watts actively encouraged differences between teams, but in some teams students found themselves confronted with a subtle form of authority. Frequently students did not want to negotiate. They just wanted to "do" or "not do" which brought differences between students and teachers to the surface. The need to secure a comfortable environment for all was obvious, but in the contract system the tutor was frequently the stronger party. Although students found ways of pursuing their own interests in depth, it was often done subversively because of the need to go outside the contract. One should not make too much of this issue because many tutors saw little that was binding in the contract. However, the lack of faith by some teachers in what had supposedly been a commitment to human freedom reveals that Countesthorpe was not a libertarian school; it was a progressive institution where libertarians and libertarianism exercised an influence, no more.

The Moot was the body around which democratic organisation and mutuality in learning pivoted; it represented the progressive aims of the College. It was open to everybody, teaching staff, cleaners, students and caretakers, although in practice it was usually dominated by teaching staff.

No Master High or Low

The development of teams, guidelines on the role of the tutor, the allowances policy, the use of first names - all decisions around these issues were taken in the Moot.

Frequently the Moot would delegate authority to sub-committees on, for example, staffing, space and the curriculum, but all policy decisions were taken in the Moot. Ideas on development could always be challenged in the Moot, whether those ideas were from the Principal or a probationary teacher. Students sometimes challenged the staff and were, by weight of numbers, potentially very strong.

In the mid-1970s a group of staff were interested in developing teams vertically, having students of different ages in one team instead of the traditional grouping by year. Although this was a laudable aim, and despite it having the support of the majority of staff, it was voted out by the students, who did not want to see the traditional structure done away with. This is an illustration of the way students were able to exercise their democratic rights in the College. However, as Moots usually took place after school real student involvement was limited.

The College faced a crisis in 1983 when it was told by the Authority that it had to shed at least seven staff. The students formed an action group and called a series of Moots in school time. Independently of the staff, they organised a coach to take students to a lobby at County Hall on the day when the County Budget was set. A student addressed a rally of teachers, calling on them to encourage students to set up action groups in schools across the county. In the Moots students passed radical proposals on class size and staffing. They demanded, for example, that the ratio of teachers to students in teams should be no more than 1:25, they threatened to work to rule if this did not become school policy and they sent letters to the Director of Education to this end. Sadly the proposals were never acted upon. They were considered by many staff to be "pie in the sky".

If the Moot was important then the allowances policy at Countesthorpe was one of the cornerstones of the democratic principles on which the College was founded, and was inextricably linked to its educational ideals. In order to realise the democracy, which was central to learning relationships, democracy had to operate at all levels within the College. A hierarchical system of promotion would not only have been incompatible with the openness of working relationships, but would also have worked against the entire educational philosophy of the College.

An elected Allowances Committee of nine was charged with the administration of the Allowances policy. Eligibility for a scale point was based on length of service: in the early days two years for a Scale Two, six years for a Scale Three. After length of service, low pay was then the next factor which determined the priority given to eligible teachers. In the late seventies the Moot decided that no more appointments, neither internal promotions nor posts filled externally, should be made above Scale Three. This policy remained unchanged until 1985 when there were only five Scale Fours or senior teachers, with over two-thirds of the staff on Scales Two and Three.

Countesthorpe's Allowances policy was inevitably flawed, as it was part of a very far from perfect national system of teacher remuneration. But it worked for fifteen years. It reflected and fostered the essential shared commitment of the staff; it was a central structural element in the framework of the College, without which the educational aims of the College could not have been genuinely approached.

However, whilst the Moot and Allowances policy were important to the development of the College, the libertarian influence was most evident in the development of teams. The philosophy behind teams has been well documented, but it is interesting to examine the experience of students in the College.

This *Lib ED* transcript of an interview conducted by the magazine with a student who attended the College from 1974-6 is revealing in its honesty and reflects the kind of aims that McMullen and Watts set themselves:

"***Lib ED:*** *Could you say when you began at Countesthorpe College and what your initial feelings were about going to school there?*

S: I started there in 1974 I think. Anyway it was the time when all the trouble was going on. My Dad was always going on about it what with all the stuff in the newspaper about it. I didn't want to go and my parents didn't want it either, they said it was nothing but a youth club and full of trouble. But all my friends were going there so I wasn't that bothered.

Lib ED: *That must have been a hard time then, going to a school that you and your parents were worried about. Did your feelings change at all?*

S: A little bit after a while. It was a right laugh to begin with, you could get away with anything. No uniform, no detentions, it was completely unlike my other school. The teachers were dead friendly, they called you by your first name and you could call them just about what you liked. I didn't use to do a lot of work just like my Dad said I wouldn't but I was happy enough there. You see, I hated maths and they said I didn't have to do it.

Lib ED: *That seems a bit strange saying you didn't have to do maths. Looking back on it do you think that was a good thing?*

S: I regret it sometimes but I don't blame the teachers. I can do all the maths I need, I could do it then. I just couldn't stand problems and all that. It all seemed so pointless. I suppose I regret I didn't get a qualification in maths, a decent one anyway, I got a low CSE grade but anyone could do that. The point is that I could do loads of other things that I really wanted to.

Lib ED: *Like what? You haven't really said anything about what you enjoyed there.*

S: Yes I have, I liked being called by my first name.

Lib ED: *But what else was there about the College that appealed?*

S: *I suppose it was a team really. Everybody was in a team there, a big area with no classrooms and about five teachers in it. I can't remember some of their names now but they were alright. After a time I started to do a project about my family - where they lived, where they came from, what work they did. That eventually ended up being a project about the village I lived in. I got a grade 1 for that in the exam - my claim to fame. I've still got it now. God, it took me about a year to finish it.*

Lib ED: *You worked on one project for a year?*

S: *Yes. That I suppose was what team was about. Everybody could do what they wanted. There was no history and geography and stuff. IG they called it or CW or something like that, I don't remember. I remember writing loads of stories about the village though. That got me an 'O' level in English. I've got them somewhere too.*

Lib ED: *How many exams did you take?*

S: *Five and I got the lot. Mind you two of them were CSEs and one was a grade 4, I got a grade 1 in the other through and three 'O' levels.*

Lib ED: *A lot of people would say that's not very many.*

S: *I suppose they would but it was enough for me. I got a job didn't I? And anyway I did loads of other things while I was there.*

Lib ED: *Like what?*

S: *I learned how to use a camera - take photographs and all that. One of the teachers taught me how to develop my own photographs. They're all upstairs. I didn't take an exam in that but so what, I can still do it now, well, just about I think.*

Lib ED: *So you began to like the College then?*

S: *Yes, it was a strange place for a school but I was used to strictness and all that. Team was dead good you see. There was always someone around in there to talk to. I got attached to it, I was quite sad to leave.*

Lib ED: *What about your parents? Did their attitude to the College change?*

S: *Not really, every parents' evening they were up there complaining but I really liked it. They said I got too cheeky.*

Lib ED: *Did you?*

S: *Maybe. I certainly started speaking my mind.*

Lib ED: *What about when you left?*

S: *I got a job as a hairdresser.*

Lib ED: *Do you still do it?*

S: *Off and on. I've got two kids now so I just do it evenings for some people.*

Lib ED: *Did going to Countesthorpe help you in getting a job?*

S: *I don't think so. That's what I'd always wanted to do and I knew I'd get a job, my sister did it as well you see. But there again I think the school changed me a lot.*

Lib ED: *In what way?*

S: *It made me more confident. My Mum and Dad had always told me what was best. I used to argue with them a lot.*

Lib ED: *What about?*

S: *Everything. My tutor said that was a good thing!*

Lib ED: *What do think?*

S: *That's probably why my Dad never got to like the school.*

Lib ED: *Do you still argue?*

S: *A bit, I've got my own ideas you see.*

Lib ED: *What about your children? Would you want them to go to a school like Countesthorpe?*

S: *They're not at school yet but yes I would want them to go to a freer school than the ones I went to before I went to the College. I want them to grow up to think for themselves a bit.*

Lib ED: *A lot of parents would disagree with you I think.*

S: *Not necessarily. My sister has her daughter at the College now. I think it's changed a lot but they seem to enjoy it. I think it's important that kids learn at school but it's the way they do it that's important."* [33]

The College was not without stresses, though. In the spring of 1973 a group of parents critical of Countesthorpe College, the Parents Action Committee (PAC), gained the support of the local Conservative MP, John Farr. Earlier the secretary of the PAC had undertaken a survey of parents in the College's catchment area. Sixty seven parents completed the questionnaire; the number of children they had attending the College was ninety five out of a total of 1200. With the backing of these sixty seven parents a petition was organised which attracted 411 signatures, not all parents, demanding that students at the College should be given "suitable and efficient education".

On the basis of this petition Farr demanded an enquiry. This call was taken up by Councillor Geoffrey Gibson, leader of the Tory Group on Leicestershire County Council. He charged that staff were not good enough, basic subjects were neglected, teachers were indoctrinating students with left-wing opinions, sex instruction given was offensive to parents, staff had little interest in exams, unrestrained violence was frequent and students were at a disadvantage from lack of a uniform. Gibson received support from the *Leicester Mercury* and announced that there would be an enquiry on 3rd April 1973. The date was crucial as it was in the week before the County Council elections. Margaret Thatcher, then Secretary of State for Education, refused the demand for an independent enquiry but a general inspection was carried out in October 1973.

The team of HM Inspectors reported that they did not take issue with any of Countesthorpe's educational philosophies, but that the College had tried out too may innovations at the same time. Watts and many of the staff accepted this criticism and acknowledged that attention had to be urgently paid to a number of problems. These included inadequate resources, the age-range of the students at the College and record-keeping of students' progress. Further members of the HMI team referred to the full inspection at Countesthorpe as:

"... the biggest in-service training course inspectors ever underwent." [34]

So how was the College able to avoid a full enquiry unlike many of its contemporaries? Why did the general inspection not lead to further demands for an enquiry? The answer to the second question is straightforward: the College worked. Farr, Gibson, the PAC and the *Leicester Mercury* had hardly had any real contact with the College; they knew little of what actually went on there. The inspection went against them because the College was tremendously successful. When 920 parents signed a statement in May 1973 expressing strong support for the staff and deploring the sensational publicity the school had received since beginning in 1970, the PAC campaign stalled. This was clearly influential in avoiding an enquiry.

But there were more reasons for the lack of an enquiry. Firstly, Watts was a tremendous spokesperson and propagandist for the College. He fully believed in its operation and was very influential. Secondly, the Director of Education in 1973, Neil Fairbairn, was also supportive. Thirdly, there was a supportive governing body, led by Dr Geoffrey Taylor, whose three children all attended the College. Fourthly, and possibly most important of all, the staff were completely united in their determination to resist the propaganda issued by the *Leicester Mercury*. Unlike the William Tyndale affair there was little or no opposition from within the College. Crucial to this was the appointing policy of the College. All appointments were controlled by the staff, and commitment to the College's philosophy was pre-requisite for getting a job there.

In 1973 survival was assured, but it also induced a mood of complacency. Watts maintains that it would have been difficult to carry on without local,

A Team Approach

national and international support. He was probably correct. Nevertheless it can be argued that Countesthorpe's failure to develop strong links outside the College proved to be critical in its ability to respond to the changing political climate. How would the College face the lurch away from progressivism nationally, which was to result from the Black Papers and the Labour Party's "Great Debate"? What would be the implications of the eventual arrival in the College of an unsupportive head and executive? Would it be possible to resist pressure from a governing body which began to temper its support?

Countesthorpe College in 1990 is a far cry from the College which survived 1973. The democratic organisation within the College, distinctive because of its participatory nature, has been completely destroyed and replaced by a traditional hierarchical structure, with heads of department and heads of year. The appointing policy has changed, with the executive of the school (the principal and three vice-principals) having a veto on any staff recommendations. The allowances system has been replaced by the traditional allocation of points for responsibilities, usually of a highly authoritarian nature. Most significant of all, the organisation of the teams and the nature of learning has changed completely.

The Black Papers set the scene in the mid-70s with their denunciations of modern educational trends. James Callaghan then provided the characters in the shape of Shirley Williams and the Manpower Services Commission with their inquiry into the quality of teaching in schools. Margaret Thatcher wrote the script, with assistance from Keith Joseph, in their desire to return education to the 1944 Education Act. The reality was that, by 1980, vocationalism and standards were at the centre of a new educational debate. An open curriculum with freedom of choice and some space for experiment had been left behind.

From 1980, after the new Education Act, Countesthorpe College had to operate in difficult circumstances. Suddenly attention to the needs of students as individuals was a thing of the past. What now became necessary was examination success, academic achievement, vocational training and a grasp of the new technology. Parents found themselves able to opt away from the College to more traditional schools and the College found it difficult to defend themselves against this.

The appointment of a new principal in 1982, Chris Evans, was crucial. One of Evans' first public statements was to inform the *Times Educational Supplement* that:

> "Countesthorpe should raise its academic standards"

and that he hoped that:

> "... the government's technical and vocational initiative will allow new emphases and styles of evaluation." [35]

He made little effort to build on the successful base provided by Watts and the earlier pioneers, or to stand out against the national prescriptive drift in education. He argued against the established appointments system, insisting that the executive should have private interviews with candidates. In addition there were cases where members of the executive operated a veto

No Master High or Low

on appointments, the justification being the need to buy in the "right people". Similarly, the Allowances policy was also seen as a constraint in this area and was done away with, further undermining the original philosophy of the College.

One must not fall into the trap of attaching singular blame to Evans. In many ways he was the pawn of the authority who were anxious to normalise the College in the light of national trends. One has to say, however, that he knew this when he accepted the appointment. The governors too, having been supportive of the College's organisation in 1973, played their part.

That is not to say, however, that there was no resistance. In the same way as the original conception of the College took place in an experimental space afforded by the political circumstances of the early 1970s so there is always some, albeit little, oppositional space within schools. Some teams and subject areas resisted the changes, especially those concerned with the creation of middle management. They have, though, been hampered by stress, small numbers and the lack of a support system outside the College.

Further, Evans made it clear that he would tolerate no opposition, a stance that was to prove his own personal downfall after a thoroughly destructive scandal at the college in 1987-8, and he left the college in 1990.

Sadly the resistance failed and the curtain was drawn on one of the most innovative state schools in Western Europe. The history of the school, however, remains as significant as that of any considered in this book, not least because we have a clear indication of the way in which libertarian ideas can reach into the state system and find support amongst parents, students, teachers and officialdom alike.

Subversive education at Countesthorpe: studying Shakespeare.

7. AN AFFIRMING FLAME

The Sutton Centre, (Sutton-in-Ashfield, Nottinghamshire, 1973 - Date)

In September 1970 senior officers of Nottinghamshire County Council met with the development committee of the Sutton Urban District Council to discuss the possibility of an educational and recreational complex in the town centre of Sutton-in-Ashfield. It was agreed to commission a feasibility study. Out of the study developed the notion of a community school as part of a community centre, where a leisure centre, youth services, a teachers' centre, a careers office, a day centre for the elderly and people with disabilities and the Workers' Educational Association could be combined with statutory educational provision, thereby mixing adult and child education.

The idea of a community school was by no means original, but the combination of a school in a leisure and amenity centre adjacent to a shopping precinct and market place was a unique concept. So too was the educational philosophy which was to provide the inspiration for the development of the Centre. Education was to be seen as a process of learning to live, rather than that of an elite learning to pass examinations; an activity that was not reserved for traditional school hours but that went on at all times and at all places, where people, young and old, could broaden their experience.

To understand the ethos that lay behind the development of the Sutton Centre, it is worth quoting from the feasibility study which was published in 1971:

> "It is important to realise that what is envisaged is not a school surrounded by a number of other buildings linked more or less closely to it, but an organically integrated unit, freely accessible, within which it will often be difficult to delineate a particular component. There will be no perceptible line of demarcation between school and adult education facilities, or between sixth form and youth service. The school theatre will also serve the needs of the health clinic, coffee bars and dining areas will serve the school and adult community alike.
>
> The concept may be difficult to visualise. If we think of a school as schools used to be, full of rows of desks, institutional in atmosphere, authoritarian in organisation and monastic in their seclusion, we can see no way forward. But schools must change, young people must be seen as young adults who are part of a broader community and who are capable of taking decisions about their own lives. If we can accept this, then the Sutton Centre will become a reality." [37]

The Centre did indeed become a reality and opened in September 1973. It found it difficult to integrate all areas of provision and there was not complete agreement about philosophy and practice. For example, there was conflict between those involved in the recreational provision and those in the school, the former seeking traditional forms of management and control.

However, workers in the school, the youth service and the day centre were committed to developing an authoritarian-free environment. Here people, young and old, could work together, and parts of the Centre thrived in its early years, surviving the most severe public examination. As at Countesthorpe libertarian influence is very evident.

Sutton is a town of 43,000 people situated fourteen miles north of Nottingham. Its industries are traditionally based on coal mining and hosiery, although in recent years newer industries such as plastics and light engineering have grown.

Prior to 1970, Sutton lacked facilities for recreation, cultural pursuits and social activities. That there was nothing for young people to do was a frequent complaint, but adults also suffered from the dearth of facilities. The building of the Idlewells Shopping Precinct, incorporating a Civic Hall and library, and the construction of a swimming pool went some way to addressing the problem, but the opening of the Sutton Centre was the most significant.

The joint recreation and social facilities include a community theatre, sports hall, indoor bowls hall, ice rink, squash courts and dining and bar facilities. The public use of these facilities is administered by the Ashfield District Council, who own the Centre jointly with Nottinghamshire County Council.

In the case of the dining rooms, theatre, sports hall and ice rink, the school has priority use between 8.30 am and 5.00 pm on weekdays in school term time, whilst at other times the priority is for public use. The bowls hall and squash courts are designated for public use at all times.

The recreation centre is well used by the community, but it is by no means fully integrated with the whole of the Sutton Centre. It is managed separately, and has no real commitment to the original general ethos.

In many ways it is like a traditional sports centre, but its proximity to the other areas of provision is important for the Centre as a whole. It seems to have "given up" on trying to convince the recreation management of the need for a non-authoritarian approach, and simply makes use of the facilities available. Relations between the recreation centre and most other parts of the Centre appear strained.

The Centre provides Sutton with a second comprehensive school for eleven to eighteen-year-olds. There is also provision for adult education. This includes "pay as you learn" classes, family sessions and the use of workshop sessions in addition to the more normal adult classes. Currently there are over 2000 adult education students, eighty five of whom join the school students for classes.

As far as the daytime school provision is concerned, all subjects are taught in large blocks. There are basically two periods a day, one in the morning and one in the afternoon, making a ten-session week in all. Most subjects are taught in one session a week. However, there are also eleventh sessions which are voluntary two-hour periods each evening from 6.30 to 8.30 pm, and it is in these times that the community school concept can be seen at work. Often there will be children, parents and grandparents all working and learning together.

An Affirming Flame

This structure apart, the curriculum in the school is actually quite prescriptive. There is a common curriculum including Sport and Leisure, Humanities, Community Studies and Personal Guidance, Languages, English and Drama, Creative Arts, Music, Design, Science and Maths. However, what is most striking about the school is the attendance rate, at over ninety per cent.

There are no petty school rules and students have free access to the building at all times. Students at the school feel it is very much their school. One has a definite sense of teachers being no more than peripheral.

The day centre was originally intended for the elderly and people with disabilities. The use of the Centre by such people has been a constant factor. People with disabilities speak affectionately of school students and teachers, who they claim have learned over a period of time not to abuse or patronise them. The day centre is also fully integrated into the Sutton Centre complex, with participation by the elderly and those with disabilities in community theatre, eleventh sessions and recreational activities.

Over the years, the day centre has developed considerably with officers for the Ashfield Careers Advisory Service, the Probation Service and Social Services having been made available. Also the Centre has actually been developed further, to flow into the shopping precinct, embracing at the same time the neighbouring health clinic and old people's flats, encouraging members of the community to make full use of its space.

On Monday 17th October 1977, a teacher at the Sutton Centre began a lesson by asking the question:

"Why do people swear?" [38]

Eight days later a parents' action group had been formed and was seeking support for a petition worded thus:

"We the undersigned deplore teaching pupils at Sutton Centre the meaning of swear words and slang words. We feel that this can only result in increased use of these words by pupils and a decrease in moral standards." [39]

The local and, eventually, national press launched an attack on the school. In Sutton there had always been an uneasiness about the centre. Young people had free access to the building, they called adults by their first names, they were confident and more important, the school did not do 'O' levels. In an attempt to avoid any division of students according to academic ability the school followed CSE courses.

The parents' action group never numbered more than thirty one, but it won the ear of the local Conservative Party. Within weeks it was announced that there would be an independent inquiry into the school. The school's National Union of Teachers (NUT) group immediately responded. As a result of their pressure the Local Education Authority (LEA) was forced to initiate a full inspection of the school rather than an independent inquiry, although the Authority reserved the right to set up an inquiry in the future.

An inspection took place, and eventually an enquiry. Both cleared the school of the charge of "bad education". The inspectors reported that the young people at the school were "great". They saw them as "cheerful, cheeky, helpful and happy". Their main concern was about the lack of 'O' level provision.

The story of the struggle against the parents' action group is a long one, but what is clear is that it was won as a result of staff solidarity and organisation, much like the first conflict at Countesthorpe College, in 1973. However, it had all been too much for Stuart Wilson, the headteacher, who announced his resignation at the beginning of 1978, midway through the crisis.

The new head was to be Tom King. By many he was seen as the Authority's man, somebody who would take the Sutton Centre off the radical map and stabilise the school.

Nothing could have been further from the truth. Although King was worried about the lack of 'O' level provision, A. S. Neill had been and still is his greatest influence. He worked to preserve the special challenge that the Sutton Centre was making to the educational establishment. Moreover, he worked to maintain the focus of the Centre on the community, where young people could come without fear and where they could learn alongside a variety of different age groups.

There was an uneasy period from 1978 to 1980, when King was regarded with suspicion and hostility by the school staff. He was seen as a Rhodes Boyson figure who would slowly dismantle the existing structure and educational provision. But again, this was an incorrect perception.

There were eventually several curriculum changes. 'O' levels were also introduced, although the latter had, by 1979, become County Council policy anyway. However, King retained the child-centred approach that had developed at the Centre, and carried out a vigorous public relations policy that involved the whole of the Centre.

If you walk into the Sutton Centre today, you have to be impressed by its diversity and friendliness. In the school, it is clear that the students believe in a system that befriends and encourages them, and they are aware that they have access to a school that remains fundamentally different from most others.

Staff at the Centre have held to a belief in challenging the educational establishment. In this sense, they have demonstrated that a radical educational initiative can exist in a time of reaction. They have shown:

"... an affirming flame ..." [40]

as one teacher at the Centre put it.

Whilst it is impossible to talk in terms of the Sutton Centre being a purely libertarian initiative, it has been influenced by libertarian ideas. Tom King, staff and students alike deserve some sort of recognition for the way in which they have refused to depart from the original ethos of the Centre.

8. A NON-FRONTAL APPROACH

William Tyndale School, (Islington, London, 1974 - 6)

Few schools have generated so much publicity in such a short period as the William Tyndale Junior School did in Islington between 1973 and 1976. As well as being the subject of a public inquiry, the events at, and history of, Tyndale have been the subject of writing by both the Right and the Left. The Conservative Political Centre deemed the affair worthy of a pamphlet and the Socialist Teachers Alliance journal, *Socialist Teacher*, has made numerous references to the events at Tyndale and their implications.

However, there are three major accounts of events at the school.[41] There are common factors in these works and, as Peter Lawley has suggested, this indicates a certain unanimity over the nature and uniqueness of the crisis. Each account acknowledges the particular problems thrown up by a large, working class intake, the sincerity of the teachers involved and the inevitability of the conflict between the type of educational provision at the school and the backlash produced by the Black Papers.[42]

There is no point in covering this ground in any kind of detail. What demands attention are the educational practices developed at Tyndale, the real limits to institutional reform, and the formal and informal powers available to enforce such restrictions which the events at Tyndale from 1974-76 reveal.

From January 1974, when Terry Ellis took over as headmaster, a number of changes were introduced. The school continued to be run without a set timetable, as introduced by the previous head. In addition to this, there was a new emphasis on freeing the school from a classroom-structured organisation of learning. This used a "non-frontal" approach, involving a more fluid and relaxed relationship between staff and pupils. Much of this was intended:

'... to discriminate in favour of the disadvantaged child, who lacks the family and social support most middle class children enjoy'.[45]

Another aspect of the approach to the "less able" or "slow readers" was a decision to tackle reading problems on a "broad front" rather than through a class under the responsibility of one teacher. This individual, Dolly Walker, subsequently a Black Paper contributor, was held to nurse:

"... a resentment that her remedial empire had been dismantled."[46]

Again, a change in the internal organisation within the school had been implemented, perhaps with the participation and agreement of the majority of staff, but at the cost of creating a dangerous and influential enemy.

Another overt change in the organisation of the school day lay in the introduction of an Options Scheme by Brian Haddow, an influential teacher at the school.[47] The Scheme involved a move away from the confines of a single classroom, and the use of other areas such as the hall. Twenty options were set up, including English Work, Needlecraft, and Board Games. Children from other classes were attracted to the activities, and it might be assumed that the necessarily changed role of the teacher was attractive to pupils, who were normally expected to spend their day with more conventional classroom teachers. This first Options Scheme of Summer 1974 was superseded in Autumn 1974 by a system, for two of the years in the school, which involved a choice for the pupils and a co-operative approach by teachers. Haddow acted as "co-ordinator", with three teachers. The eighty children from two year groups were split into three groups, each containing pupils across the whole age group. These three "base" groups had "closed" sessions on basic skills of Reading, Writing and Mathematics. In "open" sessions which followed, there was a choice from a wide range of activities, such as Art, Handicrafts, Games or a continuation of activities started in "closed" sessions. Robin Auld, the head of the enquiry into the school, describes and criticises this scheme, mainly for the defects in its implementation, and lack of preparation, though he admits that preoccupation with external problems probably prevented the organisers giving full attention to their teaching.[48]

Two actors from the Royal Court Theatre worked with pupils on an improvised play, and lecturers and students from a local College of Further Education helped pupils with a film-making project.[49] The latter group produced an 8mm film showing the school in action at this time (shown at public appearances by Ellis and Haddow after their suspension).

The most notable and successful project involved the setting up and development of a steel band. This was a specific recognition of a West Indian element in local culture, and the band represented the school at an Inner London Education Authority exhibition of school achievements. It was generally admitted that the band had been particularly successful at involving troublesome pupils, though there were objections that their enthusiasm for the activity prevented them following a balanced curriculum.[50]

The above practices might well be used as an example of a typical above-average primary school, with its vigorous approach to its own internal organisation, commitment to the needs of the "less able", and opportunistic use of local facilities and expertise. Such a school might be held up as an example and indeed, under its previous head, this had happened. The "progressive" methods were demonstrated on courses held in the school for other teachers in the district. Haddow had been appointed as a gifted teacher by the previous head for his recognised talents in developing such an ethos and practice.[51]

In the summer of 1975, movements within the school favoured further radical innovations in ethos and organisation. Auld suggests that this was a response by Haddow (he "over-reacted") to a hostile petition circulating in the neighbourhood. Haddow's document proposed that: from a basic structure of

A Non-frontal Approach

six mixed-ability groups, pupils should have the choice of coming into school or remaining in the playground; a teacher would be on half timetable for "continuing links" with the community;[52] the head's room was abolished as a separate entity; "sanctuary" and "remedial" facilities would be chosen by pupils rather than receive pupils directed there. There were to be no locks on stockroom and equipment cupboards, and a weekly meeting of staff and all pupils interested would have the right to decide on school policy.

This document demonstrates a development of the importance placed upon children deciding for themselves and assessing their own needs. For the first time they were being given rights to take part in the decision-making process within the school, rather than exercising freedom to choose within an environment which was pre-structured by the teachers. In the event no action was taken. Energies were diverted into facing the threat from outside.

Haddow's document, however, shows the direction the school might have taken had external factors been different:

> "The emphasis on the child's individuality in fluid and non- intimidatory relationships with adults was part of a liberal tradition in education most strongly implemented in private progressive schools such as Summerhill. The Plowden Report recognised 'the profundity of changes that have taken place since the war' in a paragraph celebrating free movement about the school, a multiplicity of formal and informal activities taking place side by side, and the lack of a school bell." [53]

Tyndale showed an emphasis on the child as an active agent in his own learning, and refused to make sharp distinctions between "work" and "play", another doctrine shared by A. S. Neill, the Plowden Report, and the Free School movement. It was only later that this broadly liberal emphasis on the recognition of the individual was extended to children's rights. One manifestation of this was the move to avoid the labelling of children as "remedial" and to allow them responsibility for assessing their own needs. This created a typical dilemma for "freedom" in schools, as it might leave the child more susceptible to destructive outside influences, and abrogated what would commonly be claimed to be a professional duty of the teacher. At one level, the move might be considered as purely practical; there was little point in running a small remedial unit designed for a minority of "remedial" children when the state of being "remedial" was typical of most of the children. Another dilemma was created, though, by Ellis's concern to discriminate positively in favour of the "disadvantaged child". In this case identification of the "disadvantaged" was involved, and a professional decision had to be taken by the person conventionally held responsible to the formal representatives of society. Evidence of a hierarchical power structure was here, even if the decisions made were unconventional.

Another reformed element in the school's thinking was to bring it closer to its local community. As with the "disadvantaged child", the teachers made a decision on what the response should be here. Ironically, they failed to enlist the sympathy of the formal representatives of the community; those with the power to shape and articulate local opinion. Competing definitions of community need were espoused by two articulate parties, both seeing themselves as guardians of a largely inarticulate local populace. As the battle developed, so the political efficacy of the two parties was put to the test. The failure of the staff, it may be argued, lay here, rather than in the efficiency of their teaching, which involved so many variables and assumptions that any conclusion is bound to be controversial.

A final reform lay in the movement towards a greater involvement of staff in decision-making. This involved the head taking part in staff meetings and acting as simply one individual among other members of staff who took decisions collectively. Gretton and Jackson note that:

> *"At the first sign of trouble the defensive vocabulary of a fledgling political bureaucracy emerged: the 'validity' of decisions by others was questioned and 'procedures' thrown into doubt."* [54]

However, this tended to be in response to outside pressures, and cannot be shown to have inhibited discussion and innovation within the school. Again, such reforms had been tried elsewhere, notably with the "Moot" at Countesthorpe College, though this had not led to criticisms of the head's lack of "leadership".

The Tyndale Affair has been used by the popular press to attack practices that were common to most primary schools. Fortuitously it came to the fore just as the swing against progressive ideas had started. It was a *"cause célèbre"*, providing a useful peg for both serious and sensationalist discussion and reactionary comment. Not only did the Tyndale teachers lack a broad-based supporting alliance, but in allowing themselves to be made an example of, they failed fully to use the vagueness and contradictions of the bureaucracy above them. They were teachers rather than politicians, and proved that a political concern with the appearance of things was essential in order to build a secure base for later innovation. Their lack of political dogmatism was one strength, but this was not turned to positive advantage, except in one libel action.

One way in which broad support could have been built up would have been to abstain from an unofficial strike. It should have been obvious at the time that the attempts of the National Union of Teachers to reduce the autonomy of its local association were designed to keep the left-wing dominated associations under central control. On the other hand, an attempt to dismiss staff, when so many urban schools were in a serious crisis, would have enabled the union to give legal support along the well-trodden lines of employment protection legislation. The union could then have claimed glory from the Left for supporting the Tyndale teachers to the end, while maintaining credibility on a broader front for protecting the security of its members' employment. The result of such an action would have been to have preserved its power base. It might have involved a reduced rate of reform, would probably have led to an increased injection of financial resources into the school, and would certainly have made it easier for Ellis and Haddow to remain in the public eye, receiving visitors to the school and lecturing in the time-honoured fashion to other heads of experimental schools.

It is easy for an outsider to be wise after the event; what was achieved was a considerable combination of innovations within a state school in a very short period of time.

A Non-frontal Approach

However, the individuals involved paid for their beliefs with their careers. In the private sector fortunes may have been lost in educational experiments, but the experiments still survive on the proceeds of fees; in the public sector, there can be no such tenuous survival against the wrath of those in authority. Sadly this should be a lasting lesson for libertarians inside the state system.

9. BEYOND PROGRESSIVISM

Libertarian Education and State Schooling, 1918 - 90

The progressive tradition in state schools has drawn the attention of a wide range of educational theoreticians and practitioners, historians, sociologists and practising teachers. The reading list is extensive. Few, though, have considered the influence and impact of libertarian ideas within this tradition.

Prestolee School, St. George-in-the-East School, Braehead School, Summerhill Academy, Countesthorpe College, the Sutton Centre and William Tyndale School are to the progressive state school tradition what the likes of Summerhill and Rowen House School are to the two progressive private school traditions considered earlier.

Historically what is revealing about these schools are the years of their formulation. Mostly they began in eras of experimentation, which lends credence to the notion of a libertarian tradition that has come and gone in waves and ripples.

As far as the schools are concerned, the nature of the libertarian influence is difficult to generalise. Prestolee was an elementary school, St. George-in-the-East and Braehead secondary modern schools, Summerhill Academy, Countesthorpe and the Sutton Centre comprehensive secondary schools and William Tyndale a junior school. For this reason there is no uniformity of approach, other than commitments to particular human rights and values. The basic respect for individual autonomy is a clear example. The hostility to authoritarian practice is another, as is the belief in self-government, often personal but occasionally corporate as in the Countesthorpe Moot, and an articulated intent to step outside and beyond the kind of education demanded in schools by legislation.

All too often it is tempting to assume that the aims of government have reached so far into schools as to make any libertarian practice impossible. This is quite clearly not the case, and British educational history affords us examples of long and sustained libertarian influence if only we choose to seek it out. It becomes clear that, despite the diversity of the libertarian tradition, there is also evidence of a common approach.

It is difficult to establish any criteria for an evaluation of the schools considered. Survival is clearly one, support another, impact and influence possibly the most important. With the exception of William Tyndale School and Summerhill Academy all the schools survived for long periods of time. This is significant, and is testament in the main to the careful attention that was paid to building support. If we take Countesthorpe as an example, the campaign that was undertaken by staff in 1973, in resisting the hostile attention of some parents and the media, stands as a clear lesson in how to gain support from a potentially hostile audience. Countesthorpe teachers were able to demonstrate the superiority of a libertarian influenced pedagogy, which produced the highest attendance rate in Leicestershire and academic achievements of a similarly high level. It was not uncommon, for example, for seventy five per cent of the school's intake in any given year between 1972 and 1978 to leave with English 'O' level or its equivalent.

The impact of these schools is very difficult to even begin to assess. They clearly had an impact on their students. The fact that all the schools were well-attended, even in the most adverse of circumstances, reflects this. In many respects their real impact remains potential, rather than actual, considering the scant attention that has been paid to them so far by educational history. But, as the history of William Tyndale shows, many lessons are there to be learned for libertarian state school aspirants and practitioners.

Most importantly the schools considered in this section had predominant working class intakes. Thus we can begin to bury the hitherto accepted notion that libertarian schools have served only the privileged children of privileged families.

NOTES

1. See, for example, Seifert, R., *Teacher Militancy*, Falmer Press, 1988.

2. Humphries, S., *Hooligans or Rebels*. Basil Blackwell, Oxford, 1981.

3. Simon, B., Quoted in Selleck, R. J. W., *English Primary Education and the Progressives 1914-39*. Routledge and Regan Paul, London, 1972, pv.

4. Harber C., and Meighan, R., *The Democratic School*. Education Now, Ticknall, 1989.

5. Illich, I., *Deschooling Society*. Penguin, London, 1973.

6. Watts, J., in Holmes, G., *The Idiot Teacher*. Russell Press, Nottingham, 1977, pxi.

7. Holmes, G., op.cit., pp49-50.

8. Watts, J., op.cit., pxvi.

9. *The Times.*, 27th September 1955, p17.

10. Gibson, T., *Youth For Freedom*. Freedom Press, London, 1951, pp16-18.

11. *The Times Educational Supplement*, 3rd August 1951, p35.

12. Ward, C., *A Teacher of Freedom*. in *Freedom*, London, 1st October 1955.

13. Foot. P., *Sins of the Fathers: The end of an educational experiment*. in *Anarchy*, Vol.7., No.12., London, December 1967, p358.

14. Foot, P., op.cit., p359.

15. Ibid.

16. Foot, P., op.cit., p366.

17. Mackenzie, R. F., *A Question of Living*. Collins, London, 1963. p94.

18. Foot, P., op.cit., p356-7.

19. *Aberdeen Evening Express*, 15th September 1968.

20. Ibid.

21. Fletcher, C., *Schools on Trial*. Open University Press, Milton Keynes, 1985, p41.

22. Mackenzie, R. F., *The Unbowed Head, Events at Summerhill Academy 1968-74*. Edinburgh University Student Publication Board, 1977, p34.

Notes

23. Mackenzie, R. F., op.cit., p37.

24. Mackenzie, R. F., op.cit., p82.

25. Ibid.

26. Ibid.

27. Mackenzie, R. F., op.cit., p27.

28. *Internal Document*, 1970. *Lib ED* archive.

29. *The Leicester Mercury*. 22nd May 1970, p5.

30. *Internal Document*. 1972. *Lib ED* archive.

31. Watts, J., (ed) *Countesthorpe. The First Five Years*. Allen and Unwin, London, 1975.

32. For the best description of the experience of "team", see Chessum, L., *A Countesthorpe Tale*. in Harber, C., and Meighan, R., op.cit.

33. *Lib ED*, Vol.2., No.1., Leicester 1986. p11-12.

34. Watts, J.,(ed) op.cit., p147.

35. *Times Educational Supplement*, 16th September 1983, p7.

37. *Internal Document*, 1971. *Lib ED* archive.

38. *Lib ED*, Vol.2., No.9., Leicester 1988, p13.

39. Ibid.

40. Ibid.

41. Williams, P., *The Lessons of Tyndale School Affair*. Conservative Political Centre, London, 1977; Mulhearn, C., and Pollock, J., *Tyndale Tapes Interview*. in *Socialist Teacher*, London, Spring 1978, pp20-2.

42. Peter Lawley has made a thorough study of the Tyndale affair and his research has been published by the Department of Education at the University of York. I am grateful for his permission to use the substance of his research in this section.

43. Auld, R., op.cit., pp73-4.

44. Ellis, T., op.cit., p11.

45. Gretton J., and Jackson, M., op.cit., pp37-40.

46. Ellis, T., op.cit., p20.

47. Auld, R., op.cit., pp60-1.

48. Auld, R., op.cit., pp148-51.

49. Ellis, T., op.cit., p101.

50. Auld, R., op.cit., p188.

51. Gretton, P., and Jackson, M., op.cit., pp55-7.

52. Auld, R., op.cit., p215.

53. *The Plowden Report*, 1967, p248.

54. Gretton, P., and Jackson, M., op.cit., p8.

55. Gretton, P., and Jackson, M., op.cit., p34.

56. Auld, R., op.cit., p52.

57. Auld, R., op.cit., pp182-4.

58. Ellis, T., op.cit., p43.

59. Mulhearn, C., and Pollock, J., op.cit., p21.

60. Ibid.

61. Ibid.

PART FIVE

City Freedom

THE FREE SCHOOL MOVEMENT

1960 - 90

1. TOWARDS ALTERNATIVE SCHOOLING

The Libertarian Debate and Movement, 1960 - 1990

The 1960s witnessed the emergence of a debate about education similar to that of the period immediately before and after the First World War. It was a debate which stemmed from a feeling that not even comprehensive state schooling could deliver an education that was fun and non-authoritarian. It looked to the experiences of A. S. Neill and to the child-centred approach to education that had emerged in various British Primary and Junior schools since 1945.[1] Its main focus was to move state education forward.

However, there was a significant body of opinion which emerged as a movement for development outside the state system. This was the Free Schools Campaign which started in October 1968 in South London. The magazine *Libertarian Education* (later *Lib ED*) announced its formation at the end of 1968.[2]

The Free Schools Campaign was committed to supporting the development of schools outside of the state system that would encourage and develop a libertarian approach to education. Roger Saddiev, one of the early secretaries of the organisation, saw the campaign as being rooted in the ideas of Illich and Neill, but believed strongly that the schools should not be fee-paying and should stand outside the state system to avoid the pitfalls of the independent progressive school tradition and the constraints inevitably imposed by Local Authorities.

However, it would be a mistake at the outset to imagine that the Free Schools Campaign was a national organisation with a coherent vision and policy out of which emerged the Free School movement. Although it had upwards of 1,000 members, the organisation was run by practising teachers and it did not provide the initiative for the creation of any Free School. On the contrary it existed to link initiatives and disseminate information and ideas. A similar function was performed by the magazine *Libertarian Education*, and later by the A. S. Neill Trust Association and the Campaign for State-Supported Alternative Schools.

Libertarian Education was first published as the bulletin of the Libertarian Teachers Association in April 1966. It was known as *Libertarian Teacher*, then *Libertarian Education* and now *Lib ED*. Apart from a gap between 1981 and 1985, publication has been regular and the magazine has campaigned for libertarian ideas both inside and outside of the state education system. In the 1970s it was committed to supporting the Free School movement.

The A. S. Neill Trust Association developed out of the A. S. Neill Trust formed in 1974 shortly after Neill's death with the prime object of raising funds to support groups who were developing libertarian ideas on Free

Schools. The Association acted as a meeting ground from 1975 to 1983 for the Free School movement, a support system and a communication network providing facilities for discussion and study.

The Campaign for State-Supported Alternative Schools was launched in December 1977 by the Advisory Centre for Education. The aim of the Campaign was to encourage the establishment of small, democratically-organised alternative schools funded by the state.[3] In this sense the organisation was different from the other bodies, because it saw its role as organisational, offering a modicum of leadership.

It is from these organisations and publications that we can learn about the Free School "movement" of the last thirty years. However, the organisations did little to actually initiate Free Schools. These schools were a more cultural phenomenon born of and influenced by a set of ideas, but rooted in the radical political climate of the late 1960s.[4] In one of the few books which examines some of the British Free Schools of the 1970s, Klaus Rodler has suggested that many of the schools were a product of the radical democratic students' movement of the 1960s. Whilst this is partly the case it is not entirely so, for as we shall see some of the schools were genuine working class initiatives, which were a product of community dissatisfaction with the education system.

By the mid 1970s there were free schools in London, Liverpool, Bristol, Birmingham, Nottingham, Brighton, Manchester, Leeds, Glasgow and Southampton. They were mostly found in working class communities, and were short of money, resources and often help. They shared, though, a common ideal, the liberation of learning.

Those committed to the Free School ideal believed that schools could not be self-contained purveyors of knowledge. They had to become open-ended centres which enabled learning to take place. Consequently they had to be small enough to restore the initiative for learning to its rightful place - with the learner. They also had to restore learning to its rightful goal - expanding human horizons, not mastering outdated disciplines.

Free Schools sought to make use of every conceivable resource. This naturally included some specialist learning resources of a traditional kind, but in the main the schools tried to develop resource banks for community use.

"Teachers" in the Free Schools were not to be the directors, only guides and enablers. The Free School ideal was such that it was inappropriate for the schools to be teacher-led. Organisation was to be shared amongst all users, including the parents of any children involved. The theory was that this would have the added advantage of linking the school with the rest of the young learners' lives, so that help with identifying their interests and needs would be more realistic.

Free Schools were not going to provide a specific curriculum and in consequence they did not seek to limit their clientele. It is interesting, though, that few of the Free Schools managed to break out of catering for young people.

All this implied a necessity for flexibility and accessibility. Consequently Free Schools were small, but nonetheless they were significant. Indeed the debate and circumstances which gave rise to them did produce a coherent Free School theory.

The central concept of Free School theory was the notion of freedom. This was not a new idea and drew on the insights of Godwin, Rousseau, Dewey, Tolstoy, Neill, other types of Free School in Israel's Kibbutzim, China's communes, Tolstoy's school and the "Friskoler" in Denmark. These "Friskoler" (or Free Schools) were permissive and informal, but stressed the development of co-operation and humanitarianism. British Free Schools were based on the principle that the pupils should have democratic freedom, and that they should play as active a role in the educational process and running of the school as the teachers and parents. In this sense Free School theory was the epitome of libertarian educational theory.

As we have seen, progressive educational philosophy wanted to train, teach and accustom the new generation to the actualities of industrial and technical life, working practically with the machinery; learning by doing. The advocates of Free Schools believed that to put these principles into practice they must do so outside the fault-ridden state system. They disagreed with learning being fragmented into arbitrary, disconnected chunks of subject matter, believing that, with guidance, whatever a child experiences is educational. Paul Goodman, one of the greatest advocates of and influences on Free Schooling wrote:

"We can, I believe, educate the young entirely in terms of free choice, with no processing whatever. Nothing can be effectively learned unless it meets a need, desire, curiosity or fantasy." [5]

In Free School practice, learning came to involve interaction between the learner and environment, and its effectiveness related to the frequency, varieties and intensity of the interaction. It hoped to break down barriers between children and adults as well as school and home:

"We must work and learn together (as a community) how we can exist non-exploitatively with each other, how we can satisfy our needs by understanding our resources. Specific educational areas must evolve in a practical way as essential knowledge directly relevant to the individual in the community." [6]

This idea replaced the principle of competition with one of co-operation. Free School theory, like much of the radical reform theory, concentrated on pedagogical questions, and generally did not attempt to broaden the critique politically. There was some intention of social change though, through the happier, free children who would be produced, with a developed autonomy and dignity as well as the full range of human potentialities. The ideal of Liverpool Free School, for example, was:

"... for our kids to become free people - instead of dependable consumers - aware of our environment and capable of working together to shape (or preserve) it. Our education must be a way of life instead of a training for subsequent living ... It must enable us to create community consciousness and control, and consequently a capacity for active social change." [7]

Freedom and relevance were stressed.

Freire once said that freedom, of necessity, entailed being useful, involved, aware of and concerned with people, and their lives and problems in society. He emphasised that real freedom exists, not in dropping out of society, but in making a positive approach to life's problems. Most Free Schools desired to "produce" individuals who understood and lived within this definition of freedom.

The British Free Schools of the period 1960-90 all had their individual characteristics, but generally they had no regular lessons, no set rules, nor permanent groupings of children. They had no teachers, nor pupils, when defined in terms of the authority of one "over" the other. They rested on the principles of self-government, education as self-fulfilment, and absence of coercion. A Free School was usually controlled by the parents, children and teachers together. This was their main distinguishing feature from the new state progressive schools of the same era, even those with a libertarian perspective.

Free Schools and Free School theory have been lamely lost to educational history, usually given no more than a passing mention in works about progressive education, though Nigel Wright has attempted a description and evaluation of Britain's most famous Free School, White Lion, and briefly considered the inadequacies of the more general Free School movement.[8] There are no studies which look in any detail at all of the free schools to consider their background and nature. This section attempts to do this and concludes with a consideration of their successes and failures, their impact and continuing relevance.

2. FREEDOM WORKING BOTH WAYS

The London Free School, (Notting Hill, London, 1966 - 71)

The London Free School established in Notting Hill in early 1966 was Britain's first urban Free School. It was very much the inspiration of Peter Jenner, who recorded in 1966 that the initial impetus for the idea was derived from the Free Universities in the United States.[9] The Free Universities were anti-universities, set up in order to counter the irrelevance and academic and political conservatism of many of the bigger establishments there. Jenner, though, believed that educational liberation had to begin in school and, with a group of friends, he set about beginning a Free School.

He chose the Notting Hill area of London, not only because he lived in the district, but also because educational provision was on the agenda of many community groups in the area. The Notting Hill Family Association, for example, had several meetings in 1965 where consideration was given to the establishment of a new community school funded by local trade unions.[10]

Notting Hill was an exciting community in the mid 1960s, with a tremendous diversity of human experience, and to Jenner and his associates it seemed very likely that they would find the variety of experience necessary to make an educational experiment work. Jenner spoke to the magazine *Lib ED* about the establishment of the school, and his words provide a vivid picture of the emergence of the first British Free School:

> "Initially we had hoped to try to present a new approach to education. We envisaged a system whereby the usual barriers between teacher and taught would be reduced to a minimum (an idea we borrowed from the Free University). We did not want to set out to teach people, rather we wanted to learn and explore, intellectually, visually and aurally, together with people. This had the result of giving some of the academics involved a chance to discover some new 'cases' they theorised about. Artists, writers and musicians also discovered new uncertainties in their traditions, or themselves, and discovered too the extent to which their preoccupations divorced and alienated them from ordinary people.
>
> The School was thus, in educational terms, envisaged as an attempt to communicate across the barriers of class and education, and in this way it was hoped that both teachers and taught would benefit in a refinement of perception and experience. Above all, it was an attempt to establish a common field of information and experience from both sides of the class barrier, rather than promote another middle-class attempt to put across middle-class attitudes and values. The teachers began by questioning what the people themselves, by their apathy, had rejected, for their

rejection at least raised the question that perhaps the uneducated were right and that existing academic traditions and artistic forms were, if only partially, irrelevant or misleading. It seemed to us fundamental that education should relate to experience, and that economics and sociology should help people obtain a clearer view of their situation and hence, how they might try, if it was possible, to improve it. It was also important to us to relate art to everyday perception, if only to make life yield more fun. Similarly, we asked, why should not music be within the reach of everyone without necessarily being trite, repetitive, staid or pious? Why, for the matter, should it only be played by musicians? These are merely some of the ideas that were flying around in the planning stages; action and participation were clearly implied in all of them.

The word 'Free' was included in the title because we wanted the freedom of the School to work both ways. The School was to be free to the student, and in return for his time the teacher was to be free to have a class on any subject of his choice with total freedom of expression; his subject matter was for him and his class to decide. Our only proviso was that the teacher should accept that he should be there to learn as much as the students.

The initial steps were made by canvassing for a public meeting to gain support for the idea of a Free School. This was held in March 1966 with an encouraging attendance. Over 50 people from the neighbourhood came along and there was a fair degree of enthusiasm. But then nothing happened. Nothing had been properly planned and, what was worse, hardly anyone from the district came to the classes. Even when they did, nobody seemed quite certain how to start a class, and we all began to feel we had simply led ourselves up the garden path. There were two important successes, however, one was a playgroup for children and the other was an embryonic teenage group.

These developments led to the need to rethink our approach. There was no evidence that the community was just waiting for education to be taken to it, there was in fact no reason why they should accept us any more than they accepted anyone else. But at the same time, where we provided something functional and useful, such as the playground, we found the demand was considerable. This led us back to one of our original ideas, namely that the Free School should be a neighbourhood school. 'Neighbourhood' then became a more dominant theme in our work than education itself, for we came to see that the failure of many aspects of formal education was only part of a much wider area of failure to meet real social need, and that, if education was projected in isolation from it, the people rapidly came to view it, as indeed they did most aspects of the state school system, as a luxury that entailed no real loss if it was dispensed with. Hence we felt that education through communication should be replaced with education through action, community action, which would also be an educational progress for all involved, both the people from the neighbourhood, and also for a number of us who are outsiders.

Freedom Working Both Ways

In this way we found we came to gain the trust of the community and at the same time we came to understand, as well as to love more fully, the neighbourhood in which we had chosen to work. Fundamentally I saw the Free School as becoming an agency of community education and action through attempts to tackle real community problems, such as where the kids could play, what could be done about housing, how to persuade the local authority to take its responsibilities to the area more seriously, and how to make life in the area at least more tolerable, and at best more positively enjoyable. In this we found we were educating ourselves and the people to understand that the only way to get things such as this done was to do them, and that if the people grouped together they could get things done that they could not get done if they were acting as isolated individuals or if they merely expressed passive forms of discontent. In other words we were trying to help create a community. But the long-term aim remained, once there was the beginnings of a community, once there was trust, then education as originally envisaged could return." [11]

In fact the community did not take very long to emerge; it was already there. The problem that Jenner had met was how to persuade people that libertarian ideas were relevant to their daily existence. This was resolved by a long series of meetings in late 1966.

By the new year the Free School was alive. It comprised a playgroup, a youth club, an elementary English group, a music group, a housing group and an entertainments committee. It was very much a school without walls, and most of the adults involved were volunteers rather than paid workers. All of the organisations were underpinned by libertarian ideas. There were no hierarchies, decision-making was by consensus and the emphasis was on free exploration. The majority of consumers were young people, but this was where the "school" met its downfall.

Anybody under fifteen attending the school during normal school hours was deemed a truant by the Local Authority. The experiment in Notting Hill was seen as a considerable threat to state education provision and pressure was brought to bear on the parents of children who were not regularly attending school. Jenner had avoided contact with the Local Authority, a lesson that was not lost on the later Scotland Road initiative in Liverpool and White Lion experiment in Islington.

After a series of crises in early 1970 the school was wound up. A lot of people involved in 1966 had moved away, including Jenner. While the initiative had prospered for several years, and had clearly been an exciting political adventure, the problem of maintaining a Free School in the face of local authority opposition was not really addressed.

The London Free School was an exciting departure. It has much to tell us about the process of putting the Free School idea into practice, it has much to tell too about the need to face up to constraints in an organised and systematic way.

3. INTO THE REALM OF REALITY

Liverpool Free School, (University of Liverpool, Liverpool, 1969-72)

Not to be confused with the Scotland Road Free School, also based in Liverpool, the Liverpool Free School was the second Free School to emerge in Britain in the late 1960s. It was a small, "spontaneous" initiative, and only existed for two-and-a-half years, but it was very much part of Free Schooling in action.

I visited the school in 1972 when it was winding down because of a lack of finance. It was based in the common room at the university. I was not very surprised to find a group of children wandering around where their whim took them, quietly doing their own thing.

The school was originally the idea of Arnall Richards, a Liverpool school teacher, who began the school on Saturday mornings with Geoff Sproson. The idea was to get the school established and then seek funding to make it possible for children to attend every day.

In one of the only records of the operation of the school, Geoff Sproson spoke to *Peace News* in the summer of 1970:

> "We started the school in February last year. The kids run it. We're hoping to move into the cellar under our place in Lodge Lane. The kids are doing it up at the moment. When we started up the kids did a lot of plays themselves but they've grown a bit tired of those at the moment. Now they've been cutting up small fish and examining them under the microscope. We've had a £25 grant from the Student Union for equipment. Before the school got its grant the children decided they ought to have some funds. A voluntary contribution of 3 pence was agreed." [12]

It is easy to dismiss the initiative as small, irrelevant, and more akin to a youth club. In fact there are more comparisons with the Liverpool Anarchist-Communist Sunday School of the early 1900s. Richards and Sproson were totally committed towards establishing an alternative school. They had a coherent philosophy that was based on offering a range of activities which children could opt to do if they chose. Both were determined to develop a non-authoritarian approach to working with children. They were aware of the limitations of their initiative, but were anxious to encourage children to think about school in a different way.

What did the children think about the school? *Peace News* recalls that they wanted the school to be open to them all the time.[13] When one child was asked to express what he felt about the school his support for the alternative is clear:

"They wouldn't let all schools be like this would they? It might be really disorganised but I like being able to learn what I want when I want." [14]

Even the small Liverpool Free School was turning the debate about Free Schooling into the realm of reality. It failed to develop into the kind of initiative that Richards and Sproson hoped, but it was significant because it offered a libertarian experience to a relatively large number of children. The School was attended by over three hundred children during its existence. The problems were mainly those of funding, an issue that was to haunt most of the Free School initiatives.

4. A VANGUARD FOR SOCIAL CHANGE

The Scotland Road Free School, (Vauxhall Community Services Centre, Silvester Street, Liverpool, 1970 - 72)

If the London and Liverpool Free Schools were the first free standing initiatives of the period 1960-90, the Scotland Road Free School was the first to have a real national impact and provide the impetus necessary for the emergence of other Free Schools.

It was the *Times Educational Supplement* of December 18th 1970 which announced the intention of two Liverpool teachers, Bill Murphy and John Ord, to open an educational establishment in one of the most dilapidated parts of Liverpool which would:

> "... have no headmaster, nor hierarchy nor recognise any central authority, but be controlled by the parents, children and teachers together." [15]

Murphy and Ord intended that the school would operate as a day school but would never close while people desired its facilities. Lessons were to be optional, the onus being on adults to stimulate attendance. Politically they saw the school as:

> "... the vanguard of social change in the area." [16]

By late 1970, eighty local parents and fifty prospective pupils (aged between four and fourteen) were supporting the project and a suitable building had been found. However, at the same time the likes of Eric Midwinter and Keith Pulham were asking questions about how appropriate a Free School was in such a depressed area.[17] This came to be a crucial issue for the Scotland Road Free School as it did for many of the other Free Schools, for Midwinter's concern was that Free Schools could easily just become synonymous with depressed urban areas and school non-attenders. This became a reality, and British Free Schooling has always suffered from the fact that it has often been equated with a strategy for dealing with truancy.

However, in 1970 Murphy and Ord had no intention of simply running a truancy centre, and the prospectus they produced to announce the school gives some insight into their libertarian ideas:

> "There will be set up in the Scotland Road - Vauxhall area of Liverpool, an alternative type of school to be known as the Scotland Road Free School. The school will be a community school which will be totally

A Vanguard for Social Change

involved with its environment. The nature of this involvement will be such that the school will be in the vanguard of social change in the area. By accepting this role, the school will not seek to impose its values, but will have as its premise a total acceptance of the people and the area.

It is felt that the organisation of education is insensitive, unaware and in content largely irrelevant to the needs of the children and their future role as adults in the society. Particularly in the Scotland Road - Vauxhall area, it has not provided for the aspirations, life and culture of the people, who have a social heritage worthy of itself which must be given an identity and expression of its own. We do not seek to alienate people from their backgrounds, but seek to enrich and intensify their lives.

Only those who are educated in the fullest sense of the word, imaginative and creative; mature and tolerant; aware and concerned can hope to cope with the pressures and complexities of modern society. It is only those schools that consciously create an atmosphere of understanding and tolerance that best allow these qualities to develop." [18]

For Ord and Murphy education could not be divorced from community and culture. They also had a revolutionary view of schooling:

"The ultimate aim of the free school is to bring about a fragmentation of the state system into smaller, all age, personalised, democratic, locally controlled community schools which can best serve the immediate needs of the area in which they are situated.

It is felt that the state system in contemplating change considers only innocuous reforms which do not question the total structure. We are obliged therefore to step outside the system in order to best demonstrate the feasibility and fulfilment of the free school ideal. Having achieved this demonstration we are sure that society will enforce the adoption of the free school idea by the state system.

These aims cannot be dismissed as impractical or Utopian as comparison with the Danish system will reveal. At this time in Denmark there are one hundred and seventy four free schools." [19]

However, it was the proposed organisation of the school which reveals the truly libertarian nature of the initiative:

"1) The School

The School will not have a headmaster or hierarchy, nor will it recognise any central authority, but will be controlled by the parents, children and teachers together. This would be achieved democratically through a school council.

2) Areas of Activity

> The school will operate as a day school but will never close whilst people desire to use its facilities. Lessons will not be compulsory, the onus will be upon the teacher to stimulate the children sufficiently to attend. At the same time the school will offer its participants a range of social and academic activities comparable with state schools. These activities will be ascertained by observation and pupil-staff consultation.
>
> During the initial months of the school's term the children will be given the free run and choice of the school's equipment to facilitate the assessment of their needs and abilities. Research in the Vauxhall area has uncovered a demand for an open school as a right. The Scotland Road Free school will be able to demonstrate how a community school can continue the educational process into all areas of life throughout life.
>
> ### 3) Recruitment of Pupils
>
> Personal contact with the people in the area has indicated that the school will be oversubscribed but if finance is forthcoming our original estimate of a 50 pupil intake could be extended to take all those pupils wishing to attend.
>
> The school will be co-educational and will admit children between the ages of seven and sixteen years. Eventually the aim would be to lower the age of entry and extend the school leaving age. It is hoped parents will run pre-school play groups in the school." [20]

So how did the school work in practice? Freedom is often defined as the antithesis of restraints, and at Scotland Road there were no rules, no compulsory attendance, no uniform, no homework, no punishment of any kind, no formal lessons, no syllabus and no permanent groupings of children assigned to any individual teacher. Not surprisingly much press attention focused on this lack of constraint.

However, the school had a positive ethos for those working there and for those attending. Relationships between children and adults were open, friendly and non-coercive. The teachers accepted the values and actions of the children that would have been strongly frowned upon elsewhere - swearing, smoking, spitting, stealing. Children were accepted for what they were and how they saw themselves. School meetings made decisions about activities, the use of buildings, but children also had significant informal power and the school ran on their day-to-day preferences.

Many glimpses of the school were reported in the national press. They were usually of the same ilk; an interesting experiment, but ... Maurice Punch and Ruth Swirsky wrote a fairly long piece for *The Teacher* after the school had closed in 1974. It concluded thus:

> "In the mornings generally little happened. The children sat around chatting, occasionally sang to the accompaniment of John Ord's guitar but more often somersaulted on an old pile of mattresses. There was little art work or handicrafts because it was claimed the equipment was too expensive - although there was always enough money available for

outings. It seems in fact that four sets of tools and paints disappeared or were destroyed. There was often an atmosphere of something about to happen, out of boredom which sometimes erupted into aggressive behaviour ... The children left their plates and cutlery wherever they had been sitting and food was often thrown around. One or two of the adults patiently did the cleaning and washing-up. There was no attempt to institute any co-operation in terms of either washing up or of most activities." [21]

This was fairly typical of press coverage and it raises important questions about Free Schooling in Britain. There have, though, been many harsh judgements about Scotland Road. Amongst others, Ian Lister believes that Ord and Murphy were politically naive:

"How else can one explain their hope that the state would give money to groups who aimed to fragment its institutions? State supported anarchism is a curious concept." [22]

He also wrote:

"The organisers of the Liverpool Free School had a utopian belief that others only needed to see their school and then they would themselves found further free schools. However, those who visited the Liverpool Free School were usually disappointed by what they saw. The building was an old church. It had broken windows and it was cold and uncomfortable. It was furnished with old and damaged school furniture. The freedom of choice, for the children, was more a fantasy than a reality - because in fact there was little to choose from." [23]

The problem about these judgements is not that they are inaccurate, but that they miss the point. Implicit in the criticism is a castigation of libertarian educational practice. It did not work in Liverpool - it does not work in general. Sadly Scotland Road became ghettoised. Its clientele were mostly school non-attenders, most of whom tended to be adolescent boys. The building was appalling, and money and resources were limited. The point is, though, that the school was attended regularly by between fifty and seventy children for a period of two years. Furthermore we have to accept that the provision of an exciting environment is often dependent on money. Similarly co-operative responsibility does not appear amongst a group of adolescent school refugees overnight.

The lessons to be learned from Scotland Road Free School are to do with funding, resources and clientele. But we have to respect and admire Ord and Murphy's ability to make school attendance attractive to a large number of discontented young people. Further, when the whole Interdisciplinary Service Group in Vauxhall wrote to the *Education Guardian* on March 12th 1974 bemoaning the death of the school on the grounds of a missed opportunity [24] - "all the hard work had been done, money was the main problem" - we have to take note. In 1974 Free Schools in Germany and Denmark were thriving in predominantly working class areas, courtesy of government funding. Such funding was never likely to be forthcoming at

Scotland Road, but we should not reject the notion of Free Schooling as a result. The main lesson to be learned from Scotland Road is essentially about funding and the amount of time necessary for a respect for personal autonomy to develop into a collective consciousness.

5. FIVE FREE SCHOOLS

**Durdham Park Free School, (Bristol, 1971 - 8);
Saltley Free School, (Birmingham, 1972 - 4);
Nottingham Free School, (Nottingham, 1972 - 4);
Freightliners Free School, (Camden, London, 1972 - 6);
Brighton Free School, (Brighton, 1972 - 3)**

Scotland Road Free School may have closed in 1972 but that same year saw the opening and development of seven new Free Schools, as well as Durdham Park in late 1971. The most significant were Balsall Heath Free School in Birmingham, Parkfield Street Free School in Manchester, and White Lion Free School in Islington, and they all deserve separate, more detailed, examination.

The history of the other five, all established within months of each other, offers an insight into how the Free School movement was developing in early 1972.

Free Schools were a new phenomenon for which there were few legal (or illegal) precedents. The law on education, embodied chiefly in the 1944 Education Act, was vague and open to a range of conflicting interpretations. The most obvious space for Free Schools was either to describe themselves as "otherwise", a facility allowed by the Act to anybody wanting to be educated out of school, or "independent", a way of establishing non-state schools. Most of the 1972 wave of Free Schools chose the latter.

Section 70 of the 1944 Act required that all independent schools be registered with the Department of Education and Science. When such schools could show attendance and admission registers, and the premises had passed the local building by-laws and fire regulations, the schools were generally given Provisional Registration.

Durdham Park Free School in Bristol opened in late 1971 and by December 1972 had Provisional Registration as an independent school. It had twenty-seven children aged five to sixteen on "the roll". In 1974 it was granted full registration and with community and parental funding was able to continue until 1978. Sadly very few records of the school have survived.

Saltley Free School opened in the Spring of 1972, growing out of a Community Association that had been established in July of the previous year. This Association, though, had been founded by young middle class parents with a vision of a new society that had developed in their heady student days in the late 1960s. They had enormous difficulty in taking the "indigenous" local population with them who, whilst dissatisfied with the education their children were getting, were realistically apprehensive about getting involved in an experiment which had no authoritative body or financial backing. So Saltley Free School opened with a large amount of enthusiasm, but was short-lived.

The same was true of Nottingham Free School. It obtained Provisional Registration as an independent school very quickly, but failed in its attempt to build a neighbourhood, community school that ran on libertarian principles. The reasons for this were largely class and cultural divisions. The group which established the school were not from the local community, they had really only arrived there by virtue of their education, and whilst the school was attended by upwards of fifty children in its early months, the founding group failed to draw in enough parents of the children to run the school as a community enterprise. The school had virtually petered out by the end of 1973.

Freightliners Free School in Camden was very different. It began as an "otherwise" project. Two sets of parents registered with the Local Education Authority in February 1972 that they were educating their children at home, under section 36 of the 1944 Act. They had the help of a trainee teacher. Her Majesty's Inspectorate (HMI) provisionally approved the arrangement for three months, provided that they worked in groups of four. Thereafter they encouraged them to set themselves up as an independent school, as only then could the Local Authority legally provide any assistance, something they subsequently did. This cautious beginning was crucial to the continuation of the school. HMI approval and Local Authority backing offered a firm base to work from and guaranteed a reasonable press. By 1974 the school had upwards of twenty-five children aged from six to fifteen.

The school was located in the basement of a large house, but it managed to offer a wide range of curricular activities and drew in a considerable amount of local help. For example, in the summer of 1974, a local building firm gave up a goods yard for use by the school and the building workers helped the school convert the yard into a play area. This received a lot of publicity in the local press under the headline: "Working together for a better Camden". However in 1976 Freightliners lost its premises and could not persuade the Local Authority to provide it with alternative accommodation.

The history of Brighton Free School was much the same as that of Saltley and Nottingham. It opened in the Spring of 1972, the inspiration of a group of ex-Sussex University students, but it failed to make successful contacts with the local community. It was short-lived, closing in 1973, as the founding group launched itself into a wider political enterprise, the *Brighton Voice*, a community newspaper.

The sketchy history of these five schools tell a lot about the state of the Free School movement in 1972. Success in terms of development came to Durdham Park and Freightliners, and it is no coincidence that these two initiatives had significant support from their local communities and local government. The other three were inspiring in their conception, but floundered amidst a lack of long-term organisation.

And yet the schools made a considerable contribution to the development of Free School theory and practice. Nigel Wright has suggested that the Free School movement did not have a coherent philosophy of education. He writes:

"In particular, little thought seems to have been given to the general question of the aims of education, to the matter of content of learning, and to how children learn. If the free schools preliminary pronouncements have little indication of what free schools were actually going to do when they got started, description of what happened once they were established showed that they were floundering - in some cases badly." [25]

However, such a perspective is misleading, and based on the obvious and well published problems that were faced by Scotland Road, and later by the Manchester Free School. In this context Maurice Punch's article in the *Guardian* in May 1973 has a lot to answer for.[26] Punch argued that Free Schools were merely symbolic protests against the iniquities and inequalities of certain parts of the education system. He saw them as disorganised and licentious. What he failed to do was try to understand their problems. In 1973 the Free School movement was barely born, let alone ready for a comprehensive assessment.

What Punch did not know, and what Nigel Wright has chosen to ignore, is that a considerable debate about the purpose of free schooling was beginning. This was to take place mostly via the *A. S. Neill Trust Newsletter* and the pages of *Libertarian Education*, and it was to come to no firm conclusions. But from 1975 onwards people who had been involved in all the initiatives considered in this section, and at Scotland Road Free School, were attending A. S. Neill Trust Meetings. The pages of the *Trust Newsletter* for 1974 and 1975 reveal considerable discussion on Free Schooling by participants attending gatherings at the Lifespan Community in Leeds and at Monkton Wyld School.[27] In the end that discussion pointed in a radical direction. The *A. S. Neill Trust Newsletter* became the only voice arguing for new methods of evaluation that lay in the hands of the Free Schools themselves.

6. OUT OF URBAN DECAY

Balsall Heath Community School, (Birmingham, 1972 - Date)

Balsall Heath Community School opened in June 1972. Its aim was simple:

> *"To establish a community school in an area of huge urban decay which will encourage children currently dissatisfied with school to attend school and enjoy learning."* [28]

In its early days it adopted a Free School model where attendance was not monitored and where activities were organised on a weekly basis. The history of how the school emerged and later developed is an intriguing one.

In 1972 there was no pre-school educational provision in Balsall Heath. Parents, single parents in particular, had to leave work and go onto welfare benefits, or risk their family being split up. A few teachers and nursery nurses who, in addition to the parents themselves, recognised the need for a solution to this problem, set up a nursery centre which combined the function of day care and education.

Equally there was no safe or educationally oriented play provision in the area's streets. So parents and teachers provided their own play facilities by creating an adventure play centre designed to help to bridge the gap between home and school.

This all took place in the early months of 1972. By the late Spring parents, especially those of children who were most clearly not benefiting from secondary school, suggested to nursery and playcentre staff that they should start a school. In two months enough money was raised and teachers recruited to start a school, a Free School.

Within three years this school was fully registered with the DES as an independent school. So what was the school like in its early years? It saw itself as specialising in children with problems, that way it found a legitimacy with the Local Authority which partially funded it. But the school was definitely not a truancy centre, at least not in the early years.

There were about twenty-five children on the roll from 1972-5. In order to attend the school you had to apply, and pupils were taken from a catchment area of a square mile. All teachers lived in the catchment area, and, through parent/teacher committees, took part in fund-raising ventures, market stalls, producing a community newspaper and an extensive list of other community activities.

The school had a timetable, but it was flexible and open to negotiation. No child was forced to pursue an activity they did not want to.

The school was registered as a charity, and its management committee and parents/teacher committee had to raise all the finances needed for salaries, educational expenditure and other running and capital costs. Therefore, quite literally, the school belonged to the community, and the community employed the teachers and administered the school with the help of the teachers. But this meant that the teachers were made responsible and accountable to the parents and the community of the children they taught. Because the teachers placed a high priority on showing parents that they needed their help in order to educate the children effectively, the parents responded. Equally the teachers responded to the needs of the parents and reorganised their own role, becoming neighbours, social workers, adult educators - and community workers, as well as teachers.

The school was a quite new and experimental venture and was libertarian in both theory and practice. The Local Authority treated it with caution, but the Conservative Chairman of the Education Committee publicly announced that:

> *"It's a very worthwhile project ... The school is undoubtedly providing a most important opportunity for the young people who are attending. We don't see any difficulty in this school existing alongside local authority schools."* [29]

However, the aftermath of the Conservative Party's election victory in 1979 and the wave of educational legislation that followed took their toll. In many ways the dangers had been apparent from the outset. Balsall Heath Community School became very close to the local authority. It saw itself as legitimate, and eventually it was forced to change: to introduce a set timetable and curriculum, and hierarchical organisation within the school.

However, for the Free School movement it remains a success story because it managed to overcome the problems of foundation and develop as an effective community enterprise. The school ran against the administrative tide. It offered children and parents a genuine choice. It did not aim to change, and then regulate the students' values and actions.

But there are lessons to learn too. Direct funding from the Local Authority led to a change in tone and philosophy. While Balsall Heath Community School is worth visiting, it is more a Local Authority school in 1990 that it was in 1980, and beyond recognition when compared with the 1972 initiative.

7. THE MANCUNIAN EXPERIENCE

Parkfield Street Free School, (Parkfield Street, 1972 - 3);
Manchester Free School, (Burlington Street, 1973 - 9)

In 1972 Parkfield Street in Manchester had the unmistakeable imprint of decay. The road which ran through Moss Side from Whitworth Park to Platt Fields was littered with all the evidence of the inner city dereliction.

But Parkfield was a friendly Street. Number 32 was an open house for any casual caller, an impromptu community meeting house, and primarily the home of Parkfield Street Free School which, by the summer of 1972, had nine permanent pupils aged between five and thirteen years old.

Asked by David Clark of the *Manchester Evening News* what went on at the school in the early days, Kevin Woodbridge replied:

> "Well it's down to the kids really. We had a piano and they took it to pieces. But by doing that they learned how a piano worked and now we have another one which they just play and play." [30]

Jim Leman, seventeen and unemployed in 1972, lived above the school and helped out:

> "The kids here don't get screwed up like they do at normal schools and like I was. They actually enjoy coming and sometimes they knock me up dead early shouting to come in." [31]

The nine children all lived in the street and once at the school they could stay there all day, most of the evening, and right through the summer holidays.

The Free School started in January 1972 as a quite different idea from the street neighbourhood school that had emerged by the summer, where the children developed their interests at their own pace.

David Graham, a mature student in economics at Manchester University and married with five children, was one of the founders:

> "Three couples and four of their children - including one of mine - were involved at first because of the use of corporal punishment in their schools and because the children were very unhappy with the rigid system. But we realised that Parkfield had to be a neighbourhood school." [32]

Kevin supported this idea:

The Mancunian Experience

"There are about fifty kids on the street and we hope to be able to expand the school to take in kids up to sixteen. If they want to take exams then that's O.K., we'll teach them. The important thing is to give them an education that is not tied by formal rules." [33]

So what was this education without formal rules? How did the Free School idea actually operate at Parkfield? David Head has provided a really negative and damning picture of it, a disordered chaos.[34] It is a completely prejudiced account and one that does not seem to balance with the picture of the workers and, more important, the children.

Consider this extract, for example, from a Parkfield School Publication:

"This is Parkfield Street School Now; in the summer of 1972. It is an insight into a week at Parkfield School written by teachers, helpers and children together.

Wednesday - 5th July

The afternoon meeting at 1pm. was not very well attended (14 present - no parents present). It was decided that some music should be got into the school, that the five smashed windows should have their panes replaced. Saucepans should be bought to help make school dinners instead of going to the chip shop. It was decided that more children would be welcome in the school.

Thursday - 6th July

Dave got chickenpox, Valerie, Christine, Roy and Gary came for the first time. Joan came instead of Dave, Audrey came too. Some did some faces and shapes in clay in the back room. Some did some cricket in the park. After dinner (which was chips etc.) Heinke, Kevin and Lucia all suddenly showed up and started painting flowers on walls and things. Kevin lit fires in the fireplaces, which was nice. Peter lit fires in most other places which was probably nice too. Then somehow Yvette, Paula, Ann, Gary, Roy and Linda were all piling round in coloured drapes and blouses and things in the middle room being witches and dogs. Later a few people did a little bit of reading by the fire in the front room.

Friday - 7th July

Bob came in today, and did some sums and things in the morning. It rained all day, so Paula mopped up and then other people mopped up and there was nearly as much water inside as outside but it got clean in the end, for a little while. Heinke painted some more flowers on another wall.

Monday - 10th July

The middle room was made the schoolroom today. Christine, Ann, Gary and Valerie and Martin did some things in there. Paula mopped the back room again and then a lot went to play rounders in the vacant site across the street. In the afternoon most people did a quick Sleeping Beauty, Red Riding Hood and a 'show' - in the back yard and in the cellar.

Tuesday - 11th July

Gay, Andrew, Ken and Bob came today. Yvette didn't. She went to visit her new school. Gay and Linda and Gary counted traffic and made a block graph with sticky paper. Valerie, Roy, Ann, Paula, Andrew and Ken did some sums between doing other things. After dinner (which Andrew, Roy, Gary and Paula cooked - soup and omelette), Bob took everyone to the baths, while Kevin, Heinke, Lucia and Andrew bought a new lock which was fixed to the front door, and five panes of glass, two of which were fixed during the evening as lots of people washed and mangled stuff in the washing machine Bob had made out of two others.

Wednesday - 12th July

Everyone went to Platt Fields in the morning and took sandwiches out with Alec in the afternoon to Lymm and Wythenshawe, and all sorts of places. Today, the meeting was at 7pm, and lots of people were there. It was decided once those windowpanes were in we could apply for registration. Also that the school would stay shut unless some older people were in with the children, and to help this a shift system was organised for the following week, including in the evening, while it was agreed that the school should stay shut during tea-time. Ada (Valerie's mother) said she would come to the school round dinner time to organise the cooking.

Wednesday - 19th July ... kids' views

VALERIE: *The school is not bad. You can do anything you want. We go out nearly every day with Bob or Andy. Yesterday Bob and Jim took us to another Free School and then to the beach.*

YVETTE: *Today we went to Platt Field Park. We went on the boats and I rowed the boat. Yesterday I did not come. On Tuesday I had to go to Whitworth School and had my dinner at Whitworth School and then I came home and went to the Free School, 32 Parkfield Street.*

CHRISTINE: *I like the school I am at. We can do anything at this school. Some times we go to the Baths with the teacher.*

PAULA: *We think the school is good but we can't afford a lot of money. If people would be more generous we might get somewhere.*

Wednesday 12th July

LINDA CHEEVERS: *Our school is very good because it is interesting. We have different teachers every day. Every Thursday we go out with*

Dave. Sometimes we go into the country. Last time we went into the country one of our girls caught a frog. Sometimes we do writing and sums and drawing that is why it is very interesting.

VALERIE: *Today we came to Platt Fields and went out on the boats. Yesterday we went to the baths with the Teachers. I like school and the teachers. You can do anything at school.*

Thursday - 28th September

SANDRA: *My name is Sandra Ashcroft and I am 14 years old and I go to Parkfield Street School and I like it a lot we do all different things like painting and writing and reading and I think that Parkfield School is the best school in Manchester because they teach us better things. They don't push us around or call us names. Any way I like Parkfield School and Ducie High School is no good because they teach you a lot of bullshit. That's all baby."* [35]

The development of Parkfield from a family to a neighbourhood school raised challenging issues of community control. "Education", and its various interpretations, raises feelings over values, aspirations and method. The subjection of the person to the end goals of "education" - namely success in society as presently structured - and educational mythology, enabled the authorities to bend parents and their children to the will of those in education, almost regardless of their ability to "educate" their charges. Parkfield therefore faced the task of establishing human relationships which would truly reflect the ideals of the teachers. At the same time they sought to encourage the energy and curiosity of the children into some of the channels which would eradicate the handicap of low literacy. Most of the children attended Parkfield because they rejected the local state schools, and had a great deal of resentment to overcome before any form of book learning would become acceptable. Many of the parents sent their children, or quite simply allowed them to come, because initially it was an easy way out of the daily grind of forcing them to state school. But soon the parents expected some academic work because they aspired for the future of their children. Hence many meetings met with some support from parents and enabled an understanding of the philosophy of the teachers to be tempered by the expectations of the parents. Likewise the parents, pleased and relieved at their children's happiness, saw the relaxation as a step towards real learning and exploration.

The sheer physical presence of the school provided a stimulus to those engaged in trying to bring an alternative society to birth. For the school on the street, at grass roots level, is a fundamental aspect of social change, and the complex mutually supportive groups, in 1972, seemed almost revolutionary. Without the support of On the Eighth Day, the alternative shop in Oxford Road which carried the main day-to-day running costs of Parkfield, together with Grass Roots Bookshop in Upper Brook Street, Magic (Manchester Alternative General Info Centre), University Community Action, and numerous individuals, Parkfield could not have functioned.

No Master High or Low

By the end of 1972, all those at Parkfield knew they had to look for new premises as Parkfield Street was due for slum clearance in 1973. But the mood in the spring of 1973 was not demoralised. The last publication from Parkfield concluded thus:

> "Our aim is to become accepted within the State Educational System, yet retain our identity and ideals. We see ourselves as acting as a catalyst to change by acting as a working model. In the meantime we shall obviously need future premises when the street is demolished next summer. We have heard of a large old house in the Whalley Range area, which is in easy reach of the new Moss Side development. Ideally the premises would house workshops and classrooms as well as a large garden. Such a building would cost in the region of £8,000, not forgetting day-to-day running costs and educational equipment. Our first newsletter resulted in £200 and a great deal of encouragement. Despite the fact that all work is voluntary, we obviously need money. If you know of anyone who may be interested please let us know." [36]

Buildings in the Whalley Range area never materialised but some of the workers at the school managed to keep the school running through late 1973 and early 1974 at the Hideaway Youth Club just outside Moss Side. Then in July 1974 the Social Services Department made the Aquarius Neighbourhood Centre at Burlington Street available for the Free School. The school started again, this time named the Manchester Free School. It was to continue until Social Services were forced to close the Neighbourhood Centre in 1979.

How did the new school operate? Basically, efficiently and actively. There was a significant amount of academic learning including English, Maths, Science and German, but it was not given a superior status. Football, swimming and ice-skating were regular physical activities. Everybody in the school, on average thirty pupils and twelve adult helpers and teachers, helped to prepare the mid-day meal. Photography, needlework, woodwork, decorating, car maintenance, guitar playing - these were also regular activities.

All kinds of outings had a prominent place in the new Free School. The community felt it important not to stay in the building all of the time, but to learn from experiences outside. Day, weekend and longer trips to the country gave opportunities for seeing wildlife, as well as giving a welcome break from the city. Many visits were made to Tottan Hall, Blue John Mines and, in August 1975, the whole school attended an education week at Laurieston Hall, a large commune in Scotland.

Support for the school came from a variety of sources: the building from Social Services, regular grants from On the Eighth Day, Grass Roots Bookshop, the Students Unions at Manchester Polytechnic and University, several branches of the Transport and General Workers Union and the Community Levy for Alternative Projects, free paper from Moss Side Press and paint from a Bury paint works.

Only the loss of its premises closed the school in 1979. Quietly and purposefully the Free School established itself between 1974 and 1979. There were no great leaders, no big names. The school was a work of love and dedication. It was also a gesture of defiance against the dehumanising process of schooling. However, the use of the word "against" was not negative. The school was very much a part of the positive tradition of libertarian schooling.

Nothing sums up the Manchester Free School better than this statement produced by the Manchester Free School Support Group in March 1975:

"We see in the Free School as but one of a series of movements which are growing in this and other countries. Embryonic as such movements are, they contain within them the seeds which can spread, develop and grow into a new society which within itself will not tolerate injustice, and outside itself will challenge the values which are generated by capitalism. We know that the Free School cannot of itself stand against injustice and change society. But do believe it can act as a catalyst and as an example to present initiatives, teachers and students. Further the Free School finances come from individuals and groups within the community - we have never received state or trust aid. And this itself is some sign of our potential strength, because the more awareness there is outside the Free School of its work and purpose then the more its understanding permeates amongst the community. We know that Free Schools have to grow as a movement together with other radical groups, so that the family, the community, its work and creativity is under its own control and direction. We know that without this growth the Free School is little more than a token, an oasis, within the desert. Our celebration of the Manchester Free School is out of joy and an awareness of what remains to be achieved. In struggling for freedom and justice we feel ourselves part of those great pioneering movements which united the oppressed and joined the fight against such oppression. The Free School ideal is one liberating force which has captured the imaginations and ideals of many people. We ask you to join in our celebration either in thought or deed. The Free School is real and part of an evolving movement. Help us to reach out and grow." [37]

8. THE LION OF ISLINGTON

White Lion Free School, (Islington, London, 1972 - 90)

White Lion Free School is probably the best known of the British non-fee-paying Free Schools. This is largely because of its long life and the amount of attention it has attracted from the media and a host of writers.

The history of the school has been problematic. There have been endless crises around funding, philosophy and organisation, but somehow the school managed to survive for eighteen years, only to be consumed in the melee after the abolition of the Inner London Education Authority (ILEA) in 1990.

With all of these factors in mind it is impossible to try to give a complete history of the school in a few pages. It is more important to provide what will only amount to a brief summary of the story of the school's foundation, how a selection of its pupils, parents and workers experienced the school, and an indication of the critical problems it has faced. In many ways a detailed and lengthy evaluation of the school remains a priority for the libertarian educational tradition.[38]

The White Lion Street School was born in 1972 in an old derelict house near London's Kings Cross Station. It was very much a part of the emergent Free School Movement, and from the beginning the idea was to create a space in which local children could learn without the regimentation, the boredom and the fear that is so much a part of traditional schooling.

As the renovation of the building progressed, children wandered in off the streets, and many stayed to lend a hand when the school finally opened in September 1972. Most of its children had not only discovered the school themselves but to some extent had physically created it.

Seven of the twenty-seven children had arrived by a different route, via Social Services. They were introduced to White Lion because each, in their own way, had previously demonstrated their rejection of traditional schools. By the middle of 1973 the number of children had risen to forty-three, and remained around that figure with usually about eight full-time workers.

From the outset there was to be no hierarchy amongst the workers, no head, no significant division of labour. Work was to be shared, or rotated, and everybody was expected to help with routine tasks like cleaning and washing up. Children were to have the same rights as adults and attendance, lessons and work voluntary.

The original school building, a two-hundred-year-old listed Georgian house was owned by Islington Council and leased for a nominal £100 a year. Initial funding came via a variety of different grants.

By 1977 the school had established a set of principles of operation. They provide a valuable insight into the way in which the school tried to operate in its early years:

The Lion of Islington

"The White Lion Street Free School sets out to meet basic social and educational needs, including the teaching of basic skills, for those living in its catchment area.

While the school aims to be flexible and informal, in the first five years certain principles of operation have been agreed, which those working in the school are expected to accept, and which cannot be changed except by unanimous decision by both the meeting and the meeting of the Council.

These are:

The school cannot charge fees for its basic activities; this does not prevent it from asking for contributions towards the cost of certain activities (e.g. residential trips, horse-riding etc.). The amount of these contributions should be decided by the school meeting.

There are to be regular meetings (normally weekly), with an open agenda and open to children attending the school, part-time and full-time voluntary workers (all of whom have been appointed by the school meeting) and parents of children attending. They are to be the main decision making meetings of the school.

The legal framework of the school, bye-laws and regulations affecting fire and health precautions and the requirement that the school and its users should be adequately insured may limit the decision-making powers of the meeting. The meeting cannot make decisions which contravene these principles of operation, or that affect the long-term stability or financial viability of the school.

Children will be encouraged, but never forced, to take part in learning activities.

The full-time workers are to be paid equally (with possible allowances to be agreed by them for particular personal responsibilities e.g. dependent children and necessary additional expenses.) Money earned through promoting the ideas embodied in the school (e.g. speaking and media fees etc.) are to be paid to the school.

All workers agree that they will not hit children or use physical violence. If they do, they will resign immediately and the parents of the child/children concerned will be told what happened. We recognise that there are times when mild physical force such as pushing may be used in order to prevent children and/or adults hurting themselves or others. Physical violence by any other member of the school community against another will be discouraged and when possible prevented.

Punishment will be avoided. This is not to prevent positive measures being used to protect people and their ability to make full use of the school, and to recover or replace stolen or damaged property without violating the legal rights of individuals.

> *Records or reports written about children, their parents and others will be shown to the subjects of them, who will also have the right to challenge and if necessary, correct anything in them. The persons about whom the report is written will have the right to control who else, apart from school workers sees these records. We will press for attendance and representation of children and families at case conferences and other meetings.*
>
> *In deciding which school age children should join the school, there should be no selection based on individual histories or characteristics, if the general criteria are satisfied (e.g. living within the catchment area and maintaining a rough age and sex balance in the school). Applicants aged 14 and over will be admitted subject to the decision of the full-time workers. Children who have joined the nursery (aged 3 to 5) but who live outside the catchment area may be refused a place in the school when they reach school age if it is full.*
>
> *A condition of school-age children being on the Free School roll is that they attend the school (or other approved activities) for a period which corresponds to the legal minimum attendance at maintained schools. When they do not, after a reasonable period of warning them and their parents (including warning in writing) they may be taken off the roll and the local education office informed."* [39]

So what was life like in the school? It is difficult to provide a complete picture but in 1986 the magazine *Lib ED* published a sample of experiences. Like the principles of operation they provide a fascinating insight into the school:

> **"1. A Day in the life of the Free School**
>
> *Most of the workers have dribbled in by nine o'clock. The office is soon crammed with letter-openers, typists, telephone callers, tea drinkers, photocopiers etc. ... Kids begin to drift in, play table tennis with each other or workers, chat ... Younger kids arrive with parents who maybe stay on for a while.*
>
> *By 10 o'clock most of the kids are in and the office workers are transformed into teacher workers. The nursery group might be listening to a story ... or sitting in a heap on top of their reader - sometimes a squashed worker, kid or parent. Some of the Blue Room children (5-8 year olds) and Lesley plan out lunch and then do the shopping for ingredients - others paint exotic pictures, themselves, each other or maybe join the school meeting with the older kids. Charlie chairs, Danny wants to organise a trip to Yorkshire, Tommy would like to borrow a school guitar, Liz suggests holding a jumble sale, no-one's been washing up again ... votes are taken, decisions made.*
>
> *Break time in the kids' cafe - only 5p for a cup of tea.*

The Lion of Islington

The middle group have a choice of music with Pete, basic skills with Liz or Pottery with Bill; older kids can do language work with Teri, maths with Kevin or maybe persuade Eddie to come up with something else.

Lunch from 12.30 till 1.30. Matt, Pete, Aaron and Bill wash up and clean the kitchen and dining room.

Trev's keys are missing, an emergency meeting is called. Where are they, who did it? ... the workers are asked to leave, kids sort it out, keys returned.

The older and middle kids combine for men's group. Liz, Teri and the girls go for a sauna.

Things begin to wind down about half past three, office work is completed, some workers go off on home visits, some work with Bob on the cleaning and tidying up. People drift off ...

2. Chris Hughes - Parent.

I remember when they were still doing up the building, they put up posters round the area advertising a jumble sale. I went along to that, talked to three or four people and was overwhelmed with joy about the place. I was thrilled to find such a place that operated in such a positive way. I'd been worried for quite a time about what I was going to do about my kids' education because I can't stand schooling. I don't think it has anything to do with education. It just seems to constrain children, control them and so a great deal of damage to their desire to learn, and the idea of corporal punishment appals me. The White Lion seemed to be a place that met every requirement I had.

My eldest child, Moraig, started there straight away. She was three then, she loved it. She stayed at the Free School until she was thirteen and then she decided that she wanted to do lots of exams and so she transferred to the local comprehensive, Islington Green. I thought it was really positive for a thirteen year old to make such an important decision for herself. There were some things she missed but White Lion had given her enormous self confidence. During her first term her year-head at Islington Green said to me, 'Gosh she's a real recommendation for the Free School system'. She got seven 'O' levels there and now she's doing three 'A' levels at a sixth form centre.

My son, Hamish, started at White Lion two years later than Moraig, when he was three. Like Moraig he eventually decided to go to Islington Green to do his 'O' levels. When he first got there his year group had to do a maths test and he came third out of the whole year, so academic standards at the Free School are obviously pretty good. My youngest child, Beth, is still at White Lion, she's 4. She's been there for a year and a half and really enjoys it.

No Master High or Low

Mother and daughter: Chris and Beth Hughes.

The Lion of Islington

I think there's so many good things about White Lion in terms of what it teaches kids about taking control of themselves and their lives, how it tries to teach kids about making decisions and taking responsibility.

3. Karen McDaid - Past Pupil.

I was one of the original kids at the school. My mum used to go to Risinghill School before it was closed down, and she liked the head Michael Duane, he recommended the White Lion for me. I was only three then so I don't really remember the beginning, but I think my mum helped to do the school up. I remember when there used to be baths on every floor and when you'd come in in the morning some of the teachers would be having a bath, sometimes kids would have baths, some of the teachers used to live in the school then. It was really more like a big family than a school.

A lot of my friends though used to say it was a backward school or for kids who'd been bad at their other school, just because they didn't know enough about it. People always do that, it's just ignorance. I liked the teachers there, they're more like friends not sir or miss, just Lesley or whatever. I used to talk to them about all my problems and they would listen. I liked the choice if you wanted to do something you just had to organise it.

I thought the meetings were good, like the way a five year old could say 'I don't agree with that' - so you're learning from an early age to be independent. Sometimes maybe a teacher wanted to get their own way and they'd start using long words or something but the kids wouldn't let it happen, they'd say, 'put it straight, say what you mean'. I don't think the teachers could get away with a lot at the meetings.

One thing I really didn't like was when the ILEA took over us they put a sign up that said 'White Lion Street Free School Centre'. I hated that 'Centre', 'cause it's not a Centre it's a School. I wrote to Frances Morrell about it but she just said it was for 'legal reasons'. Anyway I just got a brush and painted over it.

I was sad to leave the Free School. My mum saw an advert for a job as a dental nurse in the Hackney Gazette. I went for an interview while I was still at White Lion. They asked me to start on the Monday so I left before I'd had much time to think about it.

If I have kids I'd like them to have some experience of an ordinary school and some time at the Free School, so they could choose for themselves, but I'd prefer them to choose the Free School.

4. John Griffiths - Worker.

I have been a worker at the White Lion Street Free School for 2 years. I am employed as an art instructor. Official job tabs are, however,

No Master High or Low

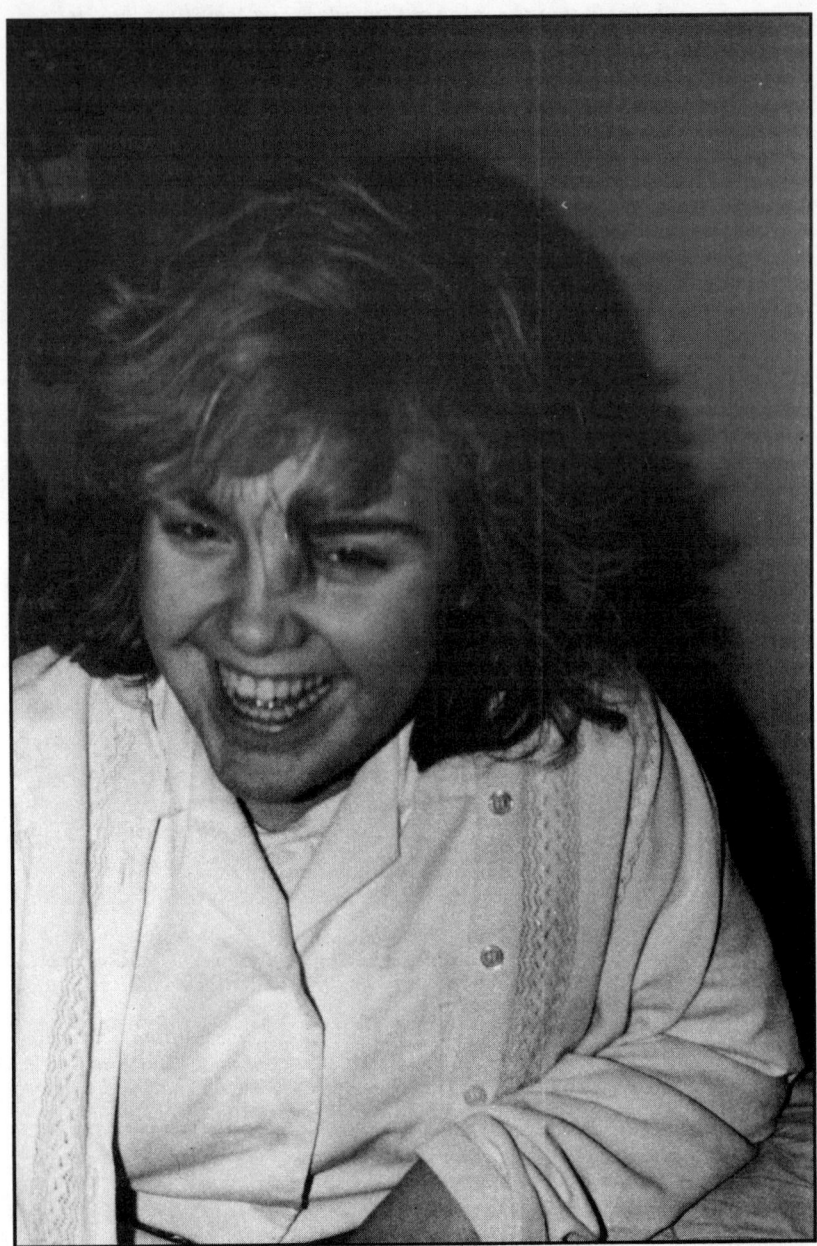

Karen McDaid: a complete education at White Lion.

unhelpful in establishing any realistic definition to the role that is expected of me within the structure that the school operates. I have, like all the other workers, not one, but many roles.

I am also during the course of the week engaged in activities which vary from cooking and cleaning to individual counselling and family visits.

My morning may well start with the making of sculpture. At 11.15, however, the priority would possibly be confronting the delicate problem of dislodging the remains of someone's supper from a malfunctioning loo. The afternoon could begin by discussing the difficulties a single parent mother has in communicating with her 12 year old son. When 3 o'clock comes round I am perhaps helping four year olds to roll dough, and taking delight with them, when a short while later we draw from the oven, like magic, a star shaped biscuit.

The expectation of the community therefore is that I will contribute to its wellbeing in ways which question the notion of 'specialisation', and subverts the oppressive distribution between different forms of human creativity.

In recent literature we have stated:

'We would like the members of the school community to feel that a human being should be valued and respected on the content of their character rather than other factors, such as society's view of their ability to earn a lot of money, their position of power over others, or their acceptance of the notions of 'men's' as opposed to 'women's' work'.

Through encouraging each individual to fully participate in all the necessary tasks of running the school, the community hopes to engender a real consciousness of equality.

Such a challenging approach demands an immense amount of commitment.

5. The Kids of '86.

HELEN: *I've always been at this school. I did visit another school once, but I didn't like it.*

JAMIE: *I like loads of things about this school. I like reading, washing up, cooking, art and pottery. I like doing photographs with Trevor, as well. You put films into a tank and then you shine this light and make pictures. I like the teachers here, they are friendly. At my other school they were all bossy boots - and you had to line up for dinner.*

RANIA: *My mummy and daddy chose for me to come here because they thought it's better than other schools. I used to go to a school in*

Highbury. I liked it there but there were lots of children in my class, it was too noisy.

TAMMY: *It's fun at the free school, we all have a laugh. Like yesterday we had a towel fight, some of the workers play but some are a bit moany. I went to another school for about a week but I didn't like it. It was too big and I didn't like the kids there too much. We go on lots of trips here like swimming, horse-riding and ice-skating. I like cooking as well.*

I made the dinner for all the kids. We had beefburgers, chips and peas. We don't like the workers' dinners much, like when Lesley makes spaghetti bolognese. The kids like kids' dinners best. I don't like the school meetings much either, it's alright if something's really a problem but mostly it's a waste of time. I don't mind our group meetings though.

DAVID: *I've been to this school since I was three so I don't know what other schools are like. It's good here. I don't like some of the older children, they nick things.*

SAM: *It's good because there's no head-teacher and you can do what you want to. I like to do maths and reading. I like to cook dinner and cakes. I think this school is big and there's too many big children, I think small children are more kind.*" [40]

So this was the school. As Karen McDaid indicates, a major change took place when the Inner London Education Authority agreed to fund the school in 1981. In becoming part of the ILEA, the Free School had to meet two immediate demands. Firstly, the Authority had no such category as "Free School". In order to satisfy the bureaucrats the school agreed to be officially designated as an "off-site unit".

The other demand was from the unions who wouldn't accept the precedent of ILEA paying qualified teachers less than the standard rates of pay. ILEA therefore paid the salaries of five teachers at the Burnham Scale Two rate. The school, however, employed eight full-time workers and shared out the five salaries between them.

The transition was therefore achieved without losing control of the school's ability to maintain its name and staffing ratio. As time passed the school retained its independence. It has kept complete control over the appointment of workers and the curriculum.

There were other problems, though. Undoubtedly the first was trying to live up to its principles of operation.

White Lion undoubtedly started with a determination to provide a learning centre for anybody in the area who wanted to use it. There were no arbitrary age limits. It stayed open in the evenings and at weekends as well as normal school hours. The adults began to come to school with the children, often to learn alongside the children. Others came mainly to use resources like tools, books or even saucepans. A general study of cities led one group of older children and adults to discuss the Council's redevelopment plan for their block of flats. The group moved on to make a video about the residents' reaction to these plans. The film was shown at a public meeting, and from that a Tenants' Association was set up.

The "allocation system" also ensured that the school maintained its roots in the community. As each child entered the school, they were allocated a worker who maintained close contact with the child's family. During home visits workers have often been asked to help with D.H.S.S. problems, unpaid bills or maybe just move furniture. Islington Council have provided financial help in recognition of this 'family support' work.

By 1986 all of the original workers had moved on, but some remained involved as "stooges". This was a group of parents, ex- workers, ex-parents and other local people who acted as a support group for the school. This structure of "stooges" helped ensure some sort of continuity, but sadly the body rarely met between 1986 and 1990.

Many schools have a hidden curriculum of fear and authority, but at White Lion underlying values and relationships were brought out and considered as part of the core curriculum. By being part of a reasonable community children learned to be reasonable.

Thus meetings were always at the centre of Free School life. It was not that meetings were held to make decisions, the meetings were seen as an education in themselves. People learned about each other and about each others' ideas and feelings and why you could not always have your own way.

Every Wednesday morning the school met as a community to discuss what anybody had written on the agenda. It could be a trip somebody was organising, it could be about washing up, personal relations or a request from somebody who would like to visit the school. This "School Meeting" has always been chaired by one of the older children and, as far as possible, decisions were always arrived at by consensus.

Every Tuesday evening there was a "General Meeting" open to children, workers and interested parties. This was the ultimate decision-making body of the school, and again children had an equal say. This meeting always tended to concentrate on longer-term principles of operation, as well as the intricacies of administration and the appointment of new workers.

During the 1970s the school, eventually with the help of the ILEA, strove to live up to its principles of operation. By the early 1980s, though, it was clear that there was considerable conflict over the principles. *Lib ED* tried to capture the essence of this conflict with an exchange of views between two ex-workers, Will Langworthy and Nigel Wright, in successive issues in 1987 and 1988. Their views are worthy of attention. Will stated:

> *"In September 1987, White Lion Free School celebrated its fifteenth birthday. There were several reasons for celebrating this occasion; amongst these is the accumulation of experience over this period, with lessons for those interested in libertarian education. One of the lessons learnt painfully at White Lion Street has been the danger of the school losing its libertarian approach. WLSFS has recently been split by a serious disagreement about the Founding Principles. Over the last five years, with new arrivals amongst the workers, a majority of them rejected the Principles and introduced an alternative Code of Practice in 1985.*

> *The Code gave workers' meeting a veto over the school meeting removing the school's principle of full democratic decision-making by all. Another principle was that the school should be rooted in the local community and that workers were there to help parents in all matters, not just the education of their children. This was undermined by the attempted abolition of the school's catchment area, previously 1000 yards with no selection, and by much greater referral of families to outside state services. Further, the introduction of selection which aimed to exclude kids not considered suitable for the school in the judgement of the workers challenged the commitment to an egalitarian school. Although the Code paid lip service to the idea of voluntary lessons a new and more coercive attitude to non-attendance was also apparent.*
>
> *After a lengthy dispute between the workers and the charitable oversight body (composed of ex-workers, parents and students), the Founding Principles reaffirmed, following which several of the workers resigned. And so September was also a rebirth of the school with a new complement of workers and its original Principles reinstated. As Britain's only state-funded free school, WLSFS has a unique role in demonstrating libertarian education in action."*

Nigel replied:

> *"It just will not do for Will to portray the recent disagreements at White Lion as a Walt Disney-like battle between good and evil. There has in fact been a legitimate debate going on at WL for several years, and all sides in the debate (there are more than two sides) have valuable viewpoints which deserve serious attention. All of these viewpoints fall within the broad libertarian tradition, and therefore I do not think it would be right for Lib ED to publish only one side of the story.*
>
> *Very briefly, the debate can be summarised in this way: when WL was founded in 1972 it described itself as an experiment. The school wrote: 'Our vision of the ideal community school is far from realisation - and will quite likely never materialise in the form we envisage. It must be firmly understood by us that we may be entirely taken by surprise by what transpires.'*
>
> *The central question is: how well has the WL experiment worked out? Those who believe that the experiment has worked well naturally conclude that WL should continue into he future along the same lines as in the past. They recommend 'more of the same.' Those who believe the experiment has not worked well have tried to identify what changes would be needed to remedy the faults they perceive.*
>
> *Thus there are two issues here. Has the school worked well? And should there be any major changes in the way the school operates? These issues have been overlaid by a third question: if there are to be any major changes who, if anyone, is entitled to make them? The school's founders? The 'stooges' (which is the nearest the school has to a council of*

management or governing body)? The workers? The parents? The children?

These are important questions. Unfortunately the school has lacked a structure within which such questions can be debated and resolved. Internally the school does have such a structure - the meeting, which is open to parents, children and workers. But this forum excludes the school's founders, the stooges, and various other people - such as myself - who would like to participate in the debate.

Sadly, and in my view dangerously, the debate has been 'guillotined'. The supporters of the 'more of the same' view went to County Hall and prevailed upon the senior ILEA officers to impose their viewpoint on the school by dictat - against the wishes of a majority of the parents and the workers. Subsequently all the workers resigned. For Will Langworthy this is a 'victory'.

If it is such, it is a Pyrrhic one because it has established the precedent that ILEA officers (not the elected members) can make decisions about the internal organisation of the school - something we tried hard to prevent when we drew up the agreements in 1982 which brought WL into the ILEA. One wonders, too, what kind of 'victory' it is for the kids to lose, all of a sudden, all the workers, with whom they had built up valuable relationships.

Of course there is very much more to the story than this brief account. The way I have described it is, certainly, jaundiced by my own conviction that in major respects the WL experiment has not worked well and that a fundamental re-evaluation of this type of libertarian practice is needed. I do not think it does any service to the libertarian cause to sweep these matters under the carpet and foreclose the debate.

I think libertarians will have to move beyond the 'hurrah-ism' of declaring that Summerhill and White Lion are perfectly wonderful. We might begin by asking this: if they are so wonderful, why haven't they been imitated on any significant scale? Could it be that there are many open-minded people who remain unconvinced that they are the right answer? And could there be any evidence to support such scepticism? I think Lib ED readers should be told." [41]

In many ways this conflict was never resolved and it is a classic example of one of the school's greatest problems. However, the greatest one was to come with the dismantling of the ILEA.

This was the biggest challenge the school had to face. Christopher Draper reported the challenge succinctly for the magazine *Freedom* at the end of 1989:

"In view of its immediate demise ILEA decided to consult the Council of London Borough of Islington, who would be expected to take over responsibility for the school, about its intention to continue funding. The

> *newly appointed Director of Education for Islington, Chris Webb, advised the Council that the White Lion should not be funded because it could not guarantee that it would inflict the national curriculum on its pupils. The Education Committee went along with his view and so it looks as if Islington will not take up the funding on the demise of ILEA in April 1990. After 17 years the end could be in sight.*
>
> *The only hope for the school lies in reverting to their Independent School status. As a private school the White Lion would not have to comply with the demands of the national curriculum but it would need to either charge fees or seek grants to cover all its expenses (or a combination of the two). The school is now drawing up a package of proposals for its continuance as a non-fee-paying independent school funded by grants. This is the same sort of structure that carried them through their first nine years but in the case of the other city free schools led to financial collapse."* [42]

Sadly the package of proposals never came together, and in April 1990 came the official end. However, the school is worthy of celebration. Its history has been tempestuous and troublesome but as *Lib ED* commented:

> *"The White Lion isn't after all the complete answer to every Libertarian's dream; it doesn't solve everyone in Islington's problems, it hasn't pioneered curriculum innovation, there's division in the school community and it takes money from the state, but it has achieved much. It has helped many kids who were failed by traditional schooling, it has supported many local families and it has demonstrated that freedom isn't just for the upper and middle classes. It has shown that Free Schools don't need idyllic rural retreats or fee-paying parents (like Summerhill and Dartington Hall) but are a real, viable alternative for all our children."* [43]

9. NEIGHBOURLY LESSONS

Leeds Free School and Community Trust, (Eldon Chapel, Woodhouse Lane, Leeds, 1972 - 4; 7, Marlborough Grove, Leeds, 1975 - 82)

There were four very distinct phases of the history of the Leeds Free School and Community Trust. The Trust opened a Free School in January 1973 after eighteen months of intensive discussions. The school was housed in Eldon Chapel, Woodhouse Lane, for about eighteen months, during which forty children were in full-time attendance, and many others used the building and adjoining adventure playground in out-of-school hours and holidays. The Chapel, though, had to be abandoned in 1974, because of lack of finance to meet statutory building requirements.

From July 1974 until July 1975 the Trust operated a network of tutorial groups. The number of children had had to be reduced from forty to twelve.

In July 1975 it was decided to set up another school, in a through-terrace house, 7 Marlborough Grove. People living nearby gradually became involved with the school, so that by December 1976 six houses in the Marlborough Grove area were committed to the school. As neighbours became more active in Free School teaching, lessons tended to be based more in their houses and less in the school.

By 1977 the Trust felt it was a natural progression to move back into tutorial groups keeping 7 Marlborough Grove open as a resource centre. This ensured that the important sense of togetherness would not be lost. Three more houses, close together in another area of Woodhouse, were also used for tutorial groups, so that the "school" had two main bases. This situation continued until 1982 when the Trust was wound up when a majority of Trustees moved out of the area.

This history makes the Leeds Free School initiative quite distinctive, because of its relatively long life and because of the development of a unique tutorial system. It warrants close consideration. Bridget Robson wrote in *Peace News* in 1974:

"School, one of the most mystifying and pervasive institutions in our society. Several of us at the receiving end of education in Leeds - parents excluded from their kids' education because they weren't professionals, kids knocking off from the classroom for the delights of playing in houses or talking to friends, teachers finding themselves unable to relate humanely to kids in the classroom because of the teacher/pupil barrier - got together to consider an alternative. Considering the examples of Summerhill and, more relevantly for us, the First Street School in New York and the Scotland Road Free School in Liverpool, the Leeds Free School and Community Trust was established in June 1972." [44]

Forty or fifty adults met through the Spring and Summer of 1972 to discuss all aspects of education and community control in the minutest detail. By September 1972 four or five people had given up their jobs and had begun work on the acquired Eldon Chapel. The Free School opened in January 1973.

The vast majority of the initial intake were school non-attenders but slowly the school began to attract children who were attending mainstream schools, but were unhappy with the experience. As Bridget Robson wrote:

> *"We believe that every child has the right to learn as s/he directs and to relate to others in a free and supportive community so Free Schools should not function as a cheap safety valve for the State, absorbing the destructive energies of frustrated working-class kids which otherwise might be creating a force for change within the schools. Free Schools are not an end in themselves, but part of a model and a step towards a de-schooled society."* [45]

So how did the school actually operate in its first phase? There was a lot of playing and getting to know one another. It was agreed to structure the school physically, rather than by a timetable. So there was always a football in the gym, a piano in the common room, paints in the art room, books in the library.

However, there were problems, which Bridget Robson openly acknowledged in the pages of *Peace News*:

> *"During the first year, I think we probably frightened many kids. An unstructured situation can be terrifying for kids used to a highly programmed day. The adults themselves were struggling to find what they could do with children in this new environment. In many ways we probably didn't organise highly enough. Having experienced the tyranny of a structure arbitrarily imposed we reacted too strongly and were frightened of taking initiatives for fear of seeming to dominate. Certainly many adults who wanted to work in the school found it difficult - we didn't seem to know how to support one another, so only people very confident in their own skills and ability to relate to the kids survived."* [46]

At this stage the loss of Eldon Chapel provided a breathing space and the development of the network of tutorial groups gave the adults a chance to explore a new type of pedagogy.

From July 1974 to July 1975 the Trust worked with about twelve children in their homes. Learning became more structured, with a timetable and set times for activities. This was not completely successful, but the twelve months provided the Trust with the opportunity to reflect and consider a new departure, Marlborough Grove. When the school reopened there in September 1975 there was a more defined organisation. Numeracy and literacy schemes were set up for younger children, project work was developed, outings became more planned, and a School Meeting took place everyday. The result was that, from 1975-77, the school became increasingly attractive to local parents and children, with the result that numbers remained consistently around fifty.

By 1977, though, the Trust felt that the school had become over-dependent on the physical space it occupied. It wanted to broaden the experience of children and move towards developing a school without walls, where children were active and learning in the local community. Hence the move back into tutorial groups and the development of the two resource centres.

A detailed description of the operation of the tutorial system was written by the Trust for the Local Education Authority in 1978. I have decided to include it here as it gives such an insight into how the system worked.

"NATURE OF EDUCATION.

(a) Co-operativeness.

Leeds Free School and Community Trust Tutorial Groups operate as a co-operative. Major decisions are taken by consensus at meetings attended by both adults and children. We deplore competition in learning and we consider it an extremely important part of education that everyone should learn to think and act together with a genuine co-operative attitude. We see this as a particular advantage of our system over most other educational establishments.

(b) Adults' Qualifications.

At present there are 16 adults working in Leeds Free School and Community Trust Tutorial Groups: seven for at least 5 years; two for at least three years; five for at least two years and two for at least a year. The time commitment varies from full-time to a couple of hours a week. Most of the adults are involved with local community projects in a typically 'deprived and run-down inner city area', such as Blenheim Residents Association and Blenheim Adventure Playground which the Trust proposes to start building this summer.

Eight adults have degrees in the following: Geography, English / Social Work, History / Politics, Maths, Law, Peace Studies, Philosophy / Psychology and Dietetics. One is fluent in three languages. Six are parents of registered children and five more are parents of under-fives. Between them, the adults have the following skills which are available to be passed on either to other adults or to the children: gardening, mechanics, plumbing, electrical work, sport, P.E., pottery, art, domestic science, basic science, typing, music and building work.

There are many sympathetic people living locally in Woodhouse who give us advice or practical help, including six qualified teachers, one of whom was heavily involved for two years and three of whom have taken the children on outings.

(c) Methods of Education.

No Master High or Low

Each of the tutors learns through experience their best level of teaching, and a wide range of teaching methods are used. There is much discussion about the differences in approach and the children are encouraged to join in these talks so they can discover individually which methods make learning easiest for them. The differences can be subdivided as follows:

(i) Structure. Some tutors, in particular with some of the more academic subjects, like to arrange lessons at the same time each week throughout a term. Others like to involve the children with what they are doing at any particular time, such as a one-off car maintenance job. Others like learning situations to develop spontaneously, often taking the form of a discussion or a game.

(ii) Group or one-to-one teaching.

(iii) Schemes of work. With such small adult-child ratios it would be difficult for a tutor not to have any scheme of work for each of the pupils coming to weekly or more frequent lessons. Sometimes this scheme is written and sometimes it is not. Some tutors rely heavily on books and some do not.

(iv) Some adults prefer work to be handed in to them by a certain day each week so that it can be marked before a tutorial. Others like the children to bring to them any problems that have occurred in work done at home during the previous week but do not insist upon a 'marking' approach. We encourage children to pursue by themselves their studies, which are often stimulated from tutorial group activities.

*(d) **Timetables**.*

We realise that there are certain basic skills necessary for the adult world, and there is a collective effort on the part of the adults to teach the children the need to develop their numeracy and literacy. However, there is a stress on the children learning what they want to learn. There is a general myth that children do not want to learn anything and so have to be forced to do so. This we have proved to ourselves not to be the case, especially with those children who have spent a few years with us. An instance of this is timetabling.

Timetables are drawn up by each child, usually at the beginning of a term, for their own benefit to remind them of what regular lessons they have arranged. If, with any particular weekly session, either tutor or child loses interest in it, then this is talked about and it is decided whether to continue with it or not. The timetables are in no way binding for any set period. Some regular lessons continue for years, others for only weeks. Examples of subjects that children have asked to learn and have followed up in this way over the past two years are: English, Maths, French, German, Spanish, History, Sex Education, Biology, Chemistry, Nutrition, Sewing, Cookery, Politics, Typing, Pottery, Art, Swimming,

Squash, Football, Mechanics, Music, Printing, and learning playleading in an under-five group.

In view of the circumstances of Teresa, for example, a timetable has been agreed upon with her for the present, though we hope that she will gradually decide more for herself exactly what it is she wants to do. She has already said she would like to be in the tutorial groups' five-a-side football team and she will be getting her football kit very soon.

An important aspect of the timetables is that they show that we do not believe full-time education is restricted to the hours 9.30 to 3.30. Whilst this might be necessary in a large state school with all the particular staff considerations, the situation is clearly different in our predominantly home-based system of education. The adults involved with the tutorial groups who are parents are in attendance for twenty-four hours a day, and we consider that education can and does take place at any time.

As far as the children are concerned whose homes are not part of the tutorial group network, we have found from experience that after a settling-in period the time spent with adults from Leeds Free School and Community Trust Tutorial Groups is at least 30 hours a week and usually much more, as was the case with Steve Beer. It could be mentioned here that the job he took on finishing his full-time education was in a restaurant about a hundred yards from 7 Marlborough Grove, where much of our activity is centred, so that he could stay close to us and continue to take part in the life of Leeds Free School and Community Trust Tutorial Groups. Could this be said about many school-leavers?

(e) Punishment.

Our approach to education in general is non-punitive and hence we take a non-punitive approach to attendance and punctuality. This does not mean that we don't care about attendance and punctuality - we care very much, but we feel that these aspects should be a reflection of the child's interest in his or her work and the child's feeling of responsibility.

We cannot, for example, force Teresa to attend, but then nobody can force her to attend any non-custodial type of full-time education. If she doesn't get on with our system then all we can do is suggest she goes elsewhere. All the children with us who are not home-based know this. In the case of one child in our history who, after a year, was still not coming to see us regularly, we contacted the Local Authority and arranged a meeting between all the parties concerned to decide upon the best next move for her.

(f) Atmosphere.

It cannot be stressed too much how we rely upon friendly relationships between everyone involved. The children learn to be friends on equal terms with adults and to trust their tutors and each other. They are not taught through competition and they do not feel guilty if they have not

> *understood something. It is precisely this type of atmosphere for example that Teresa now needs to regain her self-confidence, which has been knocked hard after the events of the last year. She is enthusiastic about coming with us on our two-week summer camp, which is in South Wales this year. Previously, this has always been a good occasion for new members of tutorial groups to establish close ties with those adults and children already involved. Even in the relatively short space of time that we have been seeing her, she has noticeably opened up. Can there be any doubt that it would be better for her to follow through this process rather than to be locked up somewhere?"* [47]

This, then, was how the Trust operated until 1982. However, by then the commitment and energy of many of the workers was waning, and tutors suddenly became in short supply. The Trust took the decision in late 1982 to close and, sadly, a considerable gap was left in educational provision in the area around Marlborough Grove.

The Leeds Free School and Community Trust was clearly successful, and won commendation from the Local Authority. As Bridget Robson suggested in the pages of *Peace News*, this was probably because it tried to tackle the difficult questions around pedagogy and structure. It also found a means to sustain a community-based initiative. And yet in the end it could not sustain it indefinitely, and Thatcher, monetarism and the advent of educational orthodoxy in the 1980s are too convenient a scapegoat.

10. FROM BARE CHURCH HALL TO THRIVING SCHOOL

Barrowfield Community School, (Glasgow, 1973 - 8)

In May 1973 Barrowfield Community School opened its doors to children from the local community. So began one of the most inspiring and forward-looking Free School initiatives. Sadly by 1978 many of the personalities involved found themselves demoralised by fatigue, a hostile media and a predatory Local Authority. The history of the school, though, is fascinating, the story of an epic struggle. I am grateful to ex-workers for their permission to use their own writings in this chapter, which are a source of considerable information, debate and inspiration.

In June 1972 a community worker from the Barrowfield area contacted John MacBeath, a lecturer in Jordanhill College, on behalf of the Tenants' Association. Many of the parents were concerned at the high incidence of truancy in the area, and were interested in examining the possibilities of a community-run or "Free School", such as they had heard about in Liverpool, London and elsewhere. At the meeting arranged, Brian Addison, a student at the College expressed an interest in working in Barrowfield with these children.

The seed of an idea was planted at that meeting and germinated in October 31st when Brian Addison, John MacBeath and George Kee (also lecturing in Jordanhill College) visited Barrowfield and initiated discussions with local community workers and parents.

From then on, after the first positive decision to act, the idea gathered momentum, and a number of local people expressed interest.

Although sympathetic, neither the Local Authority nor Jordanhill College could finance the project. By this time, those involved had come to see the immediacy of the need for support and set about trying to find suitable premises for the school, contacting firms and individuals willing to offer help. The first project was to renovate the old jail in the Gallowgate and work started on cleaning-up and planning for the adaptation of the building. As work progressed it became apparent that this would require thousands of pounds to bring it up to acceptable standards, and the idea was abandoned.

Meanwhile the school started in Christ Church hall at the end of May 1973. It began as a leap in the dark for the parents, the children and for Brian Addison in particular since at this point there were no funds for books, materials or his salary. The parents, however, voted to delay no further and to get the school under way. The only resources were the area, its considerable problems, and the dedication of a single full-time teacher and a number of helpers

When the school opened it was only after months of discussion with parents and children. There had been, over the previous few months, a number of camping trips, treks, day visits, and innumerable evening meetings at which all involved were trying to sort out basic questions of how the school would operate, to what extent parents would support it and play an active role, to what degree teachers could meet parental demands. On the day when a bare church hall welcomed its one full-time teacher and five pupils for the first time, there were no resources of any kind, no seats, or tables or books, but a group of children eager to work together to create their own school.

The first weeks, until the summer holiday, were spent in renovating the building and establishing contacts with local tradesmen and businesses to ascertain in what way they could help the school. Pupils made contacts with the local playgroup and the old-age pensioners in the area, and a number of people volunteered their services to the school.

Over the summer holidays it appeared that the school's short life might come to an end, as the Christ Church Trustees discovered that to allow their hall to be used as a school affected their status with the Local Authority concerning the payment of rates. The school pupils and teachers also felt they could find more suitable and permanent accommodation. It was not until the beginning of September, however, that a new building was found and school started the new session with a frantic attempt to make the building habitable and conducive to working in.

When the school opened in its new premises, a flat of three rooms above a taxi firm's canteen in St. Marnock Street, there were six pupils, and one full-time and five part-time teachers. The number of pupils quickly grew to ten and continued to increase as funds became available. There were a number of teachers interested in teaching part-time without pay, and a few wishing to teach full-time, but needing at least a minimum salary to be able to do so. It was felt that, while part-time teachers had a lot to offer, it was preferable to have a nucleus of two or three full-time teachers to provide the sustained individual contact which the pupils required, to be present as problems arose, and to be a resource in times of need. Brian Addison made one of the school rooms into his own home and was available in the evenings and at weekends.

Brian Addison has described how the school saw development from the outset:

> "We hope that given some source of finance the school will grow to about 40 pupils or so. We regard this as about the maximum size tolerable before a school begins to lose the advantages of close personal relationships, and begins to rely on institutional supports, rewards, sanctions, and so on. We do not think that a school of 2,000 is necessarily unworkable. We simply think it would be unworkable for us and the children we have. With 40 pupils we would hope for a minimum of four full-time staff.
>
> With the total school size kept down to this level and the teacher-pupil ratio to more than 10-1, we think it is possible to involve all children in

school meetings at which we can formulate school rules, or work out our problems and make decisions about the future. We feel quite secure in the belief that we need no hierarchies or bureaucracies in a unit of this size. We can be a community that is small enough for us to 'sort things out' among ourselves." [48]

Once open, Barrowfield attracted an enormous amount of attention from the media, beginning on 22nd June 1973 when John MacBeath was asked to write an article for the *Times Educational Supplement*. The article offers great insight into the school, and at the time raised all the crucial issues that surrounded many of the Free School initiatives. For this reason it is included in full here:

"FREE SCHOOLS FOR ACCOUNTABILITY - By John MacBeath, Lecturer of Education at Jordanhill College, Glasgow.

On the last day of May the first free school in Scotland opened its doors to its first 10 pupils. Barrowfield Community School, as it was named at a meeting of parents, pupils and teachers, rejected the name 'free school' at least partly because of the stereotypes that those two short words have come to inspire.

For some people the security of the stereotype has meant that they could dismiss this innovation in Glasgow without the need to investigate further. Others who did pursue their inquiries, made the anticlimactic discovery that the essential ingredients of the stereotype were in fact missing. Barrowfield is a representative of a new generation of free schools.

Barrowfield School has learnt a number of useful lessons from the tough-minded inner-city free schools in the United States. The first important sense in which Barrowfield is a free school is that the parents are required to pay no fees. Like Harlem Prep in New York City or the black free schools that Jonathan Kozol has worked for in Boston, it has its own interpretation of accountability.

Accountability, as originally conceived, had a great deal more to do with the hard-headed world of cost benefits than the ethos of free schools. Its language was tangible products in return for x dollars expenditure. It thereby raised questions of great significance for the free school. First of all, exactly what are schools supposed to deliver in return for that expenditure, and who has the right to hold them accountable for failure, or to evaluate that failure?

Could free-schoolers take a leaf from the book of the other independent schools with their coherent system of accountability? One might take Summerhill as a fairly good model to illustrate this. Parents have clearly defined behavioural outcomes in mind, but they do contract to pay their money, keep out of the way, and trust in the old master's magic. They are free to pull out at any time if they don't like the service and it is a fair assumption that they made a pretty informed choice from a number of alternatives in the first place.

None of this, of course, necessarily operates in state schools. As Brian Jackson has said, these schools are 'sealed off from the poor.' Such parents do not have the opportunity or expertise to hold the school accountable.

Nor is it simply that schools reinforce existing inequalities but, as Eric Midwinter has written:

'to the injury of a deprived existence is added the insult of an alien education system.'

Those apparently most in need of alternatives are caught in the vicious circle of bad service and consumer ignorance.

The well-intentioned free schoolers with their hearts, if not their heads, in the right place felt that Summerhill's only fault was its elitism and that it could offer Summerhill-type freedom to the poor and deprived. They offered the victims of the state system a more humane and less oppressive version of school for no extra payment.

But free schools, having already lost the sympathy of the right, lost the friendship of the left.

'Freeing' children from local day schools to do just as they please without the total environment of a Summerhill for the security of a middle-class backdrop (or drop back) is dangerously near a reformulation of the philosophy of keeping the peasants in their place.

When it comes to acquiring credentials, a deprived working-class child who has spent his school years following the path of least emotional resistance, escaping the drudgery of academic work and exigencies of 'O' levels, is likely to stand at the exit of the free school exactly as he did on entrance - without credentials in a highly credentialised society.

Free schools come of age when they tackle the accountability question in a more sophisticated way. Their primary accountability is clearly to children and their parents. Do they fulfil this function simply by freeing children from the oppressiveness and restrictions of ordinary schools, or by a series of easy victories over the straw men of state schooling? Those who espouse freedom must mean more than a temporary escape from bureaucracy, and begin to work out what honest promise they can hold out to parents and children who come to them for help.

The recent book by Christopher Jencks and others (Inequality Basic Books, US, 1972) concludes that 'the primary basis for evaluating a school should be whether the students and teachers find it a satisfying

From Bare Church Hall to Thriving School

place to be.' Some free schools have taken this as a comprehensive and single criterion rather than a minimum one.

Satisfaction is not at all a bad beginning as a criterion by which parents might hold school accountable, and the vision of schools as 'satisfying' places is indeed a revolutionary one: but underpinning the new school in Barrowfield is a conviction that there must be more to it than that. Accountability also means the obligation to open up possibilities, to parents and their children, that they have long ago rejected; to acknowledge right away that teachers do not always know what is best, but neither do children and their parents; that the business of the school is education, but that if it is to be realistic there is a lot of training as well.

For months now one full-time teacher and a number of part-time teachers have met with parents and pupils to thrash out these questions and policy decisions. Instead of gradually eroding parental functions until the free school becomes the surrogate mother, Barrowfield Community School continually throws the responsibility back at the parents. It is more interested in responsibility than in freedom.

An empty hall in a bleak-looking church standing among a cluster of factories, a few acres of rubble, and the skeletons of tenements edging over to accommodate a new express-way: these are the immediate resources of the school. Beyond them is the city of Glasgow. The designation 'community school' is not intended to indicate that the concerns of the school stop at the boundaries of Barrowfield, but the very first theme of study is to be the community itself - this anonymous area of the city through which tens of thousands pour every Saturday on their way to Celtic Park without an inkling of the social, historical, political implications of the way people live there.

If only the school were a primary school with the freedom to strike out along all kinds of exploratory tangents, or if only the secondary system were different! But this free school is determined not to let its pupils run blindfold against the ubiquitous 'O' level barrier. Much as most free-schoolers detest what it stands for, it is unpardonable to preach from a background of expertise and credentials that such things are not important. Those involved in Barrowfield School must convince children of the usefulness, if not the value, of the 'O' level and 'A' level game, and how to play it well. If it can short-circuit those requirements it can have time for education as well.

What has the school got that other schools haven't? Very little except two fundamental ingredients - the commitment and involvement of parents and children. The crucial question is whether it can retain those, especially as the school grows. What it has also is the understanding and respect of an exceptional teacher who has chosen to leave a good job for no financial returns in a difficult and time-consuming situation. Beside these it is felt that the total lack of money and facilities are a minor problem. Hopefully it won't be a minor problem that kills off the school just as it is coming of age." [48]

Sadly Barrowfield fell. It received no gesture of goodwill from the authorities and for this reason it took its place alongside all of the other Free School "failures". But were they really failures? This is an issue that requires attention to conclude this section.

11. AN UNSTRUCTURED TYRANNY

British Free Schooling, 1960 - 1990

Maurice Punch's article in the *Education Guardian* of 8th May 1973 entitled "Tyrannies of the Free School" remains one of the most quoted articles about the problems associated with free schooling. This is surprising considering that it was written in 1973, surely too early in the life of British Free Schooling to be a definitive assessment. It was inevitably lacking in information about British Free Schools other than Scotland Road. He wrote:

> *"I can accept the free schools as symbolic protests against the iniquities and inequalities of certain parts of our educational system ... but ... have they the ability to question the quality of the freedom they have instituted?"* [49]

Who, one might ask, were "they"? If Punch had waited, and perhaps looked beyond Liverpool, he would have discovered that there was no uniform Free School. The schools had some common characteristics and common problems, but equally a number of differences.

The Free School was an attempt to break down the barriers that have been set up between "school time" and "leisure time", between "children" and "adults", between "teachers" and "pupils", between "teachers" and other adult members of the community. This was a recognition that education, in its widest sense, takes place more outside school than inside it, that people educate themselves through experience, especially the experience of relationships with other people and that education continues throughout life.

Consequently the Free School ideal permeated far outside the walls of any building and in practice attempted to involve everybody in the community. Ultimately the Free School was the community. This was its general principle. A child learns values from its family and from the community of which that family is a part, as well as from school. Proponents of the Free School ideal believed that, in order to liberate the child, it was necessary to liberate the community. The Free School was any activity which tended to liberate the community and its children. As we have seen this included providing play facilities for children, setting up an actual "school", providing facilities and resources for community groups and community action.

Thus the Free School ideal was concerned with all the cultural and leisure-time activities of the community, in fact, all activities outside the place of work. Anybody who contributed to the development of these activities was part of the Free School.

Perhaps one of the most important activities of a community, though, is to educate its children. The advent of a national education system has led to a tendency for people to give over responsibility for this to the government and its institutions. This is particularly true among families experiencing hardships like poverty and overcrowding. People have neither the money, the space, the time nor the energy to be with their children, and to provide them with what they need. They are glad to be able to send their children to school. The Free School ideal sought the opportunity to let children feel that there were some adults who were genuinely interested in them as individuals, and to whom they could relate on an equal basis.

The "school" within the "Free School" was essentially a neighbourhood school. Children gathered in a place in conditions that were close to their normal environment. The adults in the school were people who shared that environment with them. It was not any particular features of the curriculum which made a school "free". In certain communities, the school curriculum emerged naturally from the requirements of the local population. This was not inconsistent with the idea of a free school, because the "freedom" of a Free School was an expression of its relationship to the community, not of the nature of its curriculum.

How did the Free Schools fare against the ideal? It is impossible to generalise, except to say that the Free Schools failed to make any lasting impact on their communities. However, at the London Free School, at Balsall Heath, at Parkfield and Manchester, at White Lion, at Leeds, and at Barrowfield, significant contact was made with the local community. The experience of those involved in these initiatives is a lasting testament to this.

Inside the schools, the experiences of children demonstrate the positive nature of a pedagogy that is not coercive and where learners are regarded as autonomous. Not all children left Free Schools with exclusively positive experiences and, in order to understand this, we need to search for the flaws in the schools and in the movement.

Thatcher, monetarism and the new educational orthodoxy are convenient scapegoats. It is too easy to blame the Conservative governments of the 1980s for the problems that have afflicted the Free School movement, particularly when the last five years have witnessed the emergence of new alternative schools, namely the Steiner Schools and the Small Schools.

Finance really stands at the heart of the issue. Experience seems to suggest that if Free Schools are to be a viable alternative they have to be either fee-paying, grant-assisted or state-funded. However, there are other possibilities too. One is already being developed in Steiner Schools, where parents pay what they can in cash or kind. It is also worth remembering that many libertarian schools abroad, and in London and Liverpool before the First World War, have been funded by trade unions, a source that has never really been explored by the Free Schools.

However, the whole issue of viability does not end there. Many of the Free Schools we have looked at failed to develop as collectives. In fact most of the schools, despite not actually having a head, were effectively "led" by one or two people. The style of leadership was essentially charismatic, and where the leader remained for a long time the school often survived. But charismatic leadership lacks structure, system and continuity. Instead it tends to be influenced by intuition and the mood of the moment, thus becoming unpredictable and unreliable. In these circumstances, when the

An Unstructured Tyranny

leader goes, what is there left to sustain the initiative? Ideally the community, but many of the Free Schools did not live up to their ideal.

Contrary to Maurice Punch's suggestions, the Free School movement in Britain demonstrated that, even in the face of adversity, Free Schools have much to offer. Their size, their community ideal, their belief in the autonomy of the individual child, their search for an alternative pedagogy which places learning in the hands of the learner, all give us some sort of idea of the kind of schools that could exist in an alternative society.

NOTES

1. See Jones, D. and Mason, S. *The Art of Education*. Lawrence and Wishart, London, 1988, pp95-109.

2. *Lib ED*, Leicester 1968. Vol.1, No.5, p11.

3. See Diamond, L., *Building on the failure of C.S.S.A.S.* in Harber, C., and Meigan, R., (eds), *The Democratic School*. Education Now, Derby, 1989, pp73-82.

4. Rodler, K., *Kinderbefreiung and Kinderbewusstsein, Zur Theorie und Praxis Der Freier Schule*. Frankfurt, 1983.

5. *Leeds Free School Leaflet*. 1972. *Lib ED* archive.

6. *Scotland Road Free School News Letter*. 1971. *Lib ED* archive.

7. Ibid.

8. Wright, N., *Free School: The White Lion Experience*. Libertarian Education, Leicester, 1989; and *Assessing Radical Education*. O.U.P., Milton Keynes, 1989.

9. Jenner, P., *The London Free School* in *Resurgence*, Vol.1, No.2, July/August 1966, pp16-18.

10. *Notting Hill Family Association Leaflet*. 1905. *Lib ED* archive.

11. Interview with P. Jenner. 1974. *Lib ED* archive.

12. *Peace News*, 21st August 1970, p31.

13. Ibid.

14. Ibid.

15. *Times Educational Supplement*, London, 18th December 1970, p22.

16. Ibid.

17. *Peace News*, 25th December 1970, p12.

18. *The Scotland Road Free School Prospectus*. *Lib ED* archive.

19. Ibid.

20. Ibid.

21. *The Teacher*, 13th February 1974, p586.

Notes

22. Lister, I., *The School Crisis in England 1970-1980.* Paper presented to the International Conference on Comparative Education held at Neuss, West Germany. February 1981, *Lib ED* archive.

23. Ibid.

24. *Education Guardian*, 12th March 1974, p20.

25. Wright, N., *Assessing Radical Education*, op.cit., p107.

26. Punch, M., *Tyrannies of the Free School.* in *The Guardian*, 8th May 1973.

27. *A. S. Neill Trust Newsletter*, Nos 4-6. *Lib ED* archive.

28. *Balsall Heath Community School Internal Document. Lib ED* archive.

29. Ibid.

30. *Manchester Evening News*, 7th August 1972.

31. Ibid.

32. Ibid.

33. Ibid.

34. Head, D., *Free Way to Learning.* Penguin, 1972.

35. *This is Parkfield School Now. Lib ED* archive.

36. *Parkfield - The Future. Lib ED* archive.

37. *Manchester Free School Support Group Bulletin*, March 1975. *Lib ED* archive.

38. In publishing a book by Nigel Wright about White Lion Free School *Lib ED* has apparently begun the process. We look forward to more publications from those who have experienced the school and share a genuine interest in its history.

39. *Our Principles of Operation.* in *White Lion Bulletin No.5*, p31. *Lib ED* archive.

40. *Personal Experiences of the White Lion.* in *Lib ED* Vol.2., No.2., Leicester, 1986, pp10-11.

41. Will Langworthy., *Many Happy Returns.* in *Lib ED* Vol.2., No.6., Leicester, 1987, p7; Nigel Wright, *Lion of Islington.* in *Lib ED* Vol.2., No.7., Leicester, 1988, p15.

42. Draper, C., *Free School Fights For Survival.* in *Freedom*, London, November 1989, p7.

43. *Lib ED* Vol.2., No.2., Leicester, 1986, p12.

44. Robson, B., *A Free School in an Unfree Society.* in *Peace News*, Nottingham, 7th June 1974, p8.

45. Ibid.

46. Ibid.

47. *Leeds Free School and Community Trust Bulletin 1978*. *Lib ED* archive.

48. Addison, B., *The Barrowfield Alternative*. *Lib ED* archive.

49. Punch, M., op.cit.

CONCLUSION

A Century of Libertarian Education

A THEORY, A PRACTICE, A FUTURE

1. A THEORY AND A PRACTICE

Children experience a series of prejudices from a very early age. Inside and outside the family they are objects for observation and adult gratification. Their lives are controlled by their elders, those who have to look after them. While children need some "looking after" there is a considerable difference between care and complete control. Most young children are rarely encouraged to take decisions for themselves, they are quickly slotted into prescribed gender roles, their sexuality is repressed and they experience no political, social or economic rights.

What the development of a national system of education has done, and continues to do is to build on this repression and reinforce it. Entry into the so-called educational world is compulsory and regulated. Schools are thus synonymous with education, and for most people are subsequently the only places where any learning occurs.

And yet what is learned in schools is mostly not useful knowledge, but the required values, attitudes and patterns of behaviour. Attendance and actions are monitored. Autonomy and self-determination are usually undermined and a competitive ideology prevails. Two types of child come out of schools, winners and losers, but they are bound by one characteristic, they have been schooled. They are prepared to slot into a society that is similarly schooled. There is a direct relation between the way in which children are perceived, reared and schooled, and the reality of modern industrial economics. Yesterday's children are tomorrow's factory, office, shop and training fodder.

Libertarian education is a theory and practice that recognises these controlling tendencies of national state systems of education. In 1791 William Godwin warned the campaigners for a national system of education in Britain that government would take it over and use it for its own ends. His predictions came true. While we cannot ignore the passion and commitment with which working class people fought for a state system of education that was equal to that of their upper class peers throughout the twentieth century, the fact still remains that it is government who owns the educational system, not the people.

Evidence of this emanates from almost every piece of government educational legislation introduced since 1870. In this context a reminder of the works of a senior official in the Department of Education and Science, speaking after the 1981 inner-city riots, is illustrative:

> *"We are in a period of considerable social change. There may be social unrest, but we can cope with the Toxteths. But if we have a highly educated and idle population we may possibly anticipate more serious social conflict. People must be educated once more to know their place."* [1]

This was the backdrop to the Conservative Government's legislation of the late 1980s, the Local Government Act and the Education Reform Act.

There were those who believed that the legislation would give those seeking choice in education far greater opportunities. Some, indeed, anticipated an emergence of more libertarian alternatives. Yet it soon became clear that a concentration of power in the hands of the Department of Education and Science was the primary objective.

Libertarian education also has strong roots in basic human rights. It apportions to learners a degree of independence and autonomy that libertarians seek for everybody. Furthermore it is a set of educational beliefs that seeks to break down the boundaries between teachers and learners, that is grounded in a desire to construct non-coercive and anti-authoritarian pedagogies, and that is not concerned with systems of reward and punishment. It is an all-embracing philosophy of education and learning that is compatible with anarchist views of freedom.

There is a rich tradition of libertarian educational practice in schools in Britain since 1890. This libertarian practice and development has been in the first instance, a product of particular historical circumstances. This is evident in three particular eras: the period immediately before and after the First World War, a similar period between 1940 and 1950, and the late 1960s and 1970s. All three eras witnessed a considerable debate about the purpose and nature of education, a debate which mirrored a more general and profound questioning of social values.

Considering Louise Michel's International School (1891), the International Modern Schools of London and Liverpool (1906-22), Summerhill (1924), Beacon Hill (1924), Dartington Hall (1928), the Forest School (1929), the Caldecott Community (1911), the Little Commonwealth (1913), Sysonby House (1914) and Prestolee School (1920), they were all born of an idealism that was critical of imperialism, of war, of inequality and that sought a new era. They were also products of communities and individuals who were self-determining, who saw progress lying in their hands, who sought to put into practice policies and values that society as a whole apparently feared.

Similarly when considering Burgess Hill (1935), Monkton Wyld (1940), Kilquhanity (1940), Red Hill School (1934), the Hawkspur Camp (1936), the Barns Experiment (1940) and St. George's-in-the-East School (1945) then we find another set of projects which emerged in an era that began and ended with fundamental questions about the horrors and repercussions of fascism. On this John Aitkenhead recalls:

> *"Similar ideas, similar idealism were motivating soldiers and pacifists alike only the soldiers had been proved so wrong, and so recently. At Kilquhanity we were agin the war but not agin the soldiers, we were agin the government too, and several of us went to jail for refusing to accept the conditions laid down by tribunals for conscientious objectors. An exciting, stimulating time! Our aim was simple: a school that would be international, co-educational and non-violent."* [2]

Then, in the late 1960s and early 1970s, as the young took to the streets in opposition to the Vietnam war and to the constraints of highly prescriptive university courses, there was a similar tide of idealism. This was accompanied by a fundamental examination of the purpose and nature of education. This led to the emergence of libertarian practice in state schools and to the creation of a significant number of new, free-standing initiatives, the Free Schools. As James Jupp wrote at the time:

> *"The whole western world is experiencing a phenomenon which had its origins in the United States, the creation of an autonomous 'youth culture'. The basic features of this culture are: that it rejects the adult world, that it is confined effectively to those between puberty and thirty, that it creates its own trends and symbols, that it demands 'liberation', that it requires less and less adult co-operation for its sub-society to function, that it frightens the adult world to death, and that it is basically harmless despite a dangerous and ever self-destructive aspect."* [3]

"Be realistic, demand the impossible", "Put imagination in power" - these were the slogans of the Situationists of 1968, they could also have been written over the doors of the libertarian educational projects of the same era.

On turning to the nature of the projects described, we find enormous diversity. The libertarian tradition of education and schooling has produced no uniform school, no blue-print, projects have been the inspiration of individual adventurers and whole communities. They have served different "categories" of child, different classes, different ages, different cultures. They have though been bound by a common approach, a common understanding. At the heart of all the projects examined in this study has been the belief in the capacity of the learner to determine and direct their own learning.

This belief has, in practice, taken many forms. It dispensed with formal, rigid timetabling. It is displayed in the varying systems of self-government, where the emphasis has been placed in enfranchising learners in decision-making processes. It has rejected common incentives towards and deterrents against so-called "good" and "bad" behaviour, indeed the whole concept of reward and punishment. It has been tied together by a fundamental belief in human virtue.

To attempt a general evaluation of the projects is complex. It is necessary to be aware of the principles they have been based on, to understand the possibilities, to search for and be aware of the problems and to consider their impact.

The principles are clear, they are rooted in the libertarian educational theory that stands at the heart of this study. A succinct summary of these principles was included in the pages of the early issues of volume two of the magazine *Libertarian Education*:

*"**1.** Libertarian Education is against authority.*

*****2.** Schools and Colleges use their authority to grade and to discipline in order to transform the learners into the sort of products the state demands.*

*****3.** In contrast libertarian education sees education as liberation. The learner young or old is the best judge of what they shall learn next. In our struggle to make sense out of life, the things we most need to learn are the things we most want to learn. The liberated learner controls the process - no longer the victim."* [4]

What of the possibilities? Clearly libertarian educational practice has not made inroads into the educational system in Britain, nor into popular educational ideology. Possibilities have emerged, in free-standing initiatives that have been largely self-financing, in independent fee-paying schools, in schools for the unschoolable and in some state schools. Most projects have existed outside of the mainstream, often tolerated rather than accepted.

It is here that the problems of libertarian educational experimentation in Britain lie. While Britain has not had a uniform state educational system, due to the decentralisation of responsibility to local government, it has never afforded much state support for alternatives. Consequently funding and support have always been a problem for any projects. This is very different from other European Countries, like Denmark and Germany, where state-funded alternatives have been, and are, more common. This has led to other predicaments, namely the exclusive nature of private ventures like Summerhill, or the relatively short lives of the urban Free Schools.

Many of the projects have dispensed with traditional notions of leadership, and have sought to organise themselves as collectives, without formal hierarchies. This has led to problems of its own; an increased work load for teachers, the accompanying stress and the need to engage in detailed and time consuming processes of induction for new teachers and children.

The pressures on teachers have often led to a failure to address the most basic of questions, particularly pedagogy. As Nigel Wright's book on the early history of White Lion Free School suggests, issues of pedagogy often took a back seat as the day-to-day running of a taxing project took its toll on workers and children alike.[5]

There have been significant issues concerning accountability as well. While virtually all the libertarian educational projects sought to enfranchise all "participants" in decision-making processes, in the end it was often the teachers who held sway. For example, in 1982 at Monkton Wyld, while a majority of workers in the school saw closure as the only viable prospect, the children and parents were adamant that the school should continue. In the end, though, the power lay with the teachers and the school closed.

Perhaps the greatest problem of the libertarian projects was their isolation, both from each other and from other potentially supportive agencies. Few of the projects did not face some fundamental crisis in their history. Few of those that did had an extensive network of support. This led to the existence of a tradition of libertarian education and schooling, but never a real movement.

Yet apart from all of these problems, what is clear is that the projects have had a considerable impact. In the first instance this has been confined to the participants, particularly to the children. While this study does not pretend to have researched the experiences of all the children who attended all of the different institutions, it has tried where possible to capture the experiences of as many children as possible. From the International Modern Schools, to the Free School initiatives of the 1960s and 1970s, child after child has found their experience of libertarian education a liberating one.

On a wider scale while very little research has been done, in the 1970s Ray Hemmings circulated a questionnaire to 102 school heads on the influence of A. S. Neill on their educational ideas. Seventy-five percent replied. Hemmings published the results of his research in *Fifty Years of*

Freedom. They make interesting reading, providing a quantitative assessment of the impact of libertarian ideas in state schools.[6]

However, in exploring the real significance of libertarian educational theory and practice, the most revealing and useful thing is to look at the emergence of new projects, showing that the tradition is alive and well, and to consider the relevance of the ideas in the current educational debate.

Recent years have seen the emergence of a new non fee-paying free school in Northampton, a new private school born out of the ashes of Dartington Hall in Ashburton, Devon, a new, albeit short-lived, libertarian influenced state school in Groby, Leicester, and an interesting project for the "unschoolable" in Leamington Spa. In addition there is an extensive network, Education Otherwise, where children are educated out of school.

2. A FUTURE

Blackcurrent, (Northampton)
Sands School, (Ashburton, Devon)
Lady Jane Grey School, (Groby, Leicestershire)
Bath Place School Unit, (Leamington Spa, Warwickshire)

In a row of terraced houses in Northampton there is the seed of a project that could grow to provide a model of a school without walls. What makes it different from other projects is that it is not only a learning project, but a housing co-operative that hopes to expand to become a workers co-operative eventually:

> "As well as being primarily concerned with provision of housing for the learning centre and similar educational initiatives, we also hope to promote this form of housing within the local community and further afield, eventually making loans to newly forming co-ops to enable them to buy their first property.
>
> As a co-op it is as much our concern to encourage a socially useful livelihood for tenants as it is to provide co-operative housing."[1]

Blackcurrent acknowledge the influence and help of Education Otherwise, particularly in regard to satisfying the authorities. However, what distinguishes it from many other Education Otherwise projects is its political basis in anarchist thought, its practical basis in shared property and its declared impetus to expand.

> "We do number based around practical things; shopping, games and doing a shared tapestry frame. This last had all sorts of maths experiences in it - such as sharing out the threads equally.
>
> 'Sometimes we do some sums for a treat,' said Emma, holding up a page after page of correct calculations done by the kids, 'I suppose they'll be useful to show if any inspectors call!'
>
> Joseph now loves reading. He hated it when he was at ordinary school. He now has time to read and write and go to the library.
>
> Jo was buried deep in a book about computers.

A Future

'The other school I went to was not all bad,' said Jo, 'but I can do what I want here. I was a bit worried about making friends because we moved house at the same time; but that's coming along now!' "[8]

Ironically the project seems to take in most of the areas of learning specified in the National Curriculum.

Physical exercise comes from using swimming baths, parks and skateboarding areas. Musical activities are part of life at Blackcurrent, and they are getting a piano soon.

" 'In Local Education Authority schools the children are not free to come and go as they think reasonable. The imposition of the National Curriculum is bad enough - but it is the testing that I don't want forced on the children,' said Emma.

'We are political', say Blackcurrent." [9]

What is important about Blackcurrent is that it has shown that the Free School idea is not dead and that new directions that draw on the experience of the 1960s and 1970s are possible in the current educational climate.

Sands School is one of the few private schools today that can really call itself libertarian. It was set up in 1988 by three teachers who had been together at Dartington Hall School when that was closed by its trustees.

At the time, David Gribble, now "head" at Sands, wrote in *Lib ED*:

"You cannot have a school based on respect for the individual if the ultimate governing system is authoritarian. A school must be run from within, because when you are outside you cannot really see what is going on. To give people authority over an institution is to make them believe that they understand it. Only people inside the school, seeing the many children who succeed without problems, seeing the children with difficulties change and progress, can form any true picture of its merits." [10]

How many students would talk of their school in the glowing terms that Matthew Marmot uses?

"This is the best school in the world! The learning is made fun which I think is important, and the teachers and pupils can talk as friends. The pupils are given responsibility so they become responsible. And as there are no set rules we use common sense in what's allowed and what's not allowed." [11]

Situated on the edge of Dartmoor in the small town of Ashburton, the school has thirty-three students aged between eleven and sixteen. There are now a further four part-time and one full-time staff members, in addition to the original three. The fees are £745 a term (1989/90) but they have schemes to help parents who would not otherwise be able to afford the school.

Jan Bryant, another student, describes it:

"Sands is situated in a large building called Greylands. It has grounds which extend to two acres at the back of the building. This includes an astro-turf tennis court, an old chapel, lots of grass, plenty of large trees and a vegetable garden, all of which we look after ourselves." [12]

Every Wednesday, the school community of teachers and pupils meets to make decisions about the running of the school. It was the school meeting that introduced reports and then decided how they would be handled. It is the meeting that makes any rules that may seem to be necessary. For instance, the school has a policy that children are allowed to swear, but that teachers are not. A meeting earlier this year discussed the discrepancy:

" 'I think teachers should be allowed to swear because we swear.'

'I usually swear more at things than people.'

'I think if students swear at teachers they should be allowed to swear back.'

'Is there any point in swearing?'

Someone suggested a resolution, that everyone should try and swear a bit less. This was followed by a discussion on the differences between malicious and non-malicious swearing.

'I wouldn't go up to my mum and use the f word. I'd be dead.'

'I think we should do as we like. I don't want rules made to stop me doing something.'

'Nice people don't do it'

'Rubbish!' " [13]

The meeting delegates a lot - financial matters, for instance, or advertising for staff - but staff are only appointed on the advice of the meeting. The meeting, chaired by one of the pupils, has absolute authority and the duty of the head is to make sure the school is run in accordance with the wishes of the meeting. Once a year the school discusses whether the present head has been fulfilling this function properly.

Each child chooses a tutor from the full-time staff. The children then decide in consultation with their tutor what subjects they will do. The range of subjects is conventional: English, Literature, Humanities, French, Human Biology, Integrated Science, Maths, Art, Crafts, Drama and PE, but there are also opportunities for other interests. The younger group are expected to start with a full timetable, but this includes some days when all children have time to work on their own at something which is important to them. The older students prepare for GCSE exams, if they wish:

A Future

"We are normally taught in classrooms, but if you have a project of your own you can go wherever you feel is best. This summer I've spent most of my time in the garden writing poems, drawing and writing book reviews.' Jeanett Uhrenholt relates." [14]

Nihad Alfulaij sums up Sands:

"In this school our work is only part of life and not the be all and end all which is what it's like at most schools. We work at our own levels and up to our own standards. The staff are always willing to help us and they all have trust in us and their lessons are enjoyable." [15]

Opened in 1988 Lady Jane Grey was a new primary school in Groby, Leicestershire, England. The school was built in Groby to accommodate the growing number of children in the village as affluent couples have fled from the suburbs of Leicester, only ten minutes away down the A50.

The Local Authority appointed a headteacher who had demonstrated, whilst a deputy, his ability to work within the County's long tradition of liberal education.

This head then appointed a staff committed to enquiry-based learning. He also decided, within the obvious constraints, to try to create an enabling environment for children in a non-authoritarian way.

The school was also committed to giving respect to children, valuing their opinions and engaging in honest discussion with them. To an extent the curriculum was negotiated with the children, and they learned to take responsibility for their own actions.

There was an emphasis in the school on community involvement. The philosophy was to empower parents and children, through democratic means, to have a voice of their own.

However, there has been a furore in the local papers, an unhelpful article in the *Daily Mail*, and unwelcome attentions from Midlands radio and TV networks.

Some parents moved their children away and the possibility of a general inspection was raised. As a result the head was forced to resign, leaving a demoralised staff.

Bath Place School Unit has been in existence since 1977. It has taken pupils from most of the local schools, generally for the whole of their fifth year of secondary education. The students have normally been long-term truants, or excluded or suspended from their previous schools, and have been referred to the school through the Education Office, towards the end of their fourth year.

The school plays an integral part in the community centre in which it is located. This collectively run organisation incorporates a housing advice centre, coffee bar, playgroup, a youth work project, a women's room, and a welfare rights advice centre.

The school aims to create a structure and environment which enables young people to learn and interact together in a co-operative way and to relate to each other as individuals and as members of the community. It seeks to:

No Master High or Low

The playgroup at Bath Place.

"... prepare pupils in their final year of schooling for leaving school, establish support systems with their involvement and devise a curriculum suitable for their immediate and future needs.

Structure a class which keeps the balance between the sexes and deters individuals from dominating others.

In a small group setting develop a strong sense of responsibility towards all, both fellow pupils and teachers." [16]

The curriculum includes Maths and English which may be taken at City and Guilds level. School work is based on mutual help rather than competition. Those who are academically inclined are encouraged to go to college once they have left Bath Place School.

Young people who have experienced severe problems at school need time and support to work through their difficulties and the programme allows time for this work, both individually and in groups.

The School operates within the framework of a social education programme so that subjects and skills such as Photography, Art-work, Social Studies And Cookery are not seen as an end in themselves, but as having real relevance to the community around them.

Community work in the centre is seen as an important part of the timetable and provides a valuable opportunity to build constructive relationships. Work experience placements are arranged outside the centre for pupils who feel ready for this.

From the time a young person is referred to Bath Place contact is made, and maintained frequently, with parents and guardians. The roles of the teachers in the school are to take on not only the function of pastoral care, but to supplement the functions of educational social workers and social worker when necessary.

The school's location in a community centre enables parents to drop in for coffee, a chat, or to use the facilities of the building. Family support has always been an essential ingredient of the school and effort is spent on maintaining links consistently rather than just at times of crisis.

The Unit is an interesting example of a state-funded school for the "unschoolable" that has a clear libertarian ethos.

3. A CHALLENGE

Alternatives to the New Educational Orthodoxy

The libertarian tradition lives on, but still with familiar problems. The significance and impact of libertarian educational theory and practice probably remain more potential than actual. With this in mind it is important to return to the current state of state schooling for, whilst the need for alternatives remains, it is still the state system that will serve most children in the foreseeable future. Libertarians cannot and should not turn their backs on this system.

The Conservative governments of the 1980s, under the premiership of Margaret Thatcher, set about defining the educational debate in the terms of the once discredited Black Papers. The new buzz phrases in the debate are "Parental choice", "Opting out", "Discipline", "Standards", "Basic skills", "Benchmark testing", "A relationship between schools and industry", "The National Curriculum". David Jackson and Geoffrey Johns examined these crucial phrases and key ideas in an article in *Lib ED* magazine in 1989. In the current situation their work illustrates the need for a libertarian approach to state schooling:

"All the talk of greater 'openness, choice, variety, freedom' numbs the listener's active intelligence, and effectively conceals the hidden agenda buried beneath the words. If there are to be any adequate alternatives, it is necessary to see beneath this camouflage and make clear what is really meant.

Parental choice really means giving privileged parents the right to maintain inequality by choosing comfortable schools rather than run down ones, or to opt out into the independent sector, leaving the unprivileged even more deprived of resources.

Alternatively, choice can mean choice for all rather than for a thrusting, favoured few. 93% of parents already get the school of their first choice, so present arrangements need to be vigorously defended, and then extended.

This extension should include children themselves.

Opting out of Local Authority control is really about dismantling the power of the local authorities, preparing the ground for future privatisation, reinforcing the movement towards centralised control and dramatically increasing the dictatorial power of the Secretary of State for Education.

A Challenge

Alternatively opting in could mean the undermining of the independent sector, through taking back the public money presently given to private schools through the Assisted Places Scheme and the tax and rate concessions tied to charitable status. Comprehensive schools then might have a chance of working, without being creamed off or drastically under-funded.

Discipline really means introducing an authoritarian relationship between teachers and learners that instils the attitudes needed to run a divided society - i.e. an unthinking respect for authority, obedience and servility.

Alternatively it could mean students and teachers working together so that they can both become more critically aware of their rights and responsibilities within communities.

Standards is really Thatcherism's favourite way of attacking public education, and forcing the opposition onto the defensive. It's important to appreciate that the 'falling standards' catch phrase is not founded on factual evidence. Rather, it is an ideological offensive mounted by the New Right on the foundations of state education in this country.

Alternatively, we should recognise that raising standards for all school students does not come from an over-emphasis on drills, exercises and tests within a competitive, Grammar school curriculum. It comes from the student being emotionally and intellectually challenged. These kind of challenges come from working with, and critically on, the students' own understandings and resources in situations that are motivating and meaningful to them.

This must start with the students' own terms of reference - their own varieties of language, styles of thinking and knowing, and their own purposes. Improving standards can then be seen as the students gradually extending their immediate impressions into more fully developed meanings and understandings.

Basic skills really means reducing 'skill' to a technical competence, to be mechanically ticked off in a check-list box. Basic skills, in this sense, become a central part of social discipline.

Alternatively, skills can be viewed as social as well as technical competencies; of being able to ask questions about the seemingly obvious, about seeing the power lines within workplaces, about developing an awareness of what is going on, in whose interests and how you could change things.

Benchmark testing at 7, 11, 14 and 16 really means an intimidatory way of arranging pupils, schools and local authorities into a competitive league table of results. Not for the benefit of the children but to promote the forces of selection and privatisation in the country at large.

Alternatively formative assessment can mean a collaborative mode of profiling (a three-way dialogue between students, parents and teachers) that encourages the student to take up a self-critical responsibility for the quality, direction and pace of her own learning. It can also mean diagnostic tests that highlight remedial treatment for individual pupils rather than the destructive, comparative measurement of benchmark testing.

A relationship between schools and industry really means finding convert ways of socialising disaffected youth into the habits of deference and docility. The main strand in this is the pretence of training for non-existent work.

Alternatively it could mean developing understanding about the true nature of the job market, and introducing fresh ways of achieving collaboration between work places and schools. Such as, students having a basic right to socially useful work rather than simply fitting into a 'needs of industry' model. They should be enabled to claim the right to be decision makers in the work place and to learn from initiatives like workers' co-operatives and industrial democracy.

The national curriculum really means grabbing power away from the local authorities to reinforce the move towards a greater, centralised control.

It also means perpetuating elitist, tiered schooling by reinforcing the narrow, traditional subject-base of the foundation curricular structure. This emphasis is geared to the interests of the privileged few at the expense of the majority of average and below average children. The National Curriculum is also about social regulation in that it is an attempt by central government to control what children and people should or should not know, and what counts as valid knowledge. It is also an effective way of disciplining dissenting teachers.

Alternatively it could mean a greater respect for neglected areas of knowledge and experience, and the processes of making knowledge. (Areas like World Studies, Media Studies, Social Studies, Environmental Studies, Anti-racist and anti-sexist initiatives.) It also means an emphasis on 'really useful knowledge' - the socially-critical skills needed to understand what's going on in Britain 1988, and how you can change things through the skills of critical analysis, of seeing beyond the literal surface and purposeful activity in the outside world, rather than merely 'doing subjects' in an outdated Grammar school curriculum." [17]

The kind of educational policy that emerged in the 1980s will continue as a dominating force in British education as long as there is no alternative. As Jackson and Jenkins claim, the plausibility of the new educational orthodoxy:

"... lies in its critics newly taking up a responsive approach to its proposals reaching within the boundaries laid down for them!" [18]

A Challenge

With this in mind the challenge for libertarians today, as for the libertarian educational tradition as a whole, is to define and project an alternative terrain for education generally, and to draw on the richness of the tradition and all of its many lessons.

PART 6 NOTES

1. See Introduction.

2. See Part 2, Chapter 8.

3. Quoted in Carr Hill, R., '68-'88 What went right? in *Lib ED*, Leicester, 1988, Vol.2., No.9., p6.

4. *Lib ED*, Leicester, 1986, Vol.2., No.1.

5. Wright, N., *Free School: The White Lion Experience*. Libertarian Education, Leicester, 1989.

6. Hemmings, R., *Fifty Years of Freedom*. Allen and Unwin, London, 1972, p197-8.

7. *Lib ED*, Leicester, 1989, Vol.2., No.12., pp11-12.

8. Ibid.

9. Ibid.

10. *Lib ED*, Leicester, 1986, Vol.2., No.3., p8.

11. *Lib ED*, Leicester, 1989, Vol.2., No.12., pp12-13.

12. Ibid.

13. Ibid.

14. Ibid.

15. Ibid.

16. *Bath Place School Prospectus. Lib ED* archive.

17. Jackson D. and Johns G., *Educational Thatcherism* in *Lib ED*, Vol.2., No.11., Leicester, 1989.

18. Ibid.

Bibliography

Section 1: Archival Materials

The British Library Document Supply Centre, Weatherby, West Yorkshire.
The best collection of printed matter published in English in Britain. Citations in the notes from journals and newspapers refer to this collection.

The Commonweal Collection, University of Bradford, West Yorkshire.
The largest collection in Britain of material in the fields of nonviolent action, the peace movement and the alternative society. The collection contains extensive material on the Free School Movement in Britain.

Centre International de Recherches sur l'Anarchisme (CIRA), Geneva.
The best collection of anarchist literature in Europe.

The International Institute of Social History, Amsterdam.
Houses the foremost collection of anarchist materials in the world with considerable holdings relating to the Ferrer movement and independent progressive schooling.

The Libertarian Educational Archive, Leicestershire.
Houses extensive material relating to the libertarian tradition of education and schooling in Britain including a large tape library.

Section 2: Books, Pamphlets and Articles

ABBOTT, Leonard D., (ed), *Francisco Ferrer, His Life, Work and Martyrdom*. Francisco Ferrer Association, New York. 1910.
ADAMS, J., *Modern Development in Educational Practice*. U.L.P., London. 1928.
ARMYTAGE, W. H. G., *Heavens Below. Utopian Experiments in England 1560-1960*. Routledge and Kegan Paul, London. 1961.
ASH, M., *Who Are The Progressives Now? An Account of an Educational Conference*. Routledge and Kegan Paul, London. 1969.
ASHTON-WARNER, S., *Teacher*. Penguin, London. 1970.
AVRICH, Paul, *The Modern School Movement. Anarchism and Education in the United States*. Princeton University Press, New Jersey. 1980.
BAKUNIN, M., *Integral Education*. Cambridge Free Press, Cambridge. 1986.
BEACOCK, D. A., *Play Way. English For Today. The Methods and Influence of Caldwell Cook*. Nelson, 1943.
BERG, Leila, *Risinghill: Death of a Comprehensive School*. Penguin, London. 1968.
BLEWITT, T., (ed), *The Modern Schools Handbook*. Gollancz, London. 1934.
BONHAM-CARTER, Victor, *Dartington Hall: The Formative Years 1925-1956*. Phoenix House, London. 1958.
BOYD, Carolyn P., *The Anarchists and Education in Spain 1868-1909*. The Journal of Modern History, XLVIII. 1976.
BOYD, W., *Towards a New Education*. A. A. Knapf, London. 1930.
BOYD, W. and ROYSON, W., *The story of the New Education*. Heinemann, London. 1965.
BRIDGELAND, M, *Pioneer Work With Maladjusted Children*. Staples Press, London. 1971.
BUCKMAN, P., (ed), *Education Without Schools*. Souvenir Press, London. 1973.
CALDWELL, Cook H., *The Play Way*. Heinemann, London. 1917.
CASTLES, S. & WUSTENBURG, W., *The Education of The Future*. Pluto Press, London. 1979.
CENTRE FOR CONTEMPORARY & CULTURAL STUDIES, *Unpopular Education*. Hutchinson, London. 1981.
CHILD, H. A. T., *The Independent Progressive School*. Hutchinson, London. 1962.
CLARKE, F., *Freedom In The Educative Society*. U.L.P., London. 1948.
CLEGG, A., (ed), *The Changing Primary School*. Chatto and Windus, London. 1972.
CLEMENCEAU, G., *La Melée Sociale*. Charpetier et Fusquelle, Paris. 1895.
CORNFORTH, M., *Rebels and Their Causes: Essays in Honour of A.L.Morton*. Lawrence and Wishart, London. 1978.
CROALL, J., *Neill of Summerhill. The Permanent Rebel*. Ark, London. 1984.
CURRY, W. B., *The School*. John Lane, London. 1934.
DENNISON, George, *The Lives of Children: The Story of The First Street School*. Penguin, London. 1972.
DOLGOFF, Sam, (ed), *Bakunin On Anarchy*. New York. 1972.
EDWARDS, Stewart, (ed), *Selected Writings Of Pierre-Joseph Proudhon*. Garden City, New York. 1969.
FERRER GUARDIA, Francisco, *The Origin And Ideals Of The Modern School*. Watts, London. 1913.
FISHMAN, William, J., *East End Jewish Radicals, 1875-1914*. Duckworth, London. 1975.

Bibliography

FRANKLIN, B., (ed), *The Rights of Children*. Blackwell, London. 1986.
FRANKLIN, M. E., (ed), *Q Camp*. Planned Environmental Therapy Trust, London. 1966.
FREIRE, P., *Pedagogy Of The Oppressed*. Sheed & Ward, London. 1972.
FREIRE, P., *Education; The Practice Of Freedom*. Writers and Readers Publishing Co-op, London. 1974.
GARDENER, D. E. M., *Susan Isaacs*. London. 1969.
GARDNER, Phil, *The Lost Elementary Schools of Victorian England*. Croom Helm, London. 1984.
GIBSON, Tony, *Youth For Freedom*. Freedom Press, London. 1951.
GIROUND, Gabriel, *Cempuis: Education Integrale*. Scheicher, Paris. 1900.
GIROUND, Gabriel, *Paul Robin: Sa Vie, Ses Idees, Son Action*. G.Migrole et Starz, Paris. 1937.
GODWIN, William, *Enquiry Concerning Political Justice, and its influence on Morals and Happiness (2nd ed., 2 vols., 1976; 3rd ed., 2 vols., 1978)*. Oxford. 1971.
GODWIN, William, *The Enquirer. Reflections on Education, Manners, and Literature in a Series of Essays (1971)*. New York. 1965.
GODWIN, William, *An Account of The Seminary. (1783). Reprinted in four early pamphlets (1783-84)*. Edited by B.R. Pollin. Gainesville, 1966.
GOLDMAN, E., *Anarchism and other Essays*. Mother Earth Publishing, New York. 1911.
GOODMAN, Paul, *Compulsory Mis-Education*. Harban, New York. 1964.
GOODMAN, Paul, *Growing Up Absurd*. Random House, New York. 1960.
GORDON, T., *Democracy in One School*. Falmer, London. 1986.
GRIBBLE, David, *Considering Children*. Dorling Kindersley. 1985.
GRIBBLE, David, *That's All Folks*. West Aish Publishing. 1987.
GRAUBARD, A., *Free The Children*. Pantheon, New York. 1973.
GROSSKURTH, P., *Havelock Ellis*. Allen Lane. The Penguin Press, London. 1980.
HALL, J., (ed), *Children's Rights*. Panther, London. 1972.
HALL, John R., *The Ways Out: Utopian Communal Groups in an Age of Babylon*. Routledge & Kegan Paul, London. 1978.
HARDY, Denis, *Alternative Communities in 19th Century England*. Longman, London. 1979.
HEMMINGS, Ray, *Fifty years of Freedom*. Allen and Unwin, London. 1972.
HERRIDON, J., *The Way It Sposed to Be*. Simon & Schuster, New York. 1965.
HOLMES, E., *Give Me The Young*. Constable, London. 1921.
HOLMES, E., *In Defence of What Might Be*. Constable, London. 1914.
HOLMES, E., *The Tragedy of Education*. Constable, London. 1913.
HOLMES, E., *What is and What Might Be*. Constable, London. 1911
HOLMES, R. G. A., *The Idiot Teacher*. Faber and Faber, London. 1952.
HOLT, J., *How Children Fail*. Pitman, London. 1964.
HOLT, J., *How Children Learn*. Pitman, London. 1968.
HOLT, J., *The Underachieving School*. Pitman, London. 1970.
HOLTON, Bob, *British Syndicalism 1900-14*. London. 1977.
HUMPHREYS, S., *Hooligans and Rebels*. London. 1979.
ILLICH, I. D., *Deschooling Society*. Calder and Boyars, London, 1971.
ILLICH, I. D., *After Deschooling, What?* Writers and Readers, London. 1981.
ISSACS, S., *Intellectual Growth in Young Children*. Routledge, London. 1930.
ISSACS, S., *Social Development in Young Children*. Routledge, London. 1933.
JOLL, J., *The Anarchists*. Eyre & Spottiswood, London. 1964.
JONES, K., *Beyond Progressive Education*. Macmillan, London. 1983.
KOHL. Herbert, *36 Children*. Penguin, London. 1970.
KOZOL, J., *Death at an Early Age*. Penguin, London. 1968.
KROPOTKIN, P., *Kropotkin's Revlpoutionary Pamphlets*. Dover Publications, New York. 1970.

LANE, Homer, *Talks To Parents and Teachers*. Allen and Unwin, London. 1928.
LEBERSTEIN, Stephen, *Revolutionary Education: French Libertarian Theory and Experiments. 1895-1915*. Ph.D. Dissertation, University of Wisconsin. 1972.
MACKENZIE, R. F., *The Unbowed Head: Events at Summerhill Academy 1968-74*. Edinburgh University Student Publications Board, Edinburgh. 1980.
MACKENZIE, R. F., *Escape From The Classroom*. Collins, London, 1965.
MACKENZIE, R. F., *A Question of Living*. Collins, London. 1963.
MACKENZIE, R. F., *The Sins of Children*. Collins, London. 1967.
MACKENZIE, R. F., *State School*. Penguin, London. 1970.
MACMANN, N., *A Child's Path to Freedom*. Bell, London. 1914.
MACMANN, N., *A Path to Freedom in The School*. Bell, London, 1921.
MARSHALL, P., (ed) *The Anarchist Writings Of William Godwin*. Freedom Press, London. 1986.
McMILLAN, M., *The Child and The State*. National Labour Press, London. 1911.
MOON, Bob, (ed), *Comprehensive Schools: Challenge and Change*. Neer Nelson, London. 1983.
MUNCIE, J., *The Trouble With Kids Today*. Hutchinson, London. 1984.
NEILL, A. S., *A Dominie's Log*. Herbert Jenkins, London. 1915.
NEILL, A. S., *A Dominie Dismissed*. Herbert Jenkins, London. 1916.
NEILL, A. S., *Booming of Bunkie*. Herbert Jenkins, London. 1919.
NEILL, A. S., *A Dominie in Doubt*. Herbert Jenkins, London. 1920.
NEILL, A. S., *Carrot Broon*. Herbert Jenkins, London. 1920.
NEILL, A. S., *A Dominie Abroad*. Herbert Jenkins, London. 1922.
NEILL, A. S., *A Dominie's Five*. Herbert Jenkins, London. 1924.
NEILL, A. S., *The Problem Child*. Herbert Jenkins, London. 1926.
NEILL, A. S., *The Problem Parent*. Herbert Jenkins, London. 1932.
NEILL, A. S., *Is Scotland Educated?* Routledge, London. 1936.
NEILL, A. S., *That Dreadful School*. Herbert Jenkins, London. 1937
NEILL, A. S., *Last Man Alive*. Herbert Jenkins, London. 1938.
NEILL, A. S., *The Problem Teacher*. Herbert Jenkins, London. 1940
NEILL, A. S., *Hearts Not Heads In The School*. Herbert Jenkins, London. 1945.
NEILL, A. S., *The Problem Family*. Herbert Jenkins, London. 1949.
NEILL, A. S., *The Free Child*. Herbert Jenkins, London. 1953.
NEILL, A. S., *Summerhill: A Radical Approach to Education*. Gollancz, London. 1962.
NEILL, A. S., *Talking of Summerhill*. Gollancz, London. 1967.
NEILL, A. S., *Freedom - Not License!* Hart Publishing Co., New York. 1966.
NEILL, A. S., & RITTER, P., *Wilhelm Reich*. Ritter Press, London, 1958.
PARK, J., *Bertrand Russell on Education*. Allen & Unwin, London. 1964.
PEARSE, I. H., & CROCKER, L. H., *The Peckham Experiment*. Allen & Unwin, London. 1943.
PERRY, Leslie, (ed), *Four Progressive Educators*. Collier-MacMillan, London. 1967.
PETERS, R. S., *Authority and Responsibility in Education*. Allen and Unwin, London. 1959.
PURDY, B., *Girls will be Grils*. The Laneill Press, Belper, Derbyshire. 1989.
PUNCH, M., *Progressive Retreat*. Cambridge University Press, London. 1977.
RAWSON, W., *The Freedom We Seek*. New Education Foundation, London. 1937.
REIMER, E., *School is Dead*. Penguin, London. 1971.
RICHMOND, W. K., *The Free School*. Methuen, London. 1973.
ROCKER, Rudolf, *The London Years*. Robert Anscombe, London. 1956.
ROGERS, C., *On Becoming a Person*. Constable, London. 1961.
ROGERS, C., *Freedom to Learn*. Merrill Publishing Co., London. 1969.
RUBENSTEIN, D., & STONEMAN, C., (eds), *Education For Democracy*. Penguin, London. 1970.
RUSSELL, B., *Autobiography, Vol II*. Allen & Unwin, London. 1968.
RUSSELL, B., *Education and The Social Order*. Allen and Unwin, London. 1968.

Bibliography

RUSSELL, B., *On Education*. Allen and Unwin, London. 1926.
RUSSELL, B., *Principals of Social Reconstruction*. Allen and Unwin, London. 1916.
RUSSELL, B., *Unpopular Essays*. Unwin, London. 1976.
RUSSELL, Dora, *The Tamarisk Tree*. Elec Penlenton, London. 1975.
RUSSELL, Dora, *The Tamarisk Tree 2: My School and The Years of War*. Virago, London. 1980.
RUST, Val D., *Alternatives in Education*. Sage Publications, London. 1977.
SELLECK, R. J. W., *English Primary Education and The Progressives 1914-1939*. Routledge and Kegan Paul, London. 1972.
SELLECK, R. J. W., *The New Education 1870-1914*. Pitman, London. 1968.
SHAW, Neillie, *Whiteway: A Colony in The Cotswolds*. C. W. Daniel, London, 1935.
SHAW, Otto, *Maladjusted Boys*. Allen and Unwin, London. 1965.
SIMON, B., *Education and the Labour Movement. 1870-1920* Lawrence and Wishart, London. 1965.
SKIDELSKY, R., *English Progressive Schools*. Penguin, London. 1969.
SMITH, M. P., *The Underground and Education*. Methuen & Co., London. 1977.
SMITH, M. P., *The Libertarians and Education*. Methuen, London. 1980.
SNELL, Reginald, *St. Christopher School. 1915-75*. Aldine Press, London. 1975.
SPRING, Joel, *A Primer of Libertarian Education*. Free Life Editions, New York. 1975.
SPRING, Joel, *Anarchism and Education: The Dissenting Tradition*. Libertarian Analysis, London. 1971.
STIRNER, Max, *The False Principle of Our Education*. Ralph Myles, London. 1967.
STEWART, W. A. C., *Progressives and Radicals in English Education 1750-1970*. MacMillan, London. 1972.
TAWNEY, R. H., *Secondary Education For All*. Allen & Unwin, London. 1922.
THOMAS, Edith, *Louise Michel*. Black Rose Books, Montreal. 1981.
TOLSTOY, L., *On Education*. University of Chicago Press, London. 1967.
TROYAT, H., *Tolstoy*. Penguin, London. 1970.
VAN DER EYKEN, W., & TURNER, B., *Adventures In Education*. Allen Lane, London. 1969.
WALVIN, James, *A Child's World*. Penguin, London. 1982.
WARD, C., *Anarchy in Action*. Freedom Press, London. 1982.
WEEKS, A., *Comprehensive Schools: Past, Present and Future*. Methuen, London. 1986.
WILLS, W. D., *The Barns Experiment*. Allen & Unwin, London. 1945.
WILLS, W. D., *The Hawkspur Experiment*. Allen and Unwin, London. 1967.
WILLS, W. D., *Homer Lane: A Biography*. Allen and Unwin, London. 1964.
WILLS, W. D., *Throw Away the Rod*. Gollancz, London. 1960.
WOODS, A., *Educational Experiments in England*. Methuen, London. 1920.
WRIGHT, N., *Free School. The White Lion Experience*. Lib ED, Leicester. 1989.
WRIGHT, N., *Assessing Radical Education* Oxford University Press, Milton Keynes. 1989.
YOUNG, Michael, *The Elmhirsts of Dartington: The Creation of a Utopian Community*. Routledge & Kegan Paul. 1982.
ZELDIN, D., *The Educational Ideas of Charles Fourier*. Frank Lass, London. 1969.

Section 3: Journals, Newspapers and Periodicals

The Alarm. Chicago, New York, 1884-1889.
A. S. Neill Trust Newsletter. Leicestershire, 1973-1979.
Childrens Rights Newsletter. London, 1973-1975.
L'Ecole Renovée. Brussels, Paris, 1908-1909.
Freedom. London, 1886-1990.
Labour Annual. London, 1900-1905.
Labour Leader. London, 1895-1914.
Lib ED. published by **Libertarian Education**, Leicestershire, 1966-1990.
Liberty. Boston, 1881-1908.
Marxism Today. London, 1984-1990.
Mother Earth. New York, 1906-1918.
New Era. London, 1918-1939.
Peace News. Nottingham, 1960-1980.
Quarterly Review. London, 1867-1870.
The Sheffield Anarchist. Sheffield, 1890-1895.
Les Temps Nouveaux. Paris, 1845-1914.
The Times Educational Supplement. London, 1910-1990.
The Voice of Labour. London. 1907; 1917-1916.

INDEX

A

A. S. Neill Trust	217
A. S. Neill Trust Association	201 - 202
A. S. Neill Trust Newsletter	217
Abbotsholme School	9, 23 - 24, 69, 72
Brian Addison	245 - 246
Advisory Centre for Education	202
Advisory Committee on Education (ACE)	7
John Aitkenhead	75, 95, 109, 111 - 116, 121, 260
Morag Aitkenhead	109, 115 - 116
Clifford Allen	74
Anarchist-Communist Sunday School (Liverpool)	62, 208
Anarchist-Socialist Sunday School (Jubilee St, London)	36, 39
Anarchy	141
Anti-Conscription League	55
Helena Applebaum	57 - 58, 62
Lou Appleton	58 - 59
Arbeter Fraint	36 - 37
Michael Armstrong	9
Ashburton House	54 - 55
Assisted Places Scheme	114 - 115, 271
Robin Auld	190
L'Avenir Social	26

B

Baden Powell	75
Michael Bakunin	34
Arthur Balfour	5 - 6
Balsall Heath Community School	215, 218 - 219, 252
Barns Experiment	131, 145 - 148, 260
A. T. Baron	144
Barrowfield Community School	245, 247, 249 - 250, 252
Bath Place School Unit	264, 267, 269
Jean Battola	35
Beacon Hill School	16, 24, 72, 74 - 75, 82, 88 - 92, 94, 120, 154, 260
Heiner Becker	41
Bedales School	9, 23, 69, 72, 82
Henry Betloff	33
Peter Bide	101
Black Papers	183, 189, 270
Blackcurrent	264 - 265
Lyn Blackshaw	85 - 86
T. Blewitt	69, 154
Alex Bloom	162, 167 - 168, 171

Board Schools	3 - 5, 34
Fred Bowers	44 - 45
Rhodes Boyson	188
Braehead School	16, 162, 169 - 172, 194
Maurice Bridgeland	133 - 134, 142, 154
Brighton Free School	215 - 216
Brighton Voice	216
Hamish Brown	170
Ferdinand Buisson	25
Burgess Hill School	16, 76, 95 - 97, 99, 101, 107, 118, 120 - 121, 260

C

Victor Cailes	35
Caldecott Community	130 - 131, 133 - 134, 138, 260
James Callaghan	183
Campaign for State-Supported Alternative Schools	201 - 202
Cempuis	25 - 26
Centre for Contemporary Cultural Studies (CCCS)	10
Fred Charles	35
H. A. T. (Hubert) Child	69, 85, 96, 154
Lois Child	85
Children's Rights	30
Circular 10/65	8
Georges Clemenceau	33
Arthur Cobb	94
Cockerton Judgement of 1901	5
Conference of Educational Associations	139
Conservative Party	106
Coue	73
M. Coulon	35
Countesthorpe College	16 - 17, 85, 121, 162 - 163, 174 - 184, 186, 188, 192, 194
Jonathan Croall	74, 77
Bill Curry	72, 74, 82 - 85, 89, 95, 115, 130, 164, 169

D

Dartington Hall School	16, 24, 72, 74 - 75, 82 - 86, 88 - 89, 91 - 92, 94, 120 - 121, 154, 169, 238, 260, 263, 265
Ethel Davies	134
Marcel Degalves	26
Deschooling	163
John Dewey	8, 203
James (Jimmy) Dick	27, 42 - 47, 49 - 52, 55, 62, 70

Index

Nellie Dick	15, 37 - 39, 49, 51 - 52, 55, 62, 70, 130
Douglas Social Credit Movement	75
Christopher Draper	237
Michael Duane	231
Durdham Park Free School	215 - 216

E

Jimmy East	98
L'Ecole Renovée	28 - 29
Education Act (1870)	iv - v, 14
Education Act (1902)	5 - 6, 32
Education Act (1921)	133
Education Act (1944)	v, 7, 140, 183, 215 - 216
Education Act (1980)	259
Education Act (1981)	106 - 107, 183
Education Act (1988)	v
Education Guardian	213
Education Otherwise	263 - 264
Edwardian Green movement	74
Elementary education	2 - 3
Elementary Schools	23
Eleven-plus	7
Terry Ellis	177, 189 - 191
Leonard and Dorothy Elmhirst	72, 74, 82
Lord Elton	161
Beatrice Ensor	24, 70 - 74, 130
Escuela Moderna	11, 27 - 28
Chris Evans	183 - 184

F

Fabian Society	6
Neil Fairbairn	182
John Farr	181 - 182
Chris Fassnidge	101
Sebastien Faure	26 - 29, 33
Francisco Ferrer	11 - 12, 15, 26 - 29, 38, 41, 43, 45, 52, 57, 61, 70
Ferrer School (Commercial Road East, London)	49 - 50
Ferrer School (Stelton, U. S. A.)	59
Ferrer Schools	31
Jules Ferry	25
First International	25
Paul Foot	169, 171
Ford Republic	135
Forest School	16, 74 - 75, 92 - 94, 120, 169, 260
W. E. Forster	3
Fortnightly Review	46
Charles Fourier	13, 29

Marjorie Franklin	143
Free Educational Group	57
Free Schools Campaign	201
Free Universities	205
Free Universities (US)	205
Freedom	29 - 31, 41, 43, 46, 49 - 51, 57 - 58, 168, 237
Freightliners Free School	215 - 216
Paulo Freire	164, 204
Sigmund Freud	73, 169

G

Philip Gardner	v, 14, 62
Geoffrey Gibson	182
Tony Gibson	97, 99, 167
William Godwin	iv - v, 11 - 12, 146, 203, 259
Emma Goldman	25 - 26, 37
Paul Goodman	203
Tuula Gordon	8
David Graham	220
Jean Grave	26 - 27
Mary Gray	9
David Gribble	82, 86, 121, 265
Grith Pioneers	143
The Guardian	217
James Guillaume	13
J. M. Guyan	30

H

Brian Haddow	177, 190 - 191
Clive Harber	162
Hargreaves Group	75
Hawkspur Camp	131, 143 - 148, 154, 260
William Heaford	28, 43, 138
Ray Hemmings	71, 73, 77, 120, 262
Russell Hoare	130, 138 - 139
Ivor Holland	140
Edmond Holmes	23 - 24, 70, 72, 130, 164 - 165
Bob Holton	43
Homer Lane Trust	147
Houndsditch Affair	45 - 46
Stephen Humphries	v, 62, 161
William Hunt	130

I

Ivan Illich	163, 201
Independent Labour Party	31, 43, 45 - 46

Index

Independent Progressive School movement	101
Inner London Education Authority	226, 234 - 235, 237 - 238
Integral education	13, 25 - 26, 29
International League for the Rational Education of Children	11, 28, 30, 43, 61, 138
International Modern School (Cambridge Road East, London)	56
International Modern School (Commercial Road East, London)	50 - 51
International Modern School (Fieldgate St., London)	35, 57 - 60, 62
International Modern School (Liverpool)	45 - 47, 260
International Modern School (London)	57, 260
International Modern School Movement	131, 138
International Modern School Movement (America)	56, 61
International Modern Schools	15, 31, 52, 61 - 62, 70, 161, 168, 262
International School (London)	33, 35 - 36, 62, 260
Anthony Ivins	94

J

Brian Jackson	248
David Jackson	270, 272
Emile Janvion	26
Christopher Jencks	248
Geoffrey Jenkins	272
Peter Jenner	205, 207
Jewish Anarchist Education League	51
Geoffrey Johns	270
Ken Jones	7 - 8, 10 - 11
Will Jones	45
Keith Joseph	6, 183
Jubilee Street Club	138
James Jupp	261

K

Mat Kavanagh	41, 44 - 45, 49
George Kee	245
Thomas Keell	41
Kilquhanity House School	16, 75 - 76, 95, 109, 111 - 116, 120 - 121, 260
King Alfred's School	9, 23, 69, 72
Tom King	188
Kirkdale School	16, 76, 78, 107, 117 - 118, 120 - 121, 162
Jonathan Kozol	247
Peter Kropotkin	26, 29, 37, 59, 75

L

Labour Annual	31
Labour Party	v, 7 - 8
Lady Jane Grey School	264, 267

Homer Lane	16, 62, 70, 73, 77, 129 - 131, 135 - 136, 138, 140 - 141, 147 - 148, 154
Will Langworthy	235, 237
Laurieston Hall	224
Peter Lawley	189
John Lawson	6
Frank Lea	96
League for Libertarian Education	26
League for the Rational Education of Children	61
Leeds Free School and Community Trust	239 - 241, 243 - 244, 252
Leicester Mercury	176, 182
Lib ED	11, 17, 79 - 81, 109, 113 - 115, 131, 151, 179 - 181, 201, 205, 217, 228, 235 - 238, 261, 265, 270
Libertarian Sunday Schools	25, 28, 43
Libertarian Teachers' Association	201
Liberty	26
Lifespan Community	217
Ian Lister	213
Little Commonwealth	16, 77, 129 - 131, 135 - 138, 148, 154, 260
Liverpool Anarchist-Communist Sunday School (Liverpool)	43 - 44
Liverpool Daily Post and Mercury	45 - 46
Liverpool Free School	203, 208 - 210, 213
Liverpool Weekly Mercury	45
Liverpool Weekly Post	45
London Free School	205 - 207, 210, 252
Robert Lowe	2
Lord Lytton	70

M

John MacBeath	245, 247
R. F. MacKenzie	93, 169 - 174
Margaret MacMillan	133
Tim McMullen	175 - 176, 179
Norman MacMunn	70, 73
Makhnovists	61
Enrico Malatesta	37, 41
Manchester Free School	217, 220, 224 - 225, 252
Bernard Mandeville	4
Manpower Services Commission	183
Marsh House	55, 57
Carolyn Martyn	10
Marxism Today	6
Stewart Mason	175
Roland Meighan	162
Ernestine Meunie	27

Index

Louise Michel	14 - 15, 26 - 27, 29, 31, 33 - 35, 37, 57, 62
Eric Midwinter	210, 248
Military Service Act	55
John Stuart Mill	3
Modern School (Cambridge Road East, London)	54 - 55
Modern School (Montreal, Canada)	54
Modern School Movement	41
Modern Schools	12
Monkton Wyld School	16, 76, 85, 95, 100 - 103, 105 - 109, 118, 120 - 121, 162, 217, 260, 262
George Montagu	135
Maria Montessori	23 - 24, 71 - 73
Robert Morant	6
William Morris	37 - 38, 49
Mundella Act	3
Bill Murphy	210 - 211, 213

N

National Curriculum	v, 162, 265, 270, 272
National Union of Teachers (NUT)	10, 187, 192
A.S. Neill	16, 24, 62, 69 - 77, 79 - 82, 84, 89, 95, 100, 109, 113 - 117, 120 - 121, 130 - 131, 140 - 141, 154, 162, 164, 169, 173, 188, 191, 201, 203, 262
Ena Neill	77, 79, 121
New Barns School	147 - 148
New Education Fellowship	16, 23, 71 - 72, 74, 91
New Education Group	58
New Era	16, 24, 69 - 74, 130
New Ideals in Education Group	24, 31, 70, 72, 130, 162, 164
New Psychology	131, 141
New Right	271
New Schools Movement	23 - 24, 69 - 70, 72
Nottingham Free School	215 - 216
Percy Nunn	131

O

Edward O'Neill	162, 164 - 166, 174
Oak Lane Country Day School	82
Ann Oakley	17 - 18
John Ord	210 - 211, 213
Order of Woodcraft Chivalry	75, 92, 94
Robert Owen	149

No Master High or Low

P

Paris Commune	13, 25, 33, 44
Parkfield Street Free School	215, 220 - 224, 252
Peace News	208, 239 - 240, 244
Naomi Ploschansky	15, 37, 42
Plowden Report	191
Lorenzo Portet	28, 43, 138
Susie Powlesland	118
Jose Prat	27
Prestolee School	16 - 17, 25, 162 - 5, 168, 194, 260
Pierre Proudhon	13
Elias Puig	27
Keith Pulham	210
Maurice Punch	212, 217, 251, 253
Bryn Purdy	131, 149, 151 - 152
Meg Purdy	131, 149, 151

Q

Q Camps Committee	143, 145

R

Herbert Read	95
Elisée Reclus	26 - 27
Red Hill School	16, 131, 140 - 142, 147, 260
Neil Redfern	149
Zoe Redhead	77, 79 - 81, 114
Reformers' Year Book	31 - 32
Wilhelm Reich	77
Leila Rendel	130, 133 - 134, 138
Arnall Richards	208 - 209
Risinghill School	231
Paul Robin	25 - 29, 33
Bridget Robson	239 - 240, 244
Mat Roche	45, 47, 50
Fermin Rocker	52
Rudolf Rocker	36 - 37, 51 - 52
Hamish Rodger	170
Klaus Rodler	202
William Ross	173
Jean-Jacques Rousseau	203
Rowen House School	129, 131, 149, 153 - 154, 194
La Ruche	26
Manuel Ruiz Zorilla	27
Alfred Russell	31
Bertrand Russell	72, 74, 88 - 89, 95, 117
Dora Russell	72, 74, 88 - 90, 95, 115, 117, 130, 164

Index

Cuthbert Rutter	75, 92 - 94, 143

S

Roger Saddiev	201
Saltley Free School	215 - 216
Jose Sanchez Rosa	27
Sands School	264 - 267
Alexander Schapiro	38
School Boards	4
Scotland Road Free School	207 - 208, 210 - 215, 217, 239, 251
Scouting Movement	75
Second International	27
R. J. W. Selleck	8
Otto Shaw	131, 140 - 142
Sidney Street Siege	45
Harold Silver	6
Brian Simon	6, 162
Situationists	261
Small Schools	252
Michael Smith	27, 76
Social Democratic Federation	10, 36, 43
Socialist Sunday School Movement	9 - 10, 47
Socialist Sunday School Union of Liverpool	47
Socialist Teacher	189
Socialist Teachers Alliance	189
Society for the Reform of School Discipline	32
Herbert Spencer	30 - 31
Geoff Sproson	208 - 209
St. George-in-the-East School	16, 162 - 3, 167 - 168, 194, 260
Steiner Schools	252
W. A. C. Stewart	8, 131
Max Stirner	13
Suffragette Movement	49, 61
Summerhill Academy	16 - 17, 93, 121, 162, 169, 171 - 174, 194
Summerhill School	16, 24, 72, 74 - 81, 83, 88, 91 - 95, 98, 111, 113 - 114, 120 - 121, 131, 140, 147, 154, 173, 191, 194, 237 - 239, 247 - 248, 260, 262
Martin Summers	118
Sutton Centre	16 - 17, 121, 162 - 163, 174, 185 - 188, 194
Ruth Swirsky	212
Sysonby House	130 - 131, 138 - 139, 260

T

R. H. Tawney	7
Geoffrey Taylor	182
The Teacher	212
Les Temps Nouveaux	26 - 27
Margaret Thatcher	6, 115, 182 - 183, 244, 252, 270
Thatcherism	271
Theosophy	70 - 72
Edith Thomas	33, 35
Paul Thompson	v
Geoffrey Thorp	96 - 98
The Times	24 - 25, 70, 167
Times Educational Supplement	85, 167, 183, 210, 247
Leo Tolstoy	26, 203
Benjamin Tucker	26

U

Carl Urban	76, 100 - 103
Eleanor Urban	76, 100 - 103

V

Madeleine Vernet	26
Voice of Labour	39, 51 - 52
Voluntary Schools	5 - 6
Voluntary Societies	3

W

Dolly Walker	189
Wallingford Farm Training Colony	130
James Walvin	4
Colin Ward	168
John Watts	164, 166, 176 - 177, 179, 182
Anthony Weaver	96, 121, 141
Sidney Webb	6
Steve Webster	101
West London Sunday School (Charlotte St, London)	41
Ernest Westlake	75, 92 - 93
White Lion Street Free School	15, 107, 204, 207, 215, 226 - 229, 231, 234 - 238, 252, 262
Whiteway Colony	44, 75
William Tyndale School	16 - 17, 121, 162, 177, 182, 189, 191 - 192, 194 - 195
Shirley Williams	183
David Wills	130 - 131, 143 - 148, 154

Index

Stuart Wilson	188
Morris Winchevsky	58
Woodcraft Folk	75
Alice Woods	133
Worker's Friend Club and Institute	36, 38 - 39, 57, 59
Working class private schools	14
Nigel Wright	204, 216 - 217, 235, 262

Z

Emile Zola	54